ISSUES IN GERMANY, AUSTRIA, AND SWITZERLAND

ISSUES IN GERMANY, AUSTRIA, AND SWITZERLAND

ELEANOR L. TURK

GREENWOOD PRESS
Westport, Connecticut • London

Library of Congress Cataloging-in-Publication Data

Turk, Eleanor L., 1935–
Issues in Germany, Austria, and Switzerland / Eleanor L. Turk.
p. cm.
Includes bibliographical references and index.
ISBN 0–313–31857–3 (alk. paper)
1. Germany—Politics and government—1900– 2. Germany—Ethnic relations. 3. Fascism—Austria—History. 4. Political culture—Austria. 5. Jewish property—Switzerland. 6. Foreign bank accounts—Switzerland—History—20th century. I. Title.
DD290.29.T88 2003
306.2'0943—dc21 2003044075

British Library Cataloguing in Publication Data is available.

Library of Congress Catalog Card Number: 2003044075
ISBN: 0–313–31857–3

First published in 2003

Greenwood Press, 88 Post Road West, Westport, CT 06881
An imprint of Greenwood Publishing Group, Inc.
www.greenwood.com

Printed in the United States of America

The paper used in this book complies with the Permanent Paper Standard issued by the National Information Standards Organization (Z39.48–1984).

10 9 8 7 6 5 4 3 2 1

To Andy,
my best issue.
With love.

CONTENTS

PREFACE

Some books are written to answer questions. This one is not. Rather, the purpose of this book is to explore some of the issues in contemporary Germanic societies for which there are many possible answers. The historian is, by training, an interpreter of the evidence, not merely a compiler of it. And the dynamic histories of the German-speaking countries—Germany, Austria, and Switzerland—give rise to many questions and a myriad of possible interpretations. The conscientious historian acknowledges the breadth of the discussion before attempting to provide the most plausible resolution of it. Indeed, it is probably too early to reach conclusions about the extraordinary changes in the Germanic countries in the final decade of the twentieth century.

There are many debates about contemporary affairs in the Germanic countries. Some of these debates are scholarly in nature; others are political and cultural. This book is designed to describe the dimensions of some of these discussions for students and general readers. The issues are contained in individual chapters, each formatted into four parts: first, a definition and background information; second, the relevant facts that explain the contemporary situation; third, the issues that must be considered in order to make a meaningful interpretation of the contemporary nation; and, fourth, a Questions and Activities section to encourage students' critical thinking for reports, papers, and classroom debate. Suggested readings for each chapter encourage the readers to do some research and to reach their own informed and logical conclusions. Where possible, I have indicated some Web sites that offer specific data or points of view and links that can keep the reader up to date on the subjects. These Web sites will probably be more accessible to students than some of the printed sources, and students can print the articles at low cost and take them home to study.

In each chapter I suggest only some of the alternative perspectives just to get the discussion going; many more might be considered. However, unlike the usual history text, this book includes no suggested resolutions. The topics under consideration emphasize the final decades of the twentieth century. Most have their roots in the more distant past, however, indicative of their complexity and persistence in history. One chapter for each country is designed to review the historical past in order to provide context for contemporary events. For the discussion of Germany the chapters on unification provide the necessary background for the other discussions of the Bundesrepublik Deutschland. Some issues, such as the Holocaust and immigration, have had almost generational variations in German society. Issues in Germany dominate this collection, but issues in Austria and Switzerland are closely intertwined. Together, these states form the crucial geographical and political center of the European continent. Examination of the issues in these states provides interesting insight into the general history of Europe. Indeed, some issues cross borders and can be understood only in that light.

It is not my purpose here to single out the German-speaking countries as particular heroes or villains on the European scene. The focus on these three countries is intended to give readers who are interested in German, Austrian, and Swiss affairs more information about issues and their impact in those nations than is usually available in the popular media, but without going into a full-fledged scholarly examination. As such, this collection is designed to be a starting place for understanding and a transition to possible future study of the various problems. For far too long historians and their students have been dealing with the history of countries and regions in isolation. It is time to take a more global perspective.

As a historian, I have long been fascinated by the incredibly energetic history of the Germanic people—the founders of the earliest western European states; the primary adversaries in the Reformation; the resolute particularists who were long unable to use normal western political means to unite into a national state; the immigrants who in the eighteenth and nineteenth centuries helped found nations all around the world; and the putative destroyers of twentieth-century civilization through their aggressive wars, fascism, and anti-Semitism.

It is axiomatic that history is written by the victors, and much of modern Germanic history is stained by the condemnations of that past. Yet these same Germans accomplished the most remarkable revolution of modern times: the peaceful and voluntary merger of the two previously hostile German states into a single, unified republic (1989–90). Without a shot being fired, with sophisticated utilization of political, diplomatic, and economic mechanisms, a new Germany has emerged as a major world power. Moreover, despite its racist past, Germany has become the most ethnically diverse state in contemporary Europe, absorbing refugees, asylum seekers, and ethnic Germans from other states in unprecedented numbers.

Historians and commentators are still analyzing the implications of Germany's new directions for Europe and beyond. This work introduces Germany with chapters focused on both the political and the economic concerns about the unification process. It also includes chapters on the legacy of the Holocaust; historians' debate over German history and identity; Germany's immigration law and the place of resident foreign nationals in German society; and the stability of postunification Germany.

Austria shared much of Germany's fate in the twentieth century. As allies in World War I, both surrendered territory, reparations, and political power as a result of the Paris peace treaties. Each was devastated by the global depression of the 1930s and followed the seductive and awful fascism of the Nazi Party. Like Germany, Austria was divided and occupied by the Allies after World War II. It won its sovereign independence with a pledge of permanent neutrality in 1955. But Austria, too, was saddled with the legacy of fascism. The war crimes accusations against Kurt Waldheim, former secretary-general of the United Nations (1971–82) and president of Austria (1986–92), renewed these concerns. The emergence of the ultranationalist Austrian Freedom Party in the 1980s, led by Jörg Haider, raised the specter of fascism again in 2000 as the party joined the governing coalition. Some have characterized popular support of these rightist views as a neofascist movement. This support has even threatened Austria's participation in the European Union.

Switzerland's historic neutrality helped it escape the devastation of World War II. It also protected its highly respected financial and banking sectors. Recent revelations indicate, however, that the banks accepted many deposits of funds stripped from European Jews during the Holocaust and looted from the countries conquered by Germany. They were slow to return these funds to rightful owners and their heirs, thus creating controversy. As part of that debate, the Swiss were further accused of assisting the Germans during World War II, thus violating the principles of neutrality that they claimed as the basis of their foreign and security policies. The issues discussed in this book have been defined by the populations of the countries discussed, so the compilation of them should not be construed as a criticism, much less an attack on any of these countries or on their governments. Indeed, I hope that the chapters convey recognition of the sincerity with which these countries work through the problems of our complex modern times.

ACKNOWLEDGMENTS

I am grateful to Wendi Schnaufer of the Greenwood Press for the invitation to undertake this challenging project and for her guidance and patience throughout the writing process. Indiana University East has been supportive by providing some reassigned time for the research and writing. Research librarian Mark Bay was especially helpful with the initial stages of my research, and IU East's interlibrary loan librarian Marcia Sloan has helped put valuable materials in my hands when I needed them. The consulates of Germany, Austria, and Switzerland have been generous with help and information. Gisela Fort, Mardi Bergen, Virginia Ratliff, Ron Carter, and George Blakey have offered sage advice, moral support, and encouragement throughout the project. Brenda Scott was my meticulous and helpful coordinator. They all have my thanks and my assurance that they are in no way responsible for any of the shortcomings of this book.

GERMANY

1

THE POLITICS OF GERMAN UNIFICATION

BACKGROUND

National Unity Has Always Been a Problem for Germany

Unlike France, Spain, or Russia, Germany did not emerge from the Middle Ages with a centralized monarchy in a territorially defined state. Instead, hundreds of separate sovereign states were headed by hereditary families or bishops or the senates of the imperial free cities, all loosely joined into the Holy Roman Empire. The number and frontiers of these states changed constantly through war, heredity, and diplomacy. In 1800 there were more than 300 separate sovereign German states, most with hereditary rulers. The Habsburg dynasty of Austria reigned over the empire from the thirteenth century until its demise in the early nineteenth century, but these emperors kept their position by not challenging the individual states' autonomy.

Napoleon and Germany

When Napoleon took over France, he used conquest, threat, and bribery to force a reorganization of the German states. The 1803 agreement, the Reichsdeputationshauptschluss (Imperial Delegations' Final Recess), reduced their number to 39, including four bishoprics and six imperial free cities. He formed them into a Rheinbund (Confederation of the Rhine) under the rule of the French Empire. The Habsburg ruler, excluded, had to change his own title to "emperor of Austria." When Napoleon was finally defeated in 1815, the Congress of Vienna convened to restore Europe to its prerevolutionary form, except for Germany. They reorganized it into 35 states joined in the

Deutsches Bund (German Confederation) under the conservative leadership of the Austrian emperor. The local hereditary rulers remained in place.

Revolutions of 1848

In 1848 a popular revolutionary movement arose across the German states to unify them into a constitutional monarchy. As the local rulers trembled and retreated before the often violent street mobs, outspoken members of the educated elite designed election processes and met in Frankfurt to write a German constitution. The unification issue actually led to defeat of this revolution. The delegates divided into the Grossdeutsch (Great Germany) and Kleindeutsch (Little Germany) factions over whether or not to include Austria with its great numbers of non-German Hungarians and Slavs. As this debate shattered and weakened the movement, the aristocratic rulers recovered their confidence. In desperation a delegation from Frankfurt offered the leadership of the proposed state to the king of Prussia. He rejected it out of hand, and the revolution was suppressed.

The German Empire (1871–1918)

The unification issue was resolved, for the first time in Germany, through the resolute militarism of Prussia's minister-president Otto von Bismarck. His contrived, almost surgical wars with Denmark (1864) and Austria (1866) contained the conflicts and established Prussian leadership in central Europe. The first step toward unification was the formation of the Norddeutsches Bund (North German Confederation: all states but Baden, Bayern (Bavaria), and Württemberg [1867–71]) out of the Prussian alliance and its conquests north of the Main River. Austria was excluded; the Kleindeutsch principle had prevailed.

The Norddeutsches Bund signed a defensive alliance with the three southern German states of Bayern, Baden, and Württemberg, who agreed to support the Norddeutsches Bund if it were attacked. Bismarck was able to provoke France into such an attack, and the German states cooperated in the Franco-Prussian War (1870–71). On 18 January 1871, when assured of final victory over France, the rulers of the German states, including the southern ones, signed the treaty that marked the Reichsgründung (founding of the German Empire) and the *Kaiserproklamation* (proclamation of the German emperor). The king of Prussia was acknowledged as the Deutscher Kaiser (German emperor). The title was deliberately selected to indicate that he was first among peers but not supreme over his fellow heads of state (emperor of Germany). The hereditary rulers retained most of their local autonomy, and the empire had considerable resemblance to the former Deutsches Bund. But now, at least, the German national frontiers were clearly defined. They included the provinces of Alsace and Lorraine, taken from France in the war, with a mixed German and French population.

In their enthusiasm for unification at last the German people accepted the lack of public participation in designing the new state. The treaty became, de facto, the Constitution of the new Deutsches Reich (German Empire). The other European powers were deeply suspicious of this newly enlarged state, especially when it began building a powerful navy and looking for colonies in Africa and the Pacific. Isolated by Britain, France, and their allies, this unified Reich joined Austria in initiating World War I. The war destroyed Europe's economy and ended in stalemate. The last Kaiser, William II, abdicated on 9 November 1918. On 11 November the combatants agreed to an armistice and cease-fire, calling for a conference in early 1919 to forge the peace.

The Weimar Republic (1919–33)

Excited and jubilant liberals of the majority Social Democrat Party proclaimed a national republic. Although the war ended with an armistice, the peacetime diplomacy of France, England, and the United States spelled diplomatic defeat for the Germans, who were not allowed to participate in the peace negotiations. The Treaty of Versailles (1919) was vengeful. It forced the Germans to accept full responsibility for the war, to pay 32 billion marks in reparations, to demilitarize, to accept foreign military occupation, and to relinquish significant frontier territory to France as well as to the new Poland. The popular outrage was so great that the republic's Nationalversammlung (National Assembly), elected to write the new constitution, had to flee Berlin for Weimar. The liberal new constitution went into effect on 11 August 1919, but the dream of political democracy was fleeting.

The Weimar Verfassung (Constitution) established a cabinet-style government that gave unprecedented new authority to the Reichstag (Parliament). Cabinet ministers had to be elected members of the Reichstag. The Verhältniswahlrecht (Law of Proportional Representation: 1 representative for each 150,000 votes cast for a party) for the Reichstag gave each political party representation according to its percentage of the total national vote. The result was the proliferation of political parties—more than 15 of them competing for 423 seats in the first election. These parties reflected not only the political spectrum from conservative to liberal, but also the regionalism that had so persistently plagued German history. The largest party in the first Reichstag gained only 165 seats, which meant that it had to bargain for support in order to build a majority coalition cabinet. Once built, the coalitions were always precarious owing to parties' threats to withdraw from the cabinet and bring down the government. During the brief history of the Weimar Republic the stalemates and paralysis of party in-fighting forced nine national elections between June 1920 and November 1933. Despite its idealistic constitution, the Weimar Republic was not able to help the Germans learn how to govern themselves.

The Reichstag proved unable to solve the problems imposed by the draconic peace, the drastic inflation of 1923, and the 1929 depression. Voters gravitated toward the parties that promised the most extreme solutions, especially Adolf Hitler's extremist Nationalsocialistische Deutsche Arbeiterpartei (National Socialist German Workers' Party, the Nazi Party) and the Kommunistische Partei Deutschlands (German Communist Party). The Reichspräsident (president) was often forced to use emergency dictatorial powers when the Reichstag was incapable of functioning.

Hitler and World War II

The Weimar Republic actually died quietly in early 1932, when the president appointed a cabinet of members who did not sit in the Reichstag. In the elections of November 1932 the Nazis gained the largest bloc of seats in the Reichstag. Ironically, Reichspräsident Paul von Hindenburg actually restored constitutional practice by appointing the Nazi Party leader, Adolf Hitler, as chancellor of Germany in January 1933. It took only a crisis, the suspicious Reichstag fire in February 1933, for Hitler to declare a state of emergency and thus to gain dictatorial powers from the legislature. He never relinquished them. Among other actions taken to establish his dictatorship, Hitler dissolved the state governments to create Germany's first totally unitary government, which became the vehicle for his terrifying military campaign to subject Germany, then all of Europe, to his Drittes Reich (Third Reich). He deliberately started World War II and presided over the genocide of the Jews, the disabled, Roma (Gypsies), Jehovah's Witnesses, and other minorities in Europe.

The Russian Counteroffensive

Although the Germans controlled much of northern Europe between 1940 and 1942, the Soviet Russian forces began a successful counterattack in 1943 along the eastern front and by April 1945 drove into the heart of Berlin itself. The Allied landing on France's Normandy coast in June 1944 opened up the western front, which crossed the Rhine in March 1945. Faced with inevitable defeat, Hitler committed suicide on 30 April 1945, and both fronts surrendered unconditionally in the following week.

Allied Occupation and Division of Germany

The Allies were determined to weaken the German state by dividing it up into zones for allied military occupation, demilitarizing it, de-Nazifying it, and democratizing it. On 5 June 1945 they sectioned Germany into four zones based on its 1937 borders. The British controlled northwestern Germany; the Soviets occupied east of the Elbe River, including the former capital, Berlin; the Americans controlled the southwestern region centered on Frankfurt and München (Munich); and the French held a Rhineland sector with the cities of Koblenz and Freiburg. Berlin was also divided into four sectors under the Inter-Allied Control Council. In addition, the German lands east of the Oder and Neisse Rivers were assigned to Poland as compensation for lands Russia took from Poland's eastern frontiers.

The Allies agreed that each occupying force was responsible for its own sector, but that, in principle, Germany would be treated as an economic whole. In reality, this unity proved to be unworkable. The Americans and British restored local political procedures and educational programs emphasizing democracy. They also encouraged local trade and a market economy.

The Soviets, on the other hand, began dismantling many factories and shipping them home as war reparations. They assigned the remainder of the property to the Soviet Military Administration for Germany (SMAD) and seized all bank assets. SMAD next nationalized more than 8 million acres of agricultural land to carve out some large cooperative farms and to distribute small plots to farmers and refugees. On 11 June 1945 SMAD completely reformed the political structure of its territories, recognizing only four "antifascist" parties: the Communist Party, the Social Democratic Party, the Liberal Party, and the Christian Democratic Party. They centralized the schools and began teaching a prosocialist curriculum. In April 1946 Communists and Social Democrats merged to form the majority Sozialistische Einheitspartei Deutschlands (SED, German Social Unity Party), which became the primary vehicle for political power. Thus, from the outset, East Germany was incorporated economically and politically into the Soviet sphere and system.

France initiated similar measures in its sectors, extracting reparations in the form of industrial plants and equipment, introducing a French-style school curriculum and ignoring the efforts of the British and American authorities to cooperate in the three western zones. They took control of the mineral-rich Saarland with the hope of eventually persuading the population to join France.

The Nuremberg Trials began in August 1945 to prosecute 22 of the major Nazi leaders for war crimes; these trials were the last major collaborative effort between the four powers in occupied Germany. At the same time in the three western zones, efforts to establish democratic government supported the reemergence of political parties. As the Social Democratic Party, Christian Democratic Union, Christian Social Union, Liberal Democratic Party, Democratic People's Party, and Free Democratic Party organized, they gained membership that crossed the zonal boundaries.

Tensions between the east and the west soon emerged. In 1946 the Americans halted deliveries of reparations from their sector to the Soviet Zone. As the occupation costs mounted, the British and Americans agreed next to merge their zones on 1 January 1947 into one economic unit, designated

Bizonia. (The French declined initially but joined later, in April 1949.) The Russians retaliated by suspending delivery of agricultural products to the western zones. When the western zones adopted a single currency in June 1948, the Russians blocked ground access to Berlin. The west responded with the famous "Berlin Air Lift" to supply the city until the Russians restored access after a year.

The Cold War Split Germany in Two

The Americans included western Germany in the Marshall Plan for European economic recovery (1948–52); the Soviet Union responded with the Council for Mutual Economic Cooperation (COMECON) (January 1949), integrating the East German economy with those of the other Soviet bloc states. Once France joined Bizonia in 1949, the three western zones were permitted to unify as the Bundesrepublik Deutschland (BRD, German Federal Republic, population 45 million), which adopted its constitutional Grundgesetz (Basic Law) on 23 May 1949. The Soviets, in turn, recognized the East German Deutsche Demokratische Republik (DDR, German Democratic Republic, population 18 million) with its own constitution on 7 October 1949. Each state claimed to be the sole legitimate heir to German national sovereignty.

In fact the two new states were far from independent. Each state still accommodated occupation forces. The western allies agreed in October 1954 to restore full sovereignty to the BRD. As soon as that decision was formalized on 5 May 1955, West Germany joined the western military alliance, the North Atlantic Treaty Organization (NATO). In March 1954 the Soviet Union granted the DDR full sovereignty, and the Warsaw Pact alliance of the eastern Europeans came into being on 14 May 1955; East German army contingents were authorized in January 1956.

The Two German Republics

Throughout the 1950s and 1960s the duality of German history symbolized the Cold War. Politicians in both Germanys gave lip service to reunification, but each country strove to prove that its political, cultural, and economic systems were superior to those of its rival. The BRD was praised for the "economic miracle" of its capitalist recovery in the 1950s. The DDR became a model socialist state, with collectivized agriculture, state-owned industries, centralized economic planning, and unified party government. It became the leading economy in the Soviet bloc. Soviet leader Josef Stalin's proposal in 1952 to hold all-German elections was rejected by the west. In September 1955 the West Germans announced they would sever diplomatic relations with any country that recognized the DDR. International summit conferences in Geneva (1955) and Vienna (1961) addressed German issues but produced no plan for reunification.

As the competition mounted, the East German economy suffered by comparison with the West German economy, and workers began to leave the east for higher paying jobs in the west. In August 1961 the East Germans began the construction of a wall around the western occupation sectors of Berlin and along the frontiers of the two states in order to prevent the brain drain of this skilled workforce. In 1968 the DDR revised its Constitution, and the new version held no clause providing for eventual reunification of the two German states. The separation was complete; unification appeared to be a totally lost cause. The West Germans made that explicit with the Hallstein Doctrine in September 1955. The BRD declared itself to be the only legitimate German state and threatened to break diplomatic relations with any state that recognized the DDR.

The First Efforts at Reconciliation

West German chancellor Willi Brandt's Ostpolitik (Eastern Policy) in 1970 initiated the BRD's efforts to reduce the tensions. Brandt, a Social Democrat and former mayor of West Berlin, approached the Russians, however, not the East Germans. Brandt offered to accept the Oder-Neisse River border of Poland, renouncing any German territorial claims east of that line as well as the use of force to change borders. On 7 December 1970 the two countries signed the Peace of Warsaw on those bases. The DDR was not a party to this pact, which established its eastern boundary. In 1972 Brandt and Erich Honecker, his East German counterpart, signed the Basic Treaty, through which the two Germanys agreed to recognize each other diplomatically and to establish the normal state-to-state relations of sovereign nations. Honecker introduced his Abgrenzung (Separation Policy), which emphasized the historical and territorial differences between the two states and affirmed the DDR's close association with the Russians. Nevertheless, the two German states began cooperating on trade, and the East Germans began to permit family visits across the boundaries. But after the Helsinki Human Rights Agreements of 1973, the DDR government still denied travel permits to more than 120,000 of its citizens.

Gorbachev's Glasnost and Perestroika

By the 1980s the entire eastern European bloc began an economic decline, unable to compete with the technology and expansion of the west. The DDR government began to pressure its labor force for higher rates of productivity, which created unrest. Some workers invaded foreign embassies, demanding asylum until they could emigrate. In the Soviet Union Mikhail Gorbachev assumed power in 1985. A Communist who was a generation younger than all his predecessors, he believed that the time had come to reform the centralized state economy. He called for analytical discussion (glasnost) of these systems in order to restructure them (perestroika) for greater efficiency and productivity. Although he intended these processes to be led by his Communist Party, the critique expanded widely through the state. Gorbachev realized that the Soviet Union had to encourage its satellite states to reform, too. This challenge led to surprising changes that resulted ultimately in the collapse of the Soviet system and the unification of the two German states.

Glasnost in the DDR

In the DDR protests mounted against the travel restrictions and called for freedom of the press and religion and for other civil liberties in general. Honecker's government only took a harder stand. Thus, in spring of 1989, when Hungary and Austria agreed to open their mutual border, hundreds of East Germans applied for travel permits to eastern bloc cities, where they asked for asylum. When Hungary opened its border in August, more than 24,500 East Germans sped across it into Austria. Others who remained in the DDR formed new opposition political groups to demand government reforms. Significantly, this political opposition was not a revolutionary movement to overturn the government, but a popular demand for glasnost and perestroika efforts locally.

The Fall of the Berlin Wall

When on 7 October 1989 the DDR celebrated the fortieth anniversary of the nation's founding, Gorbachev was on hand to hear Honecker state that the republic was still a "bulwark against imperialism." But throughout the DDR people were demanding free elections. They held peaceful candlelight vigils that filled the streets with hundreds of thousands of participants. Shocked by the size of the movement, the ruling SED Party replaced Honecker with Egon Krenz, who announced that die Wende (the change) in leadership would bring reform, but the candlelight demonstrations continued. Gorbachev decided not to interfere; the Russian troops were ordered to remain in their barracks instead of helping DDR police clear the streets. On 8 November Krenz reluctantly recognized the new political parties; the following day he ended the travel restrictions. On that evening, 9 November 1989, the Berlin Wall tumbled as jubilant celebrators on both sides joined hands across it.

The West German Strategy for Unification

Helmut Kohl, the chancellor of the BRD, responded quickly when the wall fell, offering aid to the East Germans if they reformed their economic and political structures. He swiftly submitted a Ten Point Plan to his Bundestag (legislature) for cooperation with the DDR to normalize transportation and communications as well as to introduce a market economy there as soon as possible. The plan, which called for a confederation of the two states, did not directly address reunification of Germany.

The East German Dilemma

In the DDR the political dictatorship of the SED crumbled as members fled to join new parties: the New Forum, Democracy Now, Democratic Awakening, and the New Left Coalition. Krenz resigned, and Hans Modrow replaced him as head of state. He met with the new party leaders on 7 December 1989 to discuss plans for a new constitution and open elections. The Soviet Union, however, indicated that it still recognized two separate republics. Addressing the Central Committee in early December, Gorbachev affirmed that the DDR was still an important part of the Warsaw Pact, although it should be possible for the two Germanys to have closer relations. He warned U.S. president George Bush against trying to achieve unification by force. But as the pro-Soviet governments across eastern Europe began to crumble, Soviet influence fell with them.

The Constitutional Issue

The West German Grundgesetz, when drafted in 1949, was considered an interim document for the period of occupation and separation of the German states. Its preamble encouraged *"das gesamte Deutsche Volk... in freier Selbstbestimmung die Einheit und Freiheit Deutschlands zu vollenden"* (all the German people, in free self-determination, to bring about the unity and independence of Germany). Accordingly, it optimistically included two options for eventual reunification: (1) either dissolve the interim BRD and write a constitution for a new unified BRD (Article 146);[1] or (2) incorporate the eastern *Länder* (states) into the existing BRD by extending the jurisdiction of the Grundgesetz to each, with their agreement (Article 23).[2] Kohl was determined to take the latter route in order to maintain the integrity of the BRD. The East German Constitution held no provision for unification; the only possible route there would be for a two-thirds vote of its Volkskammer to dissolve the DDR and join the existing western government through Article 23.

The Treaty Requirements

Technically, however, the four occupying powers still reserved the right to decide about German reunification and made this claim clear in a joint declaration on 11 December 1989. Thus, on 19 December Modrow met with Kohl, and, with the public on both sides calling for reunification, they agreed to ask the Conference for Security and Cooperation in Europe to help deal with the issue. Representatives of both NATO and the Warsaw Pact approved this method again in February 1990. Elections to the DDR Volkskammer were scheduled for March to assure that a freely elected DDR government participated in the negotiations.

The East German Response

Twenty-four political parties competed in the March 1990 elections, the first free elections in eastern Germany since 1932. The balloting was basically a referendum on unification, but the East Germans alone did not decide the outcome. The campaign was fought out among the old and new East German parties, with many candidates running under the sponsorship of West German parties. The East Germans, inexperienced in open elections, were overwhelmed by the vigorous intervention of the political veterans from the western parties. West German chancellor Helmut Kohl campaigned six times in support of the Alliance for Germany, a conservative coalition of the western Christian Democratic Union, the eastern Social Awakening, and the Democratic Social Union. West German political party organizations spent some 7.5 million marks on the DDR elections.[3] When all the votes were counted, 57.3 percent of the vote went to parties supporting unification. The premier of the new cabinet, Lothar de Maizière, who ran as a member of the Christian Democratic Union, had been actively supported by Chancellor Kohl. It is not surprising, therefore, that in his inaugural speech he spoke in favor of reunification via Article 23 of the Grundgesetz. That process provided absolutely no opportunity for the East Germans to propose revisions of the Constitution. The West Germans were similarly ignored.

Economic Issues Resolved First

Thus oriented, the first step was the negotiation of the Treaty of 18 May 1990 between the Federal Republic of Germany and the German Democratic Republic Establishing a Monetary, Economic, and Social Union the Economic Treaty.[4] By starting with economic issues, the strategy effectively preserved the BRD intact while eliminating the 40-year-old social and economic policies of the former DDR. Kohl used the economic lure of the west superbly, knowing that it was one of the major sources of tension between the East German people and their government.

The End of the DDR

The Economic Treaty took effect on 1 July 1990. In August the newly elected East German Volkskammer voted to join the BRD according to the terms of Article 23 of the Basic Law. The appropriate legislation passed in both governments, but next had to be authorized by the four Allied powers.

Young Germans run through the Brandenburg Gate in Berlin, carrying a flag decorated with the coat of arms of the 16 German states, Thursday, 3 October 1996, during a parade marking the sixth anniversary of the German unification. (AP/Wide Worlds Photo)

The western powers acted quickly. To forestall Russian concerns about a unified Germany in NATO, the NATO London Declaration of 6 July offered cooperation with the eastern European states, reaffirmed its peaceful principles, and promised a reduction in military force. Kohl then went to the Caucasus to meet with Gorbachev. On 16 July they inked an agreement that guaranteed that Germany would pay the costs of the withdrawal of the 380,000 Russian troops from Germany through 1994 and of their resettling in Russia. Kohl also agreed to reduce the total number of German troops to 370,000, with the understanding that the German military could participate in collective security actions of NATO.

With Russia's reluctant assent the two German states approved the Unification Treaty of 31 August 1990. In September the "Two Plus Four" Talks (the two Germanys and the four Allied Powers) endorsed the actions. The East German Länder (States) Brandenburg, Mecklenburg-Vorpommern, Sachsen (Saxony), Sachsen-Anhalt, and Thüringen became part of the BRD when the treaty went into force on 2 October 1990. Symbolic of this change,

Berlin was declared the new national capital. Once again Germany was united by treaty, not by a united effort of the German people. There was no review of the Constitution; there was no national referendum on the treaty. The Volkskammer, which voted to dissolve the DDR, was heavily infiltrated by the parties of the BRD. Just as in 1871, Germany had been consolidated by the largest and most powerful state.[5]

ISSUES

Unification Was Actually the BRD's Conquest of the DDR

Agree:

BRD chancellor Kohl took ruthless advantage of the political turmoil in the DDR. The protests there were not a revolution: the people had wanted to reform the government, not overthrow it. Kohl sent in well-financed conservative politicians and intervened, himself, in the political election of a separate sovereign country by promising economic benefits through unification. He and his operatives made no effort to find out what the East German people might like to retain from their society if they joined with the BRD. The March 1990 election results showed that 42 percent of the voters, a substantial core of the East Germans, were not ready to abandon the DDR. But Kohl's arrogant conservatism would permit no compromise. He detested the Soviet-style state and even induced his East German political puppet, Lothaire de Maizière, to betray it through denunciation on the eve of signing the Unification Treaty.

> We leave behind a system which called itself democratic without being so. Its stigmas were the enslavement of the spirit and enforced ideology, the wall and barbed wire, economic ruin and environmental destruction as well as ideological tutelage and fermented distrust. That tyranny has been replaced by the rule of law, democracy and human dignity.[6]

The annexation of the eastern Länder through Article 23 was an act of conquest. It totally stripped the East Germans of their political and economic structures. The utter rejection of their achievements—their success in making the DDR the leading economy of the Soviet bloc and their successful and peaceful pressure to bring down the Honecker government—further stripped them of their history and their pride. Forcing the Grundgesetz and the Economic Treaty on the unprepared DDR was a major Cold War victory. Kohl handed the East Germans a diplomatic defeat as devastating as that of the Versailles Treaty.

Kohl followed up this defeat with policies that aimed to remove tens of thousands of East German administrators and educators from their positions and to replace them with conservative employees from the BRD. The DDR was thoroughly occupied by the "Wessies" (westerners), who claimed ideological superiority and political control. Political freedom came at the expense of jobs, income, and basic necessities such as housing, as prices went up after privatization.

Kohl pressed to use Article 23 to avoid political controversy in the BRD. Some people in both the DDR and the BRD called for using Article 146 as the mechanism for unification. They argued that significant differences between the two states needed to be examined and resolved. Simple "annexation" via Article 23 would deny meaningful self-determination to the peoples of both states. Kohl got around that objection by insisting that the DDR accept the Economic Treaty first. Embedded in it were all the principles of capitalism and competition that would give the wealthier West Germans every advantage, thus preempting much of the discussion of constitutional issues. The insecure, politically compromised leaders of the DDR bowed to his pressure because there was no other option.

Disagree:

The elections of May 1990 were a clear indication that the East Germans were eager to join the BRD. But the East German Constitution offered no provision or for unification. Article 23 of the Grundgesetz offered the fastest mechanism for fulfilling their hope. Unification could be quickly implemented by the agreement of both states, and it would end the crisis situation building in the DDR. The elections of 1990 gave almost 60 percent of the vote to candidates calling for unification. The newly elected representatives in the East German Volkskammer voluntarily voted to replace their own constitution with the Grundgesetz. That can hardly be called a conquest or annexation. The Grundgesetz had proven to be a solid foundation for the BRD, in no need of significant amendment. If the Grundgesetz were invalidated, then many federal laws and rulings of the constitutional court might well come into question, which might lead to instability in both states. Thus, in the interests of speed and stability, Article 23 was the most appropriate mechanism for unification.

Unification by Treaty Rather Than by Constitutional Convention Was Antidemocratic

Agree:

In a careful analysis Peter Quint examines the constitutional issues of unification.[7] There were no public forums or constitutional decisions on the economic, social, and political structures of the newly configured state. There was no serious consideration of the abruptness of the changes to be imposed on the east. Nor was there consideration of whether some of the policies and structures of the DDR might have been introduced into unified Germany.

Quint further points out (51) that even after unification through Article 23 it would have been possible to invoke Article 146 to amend the Constitution. That is the hallmark of a democratic process. The use of treaties rather than constitutional revision meant that the 17 million Germans in the eastern Länder lost their voice in determining the nature of the new state. Not only were they forced immediately to convert to an unfamiliar system that ended their state social and economic security systems, but they also were constantly outvoted by the West German political majorities in both the Bundestag and the Bundesrat (Federal Council) when they expressed their concerns and alternatives. This preemption led to disillusionment and discontent with the unification process, and it contributed to alienation among "Ossies" (easterners) and Wessies in unified Germany. The constant monopoly of the goals of the West German majority has retarded the development of the eastern states and prolonged the tension between the two parts of Germany.

Disagree:

There was nothing secret or mysterious about the Grundgesetz. East Germans had long been familiar with it, and they eagerly sought its guarantees of freedom and equality. It was not up to Chancellor Kohl to prepare the East Germans for unification; that was the responsibility of their own government. The discussions were intense and lively after November 1989. The people voted in March 1990, and they could have voted for candidates who wanted to preserve the DDR. Instead their elective representatives expressed the popular will when they voted to dissolve the socialist state and to join the BRD.

It is illogical to say that the problems of the transitional period are a reflection of an antidemocratic process. The treaty on the economy did signal significant changes for the East Germans, but all changes had been carefully considered. Their impact was well anticipated and efforts made to prepare the East Germans for them. Prime Minister Lothar de Maizière repeated the warning and the accompanying reassurances on the eve of the unification:

> I well realize that many citizens are now faced with problems. The new currency, the economic reorganization and the introduction of a new political system naturally cause difficulties. Nevertheless, we must make the best of this opportunity in spite of what others say. We must see our problems in relation to our past—and to the incomparably greater difficulties confronting our Eastern neighbors.[8]

Most East Germans have known only a one-party dictatorial state. It is not surprising that they expected the federal government to step in and fix their complaints. The BRD government has provided substantial funding and retraining opportunities to help integrate the East Germans into the unified system. But it has many constituencies. The easterners have to learn the ways of real democracy, which requires effort to formulate a program and cooperation to achieve it.

The Western Powers Forced Germany to Abandon Its Nonmilitary Posture as Their Price for Unification

Agree:

Outvoting the Russians three to one, the western powers required the newly unified German state to become a more active partner in NATO. The unification of Germany confirmed the end of the Cold War in Europe with a victory of the west. The subsequent collapse of the Soviet Union and Warsaw Pact assured that the United States and its allies in NATO controlled the continent. Indeed, it might be said that the rationale for the North Atlantic military defensive alliance was gone. Yet the London Declaration of 6 July 1990 proclaimed the renewal of NATO and its perpetuation. The eastern European states were put on notice of this intent. They subsequently were invited to join, but only if they could meet the alliance's requirements and gain members' approval. NATO is now expanding its activities into peacekeeping operations in the Balkan regions. Since unification, German troops, which previously could not operate outside of Germany in a war zone, have come under fire as part of the peacekeeping forces in the Balkans. More recently (beginning in 2001) they have been called upon to participate in U.S. military operations in Afghanistan.

Disagree:

As a fully sovereign nation, Germany has the right to engage in active diplomacy, including the military responsibilities of an alliance. The Cold War competition between the U.S. and Soviet systems restricted that sovereignty. There were trained military forces in both republics prior to unification; there is a well-trained and equipped military now. Germany is mature and responsible enough to begin taking its share of the burden for world peace and security. The Kohl government began the process, and the Gerhardt Schröder government, despite the traditional pacifism associated with German socialism, has continued it.

To be sure, Germany's role in NATO offers the United States a firm military partner on the European continent. But from another perspective some suggest that without NATO's controlling hand Germany might be tempted once again to try to take over Europe in the future. Similarly, the international agreements prevent Germany from developing or using weapons of mass destruction. Germany is now working within the revised mission of NATO to assist with peacekeeping in the Balkans and with the antiterrorist campaign in Afghanistan. It is evident, however, that without the constraints of the Cold War, Germany is assuming a more prominent international military presence than it did in the last half of the twentieth century.

QUESTIONS AND ACTIVITIES

1. Not all Germans, in both the East and the West, favored unification in 1990. Divide into four groups. Assume it is 1989. Let two groups brainstorm reasons for and against unification from the West German perspective, and the other two groups brainstorm the same points from the East German perspective. List the reasons and some evidence to support each point of view. Conduct a debate in class and hold a secret ballot on which course to take.

2. Presume that Chancellor Kohl and Premier de Maizière had decided to unite the two German republics by convening elected representatives to write a new constitution as called for in Article 146 of the Grundgesetz. Review the current document (you can find it in both German and English versions on the Web at http://www.lexadin.nl/wlg/legis/nofr/eur/lxwedui.htm) and consider whether there are other issues in the Constitution that might be revised to make unification work better. Write a short paper listing your recommendations and your reasons for making them.

3. Make a list of the political parties with delegates in the Bundestag. Check their electoral results on the German Federal Statistical Office Web site (http://www.destatis.de) to determine whether these parties still reflect an East-West split. Determine which parties are making the best progress toward representing a national constituency. Report your analysis to the class.

4. To seat delegates in the Bundestag, political parties have to gain 5 percent of the national vote. Using data from the state elections, identify the small political parties that do not qualify for representation in the Bundestag. Check out their Web pages to find out about their party history and platform. Write a short paper analyzing which parties seem to be protesting against aspects of the unification.

5. Do some role playing. Form small groups that resemble families with retired grandparents, working parents, and teenage children. Be sure to have families from both eastern and western Germany. Hold a family discussion about the impact of unification on the lives of each generation.

6. Some of Germany's neighbors feared the rebirth of German political domination of Europe after unification. Research Germany's relations with Europe since 1990, and write a short paper using examples of policies and actions that should reassure them of Germany's intention to maintain the peace and stability of Europe.

7. The Two-Plus-Four Treaty was necessary diplomatically to end Allied control in Germany. Discuss what might have occurred if Gorbachev had decided to work with DDR premier Honecker to suppress the peaceful uprisings in September and October 1989. Would unification have occurred anyway? Would the East Germans have had a stronger or weaker voice in negotiations with the BRD and the Allies?

NOTES

1. "Artikel 146 *(Geltungsdauer des Grundgesetzes): Dieses Grundgesetz verliert seine Gültigketi an dem Tage, an dem eine Verfassung in Kraft tritt, die von dem deutschen Volke in freier Entscheidung beschlossen worden ist"* (Duration of the Basic Law): This Basic Law expires on the day on which a Constitution comes into force which was freely enacted by the German people. Ferdinand Siebert, ed., *Von Frank-*

furt nach Bonn: Die deutschen Verfassungen 1849–1949 (Frankfurt am Main: Verlag Moritz Diesterweg, 1958), 115.

2. "Artikel 23 *(Geltungsbebiet des Grundgesetzes): Dieses Grundgesetz gilt zunächst im Gebiete der Länder Baden, Bayern, Bremen, Grossberlin, Hamburg, Hessen, Niedersachsen, Nordrhein-Westfalen, Rheinland-Pfalz, Schleswig-Holstein, Württemberg-Baden und Württemberg-Hohenzollern. In anderen Teilen Deutschlands ist es nach deren Beitritt in Kraft zu setzen."* (Territory under the Jurisdiction of the Basic Law) This basic law is valid in the states of Baden, Bavaria, Bremen, Greater Berlin, Hamburg, Hesse, Lower Saxony, North Rhine-Westfalia, Rhineland-Pfalz, Schleswit-Holstein, Wurtemberg-Baden and Wurtemberg-Hohenzollern. *"In other parts of Germany it will take effect upon their joining [the Federal Republic]."* Ibid., 93, emphasis added.

3. German Information Center, *Focus on... the German Unification Process* (New York: German Information Center, 1990), 6.

4. Press and Information Office of the Federal Government, *The Unification of Germany in 1990: Documentation* (Bonn: Press and Information Office, 1991), 13.

5. Ibid., 35.

6. "[Broadcast] Address by GDR Prime Minister Lothar de Maizière on the Eve of German Unity, 2 October 1990," and "Speech by the Then Prime Minister of the German Democratic Republic, Lothar de Maizière, at the Ceremony on the Eve of German Unity, Berlin, 2 October 1990," in Press and Information Office, *The Unification of Germany in 1990,* 139, 143.

7. Peter E. Quint, *The Imperfect Union: Constitutional Structures of German Unification* (Princeton, N.J.: Princeton University Press, 1997).

8. "Speech by the Then Prime Minister of the German Democratic Republic," in Press and Information Office, *The Unification of Germany in 1990,* 142–45.

SUGGESTED READINGS

A wide variety of excellent general history texts is available for study of the first German unification. Hajo Holborn's three-volume study *A History of Modern Germany* (Princeton, N.J.: Princeton University Press, 1982), in particular volume 2, *1648–1840,* and volume 3, *1840–1945,* offers the standard historical background. Koppel S. Pinson's *Modern Germany, Its History and Civilization,* 2nd ed. (Prospect Heights, Ill.: Waveland Press, 1989), Otto Plfance's *The Unification of Germany 1848–1971* (Malabar, Fla.: Robert E. Krieger, 1979) and Eleanor L. Turk, *The History of Germany* (Westport, Conn.: Greenwood Press, 1999) also are excellent starting points. Dietrich Orlow's *A History of Modern Germany: 1871 to Present,* 3rd ed. (Englewood Cliffs, N.J.: Prentice Hall, 1986) and Arthur Rosenberg's *Imperial Germany: The Birth of the German Republic,* trans. Ian F. D. Marner (Boston: Beacon Press, 1966), offer the German perspective on the Second Empire.

David Child's *Germany in the Twentieth Century* (New York: HarperCollins, 1991) provides an excellent introductory overview. S. William Halperin's *Germany Tried Democracy* (New York: Norton, 1946), and Erich Eyck's *History of the Weimar Republic,* 2 vols. (New York: Atheneum, 1970), present the problems and tragedy of the Weimar Republic. Martin Brozat's *Hitler and the Collapse of Weimar Germany* (Leamington Spa, U.K.: Berg, 1987) and A. J. Nicholls's *Weimar and the Rise of Hitler,* 3rd ed. (New York: St. Martin's Press, 1991), discuss the awful consequences of the failure of the republic. Gerhard Weinberg's *Germany, Hitler, and World War II* (Cambridge: Cambridge University Press, 1995) offers the perspectives of the foremost academic scholar of the period.

An excellent introduction to the post–World War II occupation of Germany is John H. Backer's *The Decision to Divide Germany* (Durham, N.C.: Duke University Press, 1978). Harold Zink's *The United States in Germany 1944–55* (Princeton: Van Norstrand, 1957) and John P. Nettl's *The Eastern Zone and Soviet Policy in Germany* (New York: Oxford, 1951) sketch the different occupation strategies of the Cold War antagonists.

Mary Fulbrook's *The Two Germanies, 1945–1990* (Atlantic Highlands, N.J.: Humanities Press International, 1992) gives a concise overview of the two German republics. The political vitality of the BRD is reviewed in Tony Burkett, *Parties and Elections in West Germany: The Search for Stability* (New York: St. Martin's Press, 1975), and in Kendall L. Baker, Russell J. Dalton, and Kai Hildebrandt, *Germany Transformed: Political Culture and the New Politics* (Cambridge, Mass.: Harvard University Press, 1981). Arthur W. McCardle and A. Bruch Boenau's *East Germany: A New German Nation under Socialism?* (Lanham, Md.: University Press of America, 1984) lets the East German authors speak for themselves.

The events of 1989 that led to unification of the two republics are treated in Pekka Kalevi Hamalainen, *Uniting Germany: Actions and Reaction* (Boulder, Colo.: Westview Press, 1994), and in Dieter Brosser, ed., *Uniting Germany: The Unexpected Challenge* (Providence, R.I.: Berg, 1992). Konrad Jarausch, *The Rush to German Unity* (New York: Oxford University Press, 1994), goes into greater detail about the problems posed by unification.

Significantly, there is not yet a body of writing by East German historians, many of whom lost their academic positions as the result of unification.

The discussion over the impact of unification continues. It can be monitored in the German-language press via http://libraries.mit.edu/guides/types/flnews.German.html.

2

THE ECONOMICS OF GERMAN UNIFICATION

BACKGROUND

The German Empire

When Otto von Bismarck constructed the German Empire in 1871, he also established the strongest economy on the European continent. Unification further spurred the linking of roads, railroads, barge canals, and postal and telegraph services, and it gave the empire a single currency. In this newly consolidated trading area, commerce and industry began to flourish; workers left the farms for jobs in the cities, and the German Industrial Revolution took off.[1]

This change in the basic economy restructured the workforce as well. People left the farms for city jobs; the professions and the public-service sectors of the workforce grew in order to serve them.[2] The industrial workforce and those with "independent means" grew rapidly during these years, reflecting a growth in investment and profits from both large and small concerns, and suggesting that the expansion of commercial surpluses had created a substantial and flourishing middle class. In 1880 the population of Germany was approximately 45.1 million. By 1910 prosperity had helped it climb to more than 64.5 million.

Urbanization led to the construction of crowded and unsanitary tenements as well as stores and factories. The rapid influx of workers resulted in such a large labor pool that employers had the advantage in setting low wages and long work hours as conditions for employment. Whereas lawyers earned an annual salary of 35,000 marks per year and a primary school teacher about 1,600, a machinist earned only about 270 per year.[3] The workers responded by organizing into trade unions and flocking to the new Social Democrat Party (SPD) with its Marxist pro-labor orientation. By 1877 there were almost half a million men voting for SPD candidates for the Reichstag (Parliament).

In 1878 there was an assassination attempt against Emperor William I, and Bismarck used it as the excuse for outlawing the SPD. This was the first part of his policy toward the working classes. The SPD's committees and press were shut down, but the Constitution and election laws still made it possible to vote for SPD candidates to the Reichstag, which made the pro-working-class party seem to be somewhat dangerous to the successive conservative governments of Germany.

Thus, the other part of Bismarck's policy began to take shape in 1883 with the introduction of a health insurance bill to protect the workers. His strategy was for the government to weaken the workers' demands through a paternalistic program of social insurance. In 1884 an accident insurance bill offered workers additional medical care and a pension in the event of full disability. The capstone was legislation for old-age and disability pensions for workers. Germany was the first industrial nation to provide this comprehensive social insurance for the working classes. Thereafter, this combination of government support for industry and social welfare for the workers was a permanent fixture of German domestic politics.

Bismarck's persecution of the Social Democrats only served to fuel support for the party. Its Reichstag contingent grew from only 2 seats in 1871 to 35 seats in 1890. In the 1890 elections it garnered more votes than any other party, although failure to redistrict the Reichstag to reflect urbanization denied them a majority in the legislature. The new young emperor, William II, decided to end the Antisocialists laws. When Bismarck protested, William accepted Bismarck's resignation and initiated his own "personal regime." The Social Democrats forged ahead nonetheless. In the 1912 elections, the last Reichstag election before World War I, they amassed 4.25 million of the approximately 14.5 million votes cast. With 110 of the 397 seats in the Reichstag, they were, for the first time, the largest faction in the legislature.

World War I

The aggressive diplomacy that led the German Empire into World War I in 1914 proved disastrous for the new nation. Germany financed its war effort by bonds, draining the wealth of its economy away for weapons of war and amassing staggering government debt. Army requisitions of food and supplies took these items away from the civilian population, and the shortages led to severe inflation. The land campaigns degenerated into a stalemate of trench warfare in France. But the British imposed a blockade on Germany that deepened the latter's economic domestic crisis. The impact of the war on the civilian home front was devastating, leading to strikes, a rampant black market, and famine. With 1,808,000 war dead and 4,247,000 wounded, Germany also suffered more casualties than any of the other belligerents. Shaken by failure, the emperor abdicated on 9 November 1918, and SPD leaders proclaimed a German republic. They expected to form the national government for the first time. The armistice of 11 November 1918 ended the war and was a relief for all the combatants. The Germans hoped it would bring a return to normality. In violation of the armistice, however, the British maintained their naval blockade of Germany, technically an act of war.

The Diplomatic Campaign

Unable to win on the battlefield, France and England secured support from the United States to win the peace. When the peace negotiations opened in Paris in on 18 January 1919 (the forty-eighth anniversary of the foundation of the German Empire), the representatives of the 27 Allied powers excluded the German delegation. Although the planned focus of the discussions was U.S. president Woodrow Wilson's idealistic Fourteen Points, what resulted was the collaboration of the power-wielding Council of Four (Woodrow Wilson of the United States, Georges Clemenceau of France, David Lloyd George of England, and Vittorio Orlando of Italy) to punish their enemies, especially Germany.

The Treaty of Versailles

The German delegations were finally summoned to Versailles on 7 May 1919 to receive the treaty drafted by the "Big Four." The treaty was draconic. It forced Germany to make territorial concessions of almost 13 percent of its prewar territory to Poland, France, and Belgium. This land contained nearly 75 percent of Germany's iron ore and more than 25 percent of it coal. The treaty further stripped Germany of its colonies, turning them over to the newly formed League of Nations as "mandates" to be governed by the Allies. Article 231 required Germany to admit sole responsibility for starting the war. As a result, Germany was prohibited from having any submarines or military planes and could maintain a professional army of only 100,000. Allied armies would occupy the left bank of the Rhine for 15 years, and the right bank was to be demilitarized to the depth of 30 miles. As a further consequence of the "war guilt," Germany was to pay for the civilian damage caused by the war: it was to make immediate reparations in cash and kind to the Allies, the total amount to be identified at a future date; by turning over all of its large merchant ships and part of its fishing fleet to the Allies; by shipping large amounts of coal to France, Belgium, and Italy; and by paying the costs of the Allied occupation.

When the Germans protested the treaty, they were told that the British blockade would be maintained and that hostilities might be resumed if they did not sign. There was no option. On 7 July 1919 the German government ratified the treaty. They had lost not only the war, but control over their economy as well.

The Weimar Republic

Instead of attaining the longed-for return to normality, the new German Republic became the very symbol of continuing crisis. The atmosphere in Berlin was chaotic with political protest, rebellions, and out-of-work veterans. The delegates elected to write a new national constitution had to flee the capital city for the more peaceful environment of the city of Weimar. They wrote a very idealistic constitution and drafted a voting law specifying proportional representation for the political parties. So many parties contested the ensuing election, however, that no majority was possible. The Social Democrats won 102 seats in the 459-member Reichstag and had the largest faction, so they formed the first coalition cabinet.

It was a dubious honor because the opposition conservatives and nationalists held the working-class party responsible for all the evils of the peace. Shock and anger at the humiliating peace treaty compounded the economic collapse caused by the war. Extremists on both the right and the left attempted to overthrow the constitutional government during the early years. Against this background of political tension the government attempted to guide German recovery and compliance with the Versailles Treaty.

The Ruhr Crisis of 1923

An acute economic crisis began on 9 January 1923, when Germany defaulted on a load of reparation coal to France. Raymond Poincaré, who headed the French government, had been elected on a platform of enforcing German reparations payment. He immediately ordered the French army to occupy the coal- and iron-rich Ruhr Valley of Germany. His Belgian allies followed suit, but the British and Italians declined to participate because the treaty did not identify this type of retaliation. The German government's response to the occupation was bold, canceling all further reparations deliveries and ordering the Ruhr workers out of the mines in a demonstration of passive resistance. All of the political parties supported this policy. To make it workable, the government promised to pay both the workers and their employers for the duration of the crisis.

This policy was dramatic and disastrous. To pay the cost of supporting the Ruhr, the German government resorted to inflation and to printing money to cover it. The value of the mark plummeted from 8.9 marks to the U.S. dollar to more than 190. The currency was so unreliable in its freefall that some cities began issuing their own currencies for local use. The French tried to stir up a separatist movement in the Rhine Valley, but German pride and nationalism defeated it. Nevertheless, with the German economy spiraling downward, the government of Gustav Stresemann was forced to end the passive resistance in August. By November the exchange rate was an incredible 4.2 billion marks to the dollar. It was during this crisis that Adolf Hitler led a Putsch (rebellion) to overthrow the government in the southern state of Bayern (Bavaria).

After Hitler was arrested for this attempted Putsch on 9 November, Stresemann called for the issue of a new currency, the Rentenmark, with a theoretical collateral of the mortgage value of all German lands and an official exchange rage of 4.2 to the dollar. German citizens could trade their old marks in at the rate of 1 trillion old marks to one Rentenmark.

German Recovery

Taking advantage of the split among the Allies, Stresemann cultivated the British by beginning the Erfullüllungspolitik (Fulfillment Policy) to show that even with the most sincere effort, Germany could not meet the reparations requirements and still maintain political and economic stability at home. The United States, still hoping for repayment of war loans by the French and British, entered the scene. In 1924 American financial expert Charles Dawes proposed a revision of the economic provisions of the Versailles Treaty. Because the final total of reparations had still not been set, the allied demands on the German economy had been escalating. The Dawes Plan specified a fixed rate of payment for the next five years and also arranged for a loan of $200 million to restart the German economy. Stresemann continued his diplomatic offensive by guaranteeing the controversial western frontiers of Germany with the Treaty of Locarno (1925) and by joining the League of Nations (1926). In 1929 he negotiated the Young Plan, which set German reparations at a total of 2.5 million marks annually for the next 59 years.

On the surface the German economy stabilized, but inflation had wiped out the savings of workers and those on fixed incomes, while helping the wealthy to pay off their debts easily. Productivity rates increased dramatically as the application of new technologies displaced many workers. Once again government welfare compensated their loss.

The Depression

But October 1929 ended this stability. On 3 October Stresemann died, and three weeks later the crash of the U.S. stock market sent a shockwave through the world economy. The U.S. loans to Germany stopped abruptly. To reduce expenditures, the German government began to dismiss workers and voted to increase taxes. Unemployment skyrocketed, and major sectors of the economy began to collapse.[4]

As the distress increased, the Reichstag parties deadlocked. In the July 1932 elections the voters turned to the extremist parties: the Communists won 89 seats, but the National Socialists (Nazis) won 37.8 percent of the votes, and, with 230 representatives, became the largest faction in the Reichstag. Hitler, the head of the National Socialists at that time, was appointed chancellor on 30 January 1933.

The Third Reich

Hitler used the incident of the Reichstag fire on 27 February 1933 to declare a Notverordnung (state of emergency) the following day, which allowed him to suspend civil liberties "temporarily." The 5 March elections, for which all opposition press, organizations, and meetings were banned while the Nazis had total freedom, guaranteed Hitler a favorable majority in the Reichstag. On 23 March the legislature passed the Ermächtigungsgesetz (Enabling Act), which became the legal basis for the dictatorship: the legislature gave Hitler the right to pass legislation and constitutional amendments by decree for the duration of the emergency. In reality, this dictatorship was not revoked until Germany was defeated in World War II 12 years later.

Hitler's Economic Policies

Hitler was a fanatical nationalist. His main economic goals were remilitarization to a level of war readiness and autarchy, thus making Germany self-sufficient. He sought to achieve these goals through the policy of Gleichschaltung (coordination), bringing all economic and political activities into conformance with Nazi policy. On 2 May 1933 the labor unions were closed down, and the Deutsche Arbeitsfront (German Labor Front) proclaimed. All workers were forced to join and to accept the work assigned. The government set the wage levels. In 1935 all men and women between the ages of 18 and 25 were obligated to serve in the Reichsarbeitsdienst (Labor Service), unpaid work service to the state.

With labor under control, on 9 September 1936 Hitler proclaimed his Four-Year Plan for autarchy and rearmament. This proclamation ended the competitive market economy and imposed state-centralized planning. The plan curtailed production of consumer goods in order to revitalize heavy industry that would help rearm Germany. Approximately 20 percent of the workforce was reallocated to this sector. Businesses were allowed to remain in private hands but forced to comply with government economic plans. The government also built its own steelworks and other enterprises as foundations for rearmament. The Arbeitsfront and Arbeitsdienst began the great Autobahn (highway) system that could move troops and supplies quickly throughout the country.

Hitler totally reversed the traditional German practice of blending vibrant capitalism with paternalistic social insurance for the workers. Similarly, the dissolution of the Reichstag ended the SPD's ability to act on behalf of the workers. Yet despite losing their political representation and their freedom to choose their work, the workers were paid regularly, and the economy did begin to recover.[5] This upswing, plus the appeals to nationalism and patriotism, as well as the fear of arrest, assured support of this new economic direction.

Lebensraum

The mass mobilization of society for war added to the appearance of recovery. In *Mein Kampf* (My struggle), Hitler's personal political program written while he was in prison, 1924–25, he had proposed war to win for the Germans more Lebensraum (living space) in eastern Europe. The Slavs, whom he regarded as inferior human beings, were to be required to work for the Germans. In 1938 the Anschluss (annexation) of German Austria (in March) and the incorporation of the Germans in the Sudetenland of Czechoslovakia (in September) glorified the nationalistic concept of the greater German Reich. The annexation of the non-German remainder of Czechoslovakia in March 1939 and the invasion of Poland in September of that year confirmed the grim reality of Hitler's plan. World War II began in Europe: it could not have been avoided.

World War II and the Holocaust

Soon the world would also become aware of the intensity of Hitler's fanatical anti-Semitic program. Just as he had organized the German economy for war to control Europe, he mobilized it again during the war to implement the Endlösung (Final Solution) against the Jews. Einsatzgruppen (Mobile Killing Units) were incorporated with the frontline troops to capture and force Jews into ghettos in Poland. For example, there were 445,000 Jews in the Warsaw Ghetto, and 144,000 in the Łodź Ghetto by September 1941, massive undertakings.[6] The Einsatzgruppen simply murdered Jews on the Russian front after 1941. Men and material were then diverted to Poland to build the concentration camps, and railroads were built to empty the ghettos into them. Branches of German firms were relocated to Auschwitz and other camps in Poland to take advantage of the captive labor to prepare war materials. German railroads and railroad workers transported hundreds of thousands across Europe into the death camps and brought the armaments back to Germany.

Defeat and Surrender

Although the Germans conquered and occupied Europe from the Atlantic to the Volga between 1939 and 1942, the recapture of Stalingrad by the Russians in January 1943 spelled the beginning of the end for the Third Reich. In January 1943 U.S. president Franklin D. Roosevelt and British prime minister Winston Churchill met at Casablanca, Morocco. They agreed to continue the war until Germany agreed to an unconditional surrender. Thereafter the Germans were on retreat in eastern Europe. The 6 June 1944 landings of allied forces at Normandy, France, opened up a second front in the west. The German forces were inexorably pushed back on each front toward their homeland. The outcome was inevitable. The meeting of the "Big Three"—Roosevelt, Churchill, and Josef Stalin of the Soviet Union—in Yalta, February 1945, confirmed the principle of unconditional surrender. There they also agreed to divide Germany into occupation zones, to demilitarize and de-Nazify it, and to establish democratic forms of government. The end came quickly. In April the Soviet army was besieging Berlin, and allied forces were entering Germany in the west. Hitler committed suicide on 30 April 1945. The German armies surrendered on both fronts on 7–8 May 1945 (26 years to the day after Germany was presented with the tough Treaty of Versailles).

Division and Occupation

Once again war had destroyed a dynamic German economy. More than 50 percent of its buildings were destroyed, including more than 25 percent of the housing. Most of the railroad tracks, engines, and freight cars had been destroyed by air attacks. Canals were choked with the wreckage of freight barges; roads and bridges were impassable. Food was scarce and provided only approximately 40 percent of minimum requirements. The Germans called it "Stunde Null," Zero Hour. Soon the battered country's population was swollen with more than 10 million refugees and displaced persons, and with 6.7 million ethnic Germans who had been expelled from their eastern European homelands. In addition, approximately 8 million men in the armies and support forces of the victors occupied the country. From the outset it was obvious that the victors would have to support the vanquished. Although the British and Americans had initially imposed punitive production limits, they were seriously rethinking that policy.

The Economic Division of Germany

The Soviet Union had freed itself and eastern Europe from the Germans and had no intention of letting a hostile power invade again. It established firm control over the eastern states and eastern Germany and began to build pro-Soviet regimes along socialist lines. The British and American authorities reacted by halting reparations shipments to the Russians in May 1946. In January 1947 they merged their zones to coordinate economic and political affairs. (France declined to join until April 1949.) In June 1947, as the Cold War escalated, the United States proclaimed its willingness to fund an integrated European recovery plan. When the Soviets and eastern Europe declined to participate, planning went ahead in the west. Significantly, those plans included the western zones of Germany in the recovery program. Disagreement over economic policy led the Russians to walk out of the Allied Control Council in March 1948. The economies of both western and eastern Germany were thus irreparably separated and remained so until 1990.

West German Economic Recovery

The Marshall Plan for European recovery, passed by the U.S. Congress in 1948, required the western Europeans to collaborate on a regional plan for the recovery of basic industry, agriculture, and the infrastructure. As necessary, the plan included emergency supplies of food and raw material to get the systems going. Of the $17 billion appropriated to western Europe over the four-year duration (1948–52) of the program, western Germany received $1.4 billion. These dollars were invested to promote full reconstruction and full productivity of the economy. To facilitate this reconstruction, the western zones agreed upon a currency reform linking the mark to the U.S. dollar. The Soviets retaliated by closing all land routes to Berlin, but the city was sustained for a year by an airlift of all necessary supplies to West Berlin. The blockade failed to force the Western powers to revoke their economic policies, however, and ended quietly in May 1949. On 23 May 1949 the Basic Law became the constitution of the new Bundesrepublik Deutschland (BRD, German Federal Republic).

The Wirtschaftswunder (Economic Miracle)

The foundation of the West German economy was established through the positive encouragement of the three occupying powers and the Marshall Plan aid. Minister of Finance Ludwig Erhard established the principle of the Sozialmarktwirtschaft (social market economy). It encouraged the free play of competition among entrepreneurs, but with recognition of the social priorities of the state. This combination meant business participation in the traditional social insurance plans, while the government taxation and regulation policies provided a favorable economic environment. Table 2.1 shows the changes in West German industrial production from 1948, before the plan, to 1953, after the final year.

On this foundation the BRD's gross national product more than doubled between 1960 and 1986, despite the worldwide recession that began in 1974. By 1986 it was the world's third largest economy, behind the United States and Japan.

The Soviet Zone

The Soviet Military Administration for Germany (SMAD) was assisted by prominent Soviet-trained Germans who had been in exile in Russia: Wilhelm

Table 2.1
Index of Change in Industrial Production in the Bundesrepublik Deutschland

Industrial Sector	1948	1949	1950	1951	1952	1953	Increase (%1948–53)
General Index	63	90	113	135	145	158	151
Mining	81	96	106	117	125	129	59
Capital Goods	51	83	114	151	170	176	246
Foodstuffs	80	99	112	119	127	148	85
Power Production	112	136	154	181	199	212	89

(1936 = 100)

Source: Wilhelm Grotkopp, Heinrich Spieker, and Dorothea Kempff, eds., *Germany: 1945–1954* (Schaan-Liechtenstein: Boas International, n.d.), 171.

Pieck, leader of the German Communist Party, and Otto Grotewohl, who chaired the zonal Social Democrats. In April 1946 these two parties and the smaller zonal Liberal and Christian Democratic factions merged to form the Sozialistische Einheitspartei (SED, Socialist Unity Party). This basically one-party system made no protest as SMAD dismantled factories and collected equipment and livestock to ship to the Soviet Union as reparations. SMAD also nationalized more than 8 million acres of agricultural lands for the creation of large agricultural collectives and for distribution in small 17- to 20-acre holdings to refugees and farmers. The original owners were not compensated for their losses. What was left of the industrial sector was weak and obsolete. There were virtually no natural resources beyond the low-grade lignite (brown) coal and some potash deposits. Thus, the East Germans faced an enormous economic challenge.

On 7 October 1949 the Deutsche Demokratische Republik (DDR, German Democratic Republic) was established. The Russians organized it with the eastern European nations into the Council for Mutual Economic Cooperation (COMECON), but this council was no counterpart to the Marshall Plan. Rather, the economies of the member nations were aligned primarily to help the Soviet Union recover and only secondarily could they address their own needs. Yet despite the massive restructuring of property, the loss of contact with western Germany, and the forced integration with the more backward eastern European economies, the East German economy showed remarkable strength.

The per capita productivity of the workers grew from 5,000 East German marks (GDR) in 1950 to 18,000 GDR in 1970 and then to 29,000 GDR in 1982. The national income (gross national product less input, based on 1980 rates in million GDR) grew from 29,000 in 1950 to 201,000 in 1982. During that same period, however, the workforce grew only slightly, from 7.2 million in 1950 to 8.4 million in 1982. The average gross income for pro-

Table 2.2
Summary of East German Economic Development Indicators*

Selected Products	**1950**	**1965**	**1982**
Electricity (bil. kWhrs)	19	54	103
Petrol (1000 tonnes)	486	1,604	3,891
Rolled Steel (mil. tones)	1	4	7
Nitrogenous Fertilizer (1000 tonnes)	231	348	948
Passenger Cars (1000s)	7	103	183
Housing Construction (1000s)	208	363	940

*Currency of measurement is East German marks. *The German Democratic Republic* (Berlin: Grafischer Grossbetrieb Völkerfreundschaft, 1984), 153–54, 158–59.

duction and office workers rose from 311 GDR in 1950 to 1,066 in 1982.[7] Table 2.2 summarizes other aspects of development.

Centralized Economic Planning

State centralized planning directed the socialist East German economy. It also provided many benefits for the citizens: low rents and maintenance subsidies; education; cultural, sport, and recreation facilities; health and social services; and welfare insurance. Spending in the social sector rose from 161 billion GDR in 1971–75 to 234 billion GDR in 1976–80.[8] Indeed, despite the economic downturn of the 1980s, the DDR was the most prosperous nation in the socialist bloc in 1987. In terms of per capita income, agricultural yield per worker, and number of cars and hospital beds per 1,000 individuals, it led the Soviet bloc. It was noted that "East Germany is a major supplier of advanced technology to the other members (of COMECON). In short, it is the most modern and industrialized socialist state."[9] It ranked among the top 20 world economies in its final years. Nonetheless, thousands of East Germans fled to the West for better opportunities.

Unification

Although there had long been discussion of political unification, neither German republic had given much consideration to its economic implications. The West Germans had little knowledge about the weaknesses beginning to appear in East German manufacturing and trade. After the fall of the Berlin Wall in 1989 and the March 1990 elections in the DDR, the first step toward economic unification was the negotiation of the Treaty of 18 May 1990 between the Federal Republic of Germany and the German Democratic Republic Establishing a Monetary, Economic, and Social Union the Economic Treaty. By starting with economic issues, the strategy effectively preserved the

BRD intact while eliminating the 40-year-old social and economic policies of the former DDR. In his effort to gain the support of the East Germans and their government, Chancellor Helmut Kohl emphasized the benefits of the West German economy. The treaty was signed by the finance ministers of the two German governments. Article 1.1 clearly stated the intention:

> to introduce the social market economy in the German Democratic Republic as the basis for further economic and social development, with social compensation and social safeguards and responsibility towards the environment, and thereby constantly to improve the living and working conditions of its population....
>
> Proceeding from the mutual desire to take an initial significant step...towards national unity in accordance with Article 23 of the Basic Law of the Federal Republic of Germany.[10]

Subsequently the DDR formed the Treuhandanstalt (Trust Agency), which was charged to privatize East German enterprises. The assets and liabilities of 8,500 firms were turned over to the Treuhand so it could attract private investors and management from western Germany and abroad. The BRD continued the operations of the Treuhand after unification until 1994. By that time more than 14,000 East German enterprises were in private hands.

The July 1990 treaty on the economy was a political conquest for Western capitalism, not a blueprint for the merger of two systems; virtually nothing of the DDR's socialist economy survived. All industry, agriculture, commerce, and service enterprises in the eastern states had to be open to free-market competition. State-owned land as well as industry had to be privatized; and the western states had to foot most of the social costs for individuals displaced by the conversion.

The West German mark and the Bundesbank (Federal Bank) had sole authority over currency and money circulation. The treaty further required the East Germans to establish a system of private-sector commercial banks and corporations operating in the competitive free-market economy with private ownership and means of production. Western managers were sent in to direct them. Without a public discussion or vote the DDR's agricultural production was changed to conform to the price support system of the European Community, to which the BRD belonged. West German social insurance systems and labor laws were extended to eastern Länder. Lothar de Maizière, the last prime minister of the DDR, told his constituents to remember the "seriousness of the crisis in the [DDR's] economy."

> Not every rosy dream which some people have associated with [this] State Treaty could be fulfilled. But no one will be worse off than before. On the contrary: what country has ever been afforded as good a starting position as we have with this Treaty?
>
> We in the [DDR] must now make the best of it. Adopting a realistic view of the situation, we must set to work with a new pioneering spirit, with commitment, faith and confidence in our own strength. In doing so, we will never lose sight of social justice.[11]

Jobless Berliners protest in Berlin, March 1998. The poster reads: "Ripped off by Honi [Erich Honecker, former East German leader], then ripped off by [Chancellor Helmut] Kohl, then ripped off by ? ? ?" (AP/Wide Worlds Photo)

The New German Economy

These economic changes caused a shock to both systems. The Kohl government promised to bring the productivity in the eastern states up to that in western states. This equalization was to happen through subsidies and the encouragement of foreign investment to modernize obsolete factories and to introduce new ones. But the West Germans had the highest wages in Europe. The unit labor costs (the ratio of labor costs to productivity) rose from 61.8 percent in 1999 to 64.5 percent in 2001, but gross domestic product declined from 2.3 percent per resident to 1.7 percent in the same time period.[12] By destroying the East German economy instead of integrating it, the equalization costs escalated. Shutting down obsolete industries, closing the collective farms, and "decommunizing" the government caused unemployment to skyrocket in the east. The costs of unemployment insurance rose with it. By February 1991 the unemployment rate in the east approached 20 percent. Without income from production, sales, and taxation, the costs of maintaining basic services and infrastructure in the east increased. Some began to talk about unification as an economic disaster.[13]

The strategies for Aufbau Ost (Rebuilding the East) changed. Private investment and natural growth in a free-market economy did not occur in the new states. Between 1990 and 1994 the government pumped more than 200 billion marks into the east. The Solidarity Program implemented in 1995 began a 10-year program of sending approximately 6.6 billion marks a year to the eastern states. The Solidarity Tax of 7.5 percent on wages, imposed initially in 1991 for one year, was extended in 1995 for an indefinite period (although the rate was reduced to 5.5 in 1998). Since 1995 the government has spent some 6.6 billion annually to improve the economy of the eastern states and plans to continue at this rate through 2005.

The Postunification Elections

The poor performance of the economy following unification led to the election defeat in 1998 of Chancellor Helmut Kohl and his conservative Christian Democratic government. The new chancellor, Gerhardt Schröder, currently leads a coalition of Social Democrats and Greens, the pro-environment liberal faction. This government has been unable to resolve the stubborn unemployment problems, however. At the beginning of 1999 the number of unemployed hovered around 4.1 million. Although it declined to 3.8 million by the end of 2000, it rose again to 3.9 at the beginning of 2002. The economy was the major issue in the September 2002 national elections.

The First Decade of United Germany

On 1 January 2002, in accordance with the regulations of the European Union (EU), Germany converted its currency to the Euro, designed to circulate as the single currency of the 15 member states. The single currency reduces the problems of converting trade and financial accounts into many national currencies. The initial conversion rate was 1.95583 marks to one Euro. The European Central Bank of the EU is headquartered in Frankfurt, Germany.

Some improvement has occurred in the decade since unification (see Table 2.3). The German government reports that more than 500,000 new companies employ some 3.2 million individuals. Wages and pensions in the east were the equivalent of 91 percent of those in the west by 1999. There are 11,700 new or upgraded kilometers of highways and 5,400 kilometers of railroad lines. There are 5.7 million more telephones and 4.3 million new or repaired dwellings. The entire public education curriculum has been rewrit-

Table 2.3
Recent Economic Indicators for United Germany*

Economic Sector	1999	2000	2001 (preliminary)
Gross Domestic Product	**1,974.30**	**2,025.50**	**2,063.78**
Agriculture, Forestry and fishing	21.70	22.00	23.25
Industry	453.09	477.33	483.57
Construction	100.64	95.92	91.04
Trade and Transport	321.85	333.05	343.26
Financial and Business Activities	546.69	560.47	575.21
Other Service Activities	394.35	397.26	404.23

(Unit: Euro, billion)

*These data are identified in the new Euro denomination, the EU currency that went into effect in Germany in January 2002. Federal Statistical Office Germany, 2002, http://www.destatis.de/basis/e/vgr/vgrtab1.htm.

ten, although most of the former East German educators who taught the socialist curriculum have lost their positions to West Germans.[14]

ISSUES

Kohl's Rush to Get the Economic Treaty Signed Was a Mistake

Agree:

Hindsight suggests that the Kohl government's haste to assure its own economic and political control has contributed to many of the economic woes of contemporary Germany. No realistic analysis of either economy was made prior to the treaty. Perhaps transitional steps toward merger, rather than immediate takeover, would have been prudent.

The productivity and trade of the DDR were linked to trading with the socialist nations of eastern Europe, where technology lagged far behind the West. Their exports to the eastern countries amounted to some 95,800 million GDR in 1982, out of a total of 145.1 million GDR in foreign trade. Almost 45 percent of that trade was in durable manufactured goods of a type enjoyed in the east, if not in the west.[15] The treaty interrupted that trade and forced East German industries to compete directly with West German industries, which they could not. When the Treuhand was successful in selling properties to West German companies and foreign investors, modernization often cut the workforce, reducing local income and often sending profits and their potential local investment out of the region. Totally obsolescent enterprises were closed, again resulting in unemployment for their workers. The establishment of new firms was often delayed because of conflicting claims to the property that the socialist state had confiscated.

This cessation in employment and productivity was devastating. By 2000 unemployment in the five eastern states was 17.3 percent, contrasting sharply with the 7.8 percent unemployment rate of the western states. The government had to compensate for the lack of income with massive welfare subsidies. Productivity in the eastern states was only 60 percent of that in the western states, and exports only half of the western rate. With almost 20 percent of the German population, the eastern states contributed only 8 percent of the income from taxes. Approximately one-third of all income for the eastern states currently must come from subsidies or foreign investment.[16]

Moreover, the government made unrealistic projections for the integration of the East German economy, which resulted in unrestrained speculation in building. The bare concrete frames of Investionsruinen ("investment ruins," unfinished factories) dot the countryside. New shopping malls and office buildings are virtually empty of clients in Leipzig and other cities because of overbuilding.

Although it was supposed to be an economic treaty, the document was simply a description of the West German economy, which the East Germans were obliged to adopt. There is no credible evidence that unification would have failed to occur had more time been taken to plan a more realistic economic program. Kohl's strategy was in error.

Disagree:

It would have been a mistake to delay action on the economic conversion. The East German government was in a state of crisis and collapse. Had Chancellor Kohl waited for a group of experts to survey all aspects of the East German economy, that system would have crashed. Indeed, the economies of the eastern European states were going through similar crises and would have offered no help to the DDR during such a transition period.

Leaders in both German republics recognized the necessity of moving forward quickly. The Economic Treaty identified clear goals of privatization of property, conversion of currency and banking, and rationalization of production. Trained businesspersons and bankers from the BRD could begin immediately to link viable aspects of the East German economy with those same aspects in the West, thus sustaining and developing their employment and productivity.

It is true that not enough time was taken for an in-depth analysis, but the speed of the collapse would have made that very difficult. When the magnitude of the problems was known, Kohl's government acted responsibly to provide welfare support for the people, funds to clean up the environmental disasters created by socialist-style production, and the educational and training programs necessary to prepare East German workers for their new economy.

The Kohl government did not create the East German economic and political crises. The West German economy could not correct 40 years of socialism overnight. Kohl took the most logical route to help resolve them through the unification that both German societies wanted. Although hindsight is valuable, it never applies to current problems. Kohl's dynamic leadership prevented a deepening of the crisis through delay.

The Social Market Economy Has Become Too Expensive to Sustain since Unification

Agree:

Since Bismarck initiated the dual goals of a vigorous capitalism supported by a passive workforce, the German governments, irrespective of their politics, have had a direct hand in regulating the conditions of employment and in promoting the health and social welfare of the workforce. After the Wirtschaftswunder of the post–World War II era, West German workers became the highest paid in Europe, often working shorter hours and receiving more benefits than their continental counterparts. West German labor unions are strong and politically active in maintaining this work climate. Guaranteeing parity to the more than 8 million workers of the eastern states after unification was a wonderful promise to secure their votes, but it is proving to be an enormous burden to the state. As unemployment soars, budget deficits grow owing to unemployment insurance payments.

To increase investment and stimulate the business economy, the Schröder government in July 2000 introduced a significant tax reform. It reduced corporate income tax from 40 percent to 25 percent and eliminated the 53 percent tax on profit from selling interests in other companies. Top tax levels on private income will be reduced from 56 percent to 42 percent by 2005. Members of Schröder's own party are strongly criticizing his "enrich the rich" policy, which, they say, cannot pay for the welfare system. They are predicting the end of the social market economy.[17]

The doomsayers have strong evidence. The trickle-down tax stimulus program has not yet substantially helped the economy. In 2001, according to the World Economic Forum of Switzerland, Germany went from fourteenth to seventeenth place in the annual ratings of global economic competitiveness, and some economists are declaring that Germany is in a significant economic recession. The global economic downturn following the 11 September 2001 terrorist attacks in the United States has added to Germany's economic woes. Nevertheless, in April 2002 the government increased its liabilities as it began to create low-paying jobs with subsidized child and social security benefits.[18]

Attitudes toward the social market economy do seem to be changing. A poll reported in November 2001 indicated that 56 percent of Germans felt that unemployment benefits are too high.[19] Because of the tax cuts and rising prices for food and oil, Germany is running a budget deficit that approaches the 3 percent limit set by the EU. It faces a potential fine for exceeding that limit. Schröder and the SPD faced a strong challenge in the September 2002 elections from Edmund Stoiber, the conservative premier of Bayern (Bavaria). Bayern has attracted a number of new companies and has low unemployment, and the record may be attractive to disillusioned German voters. It remains to be seen, however, whether they will believe that he will have any better luck than Kohl and Schröder in the eastern states.

Disagree:

The unique German partnership among management, labor, and government built the strong economy in the 1870s and in the 1950s up until today. The German economy is under strong pressure to integrate the eastern states; workers in the west were asked to help through the Solidarity Tax and increased effort. They are not entirely happy with that request, but they are meeting their responsibilities. This is no time to penalize them by cutting back on the wages and benefits that they have earned over the years.

Similarly, the workers in the east should have an incentive to increase their productivity and gain those wages and benefits at the same levels as their western coworkers. The rapid conversion from socialism to capitalism destroyed the economic security to which they were accustomed. It introduced managers from the west demanding different methods; its wage rates for East Germans were lower than those for the West Germans working beside them at the same job. It took away the child care centers that enabled mothers to work. To many East Germans the new economic policies seemed to be punishing them, to be devaluing their work despite the fact that they had produced the strongest economy in the eastern bloc. If social protection is cut back now, they will see it as a new form of punishment. And even worse, West German workers will blame them for it, which will increase the "Wessie"/"Ossie" tensions that all are working so hard to reduce.

Therefore, the government has introduced the tax reductions on business to promote investment and job creation. It has reviewed education and training programs for workers and cut tuition to technical schools in order to speed up this process. It has also expanded child care opportunities. It is taking longer than was hoped to integrate the new Länder. In the interim, however, these workers and their families need to be sustained. A cornerstone of the economic policy should not be discarded because of a short-term crisis.

QUESTIONS AND ACTIVITIES

1. Using the Web and other sources, find as much information as you can on the economy of the BRD in the 10 years prior to unification. What were its major industries and businesses? How was the workforce distributed? What were the costs of benefits to the workers? How many workers were unemployed? What countries were its major trading partners, and which were its competitors? Using this information, write a short report analyzing any weaknesses in the West German economy that would be affected by unification.

2. Using the Web and other sources, find as much information as you can on the economy of the DDR in the 10 years prior to unification. For example: what were its major industries and businesses? How was the workforce distributed? What were the costs of benefits to the workers? What countries were its major trading partners, and which were its major competitors? Can you find any information on which portion of its business, industry, and housing were private? Using that information, write a short

report to indicate why the East German economy has been so slow to catch up to the West German economy.

3. Prior to unification the DDR government established the Treuhand to find buyers or investors for state-run businesses and industries in order to privatize them. Presume that you are an administrator of the Treuhand dealing with the West German administrators who are urging you to shut down these enterprises. What sorts of issues would you raise in these negotiations in order to maintain some economic continuity in the lives of the East German workers? List these issues and discuss them with the class.

4. Using the Web and other sources, find out about the role of women in the East German economy and society prior to unification. Report on the impact of unification on their work and family life. Do some in-class role playing to voice concerns they may have had or still have.

5. Unification occurred just as the West German economy was struggling to upgrade its technology. The government recently has initiated new programs to train and upgrade its workforce. Review recent government press releases and policy statements. Report to the class about the issues the government is addressing and the strategies it is using.

6. German workers have some of the highest wages and benefits in Europe. These social costs, however, must be paid for by taxes and careful budgeting. Investigate how these costs have changed since unification. Discuss the impact of these costs on the German economy in general and on the personal income and taxes of German citizens and businesses.

7. German workers have moved both east and west in their search for employment. Many immigrants have also entered Germany since unification. Find out how this internal migration has changed the population of the individual German Länder. Using a map, make a chart showing the gains or losses or both in Land populations since unification.

8. West and East German citizens alike are concerned about the ongoing economic problems since unification. On your own use the Web and other sites to identify these issues. Discuss them in class and list them in the order of their importance. (Do not forget to consider such things as the impact of the recent recession in the United States.) Try to determine whether these economic problems were the product of unification or were issues that existed prior to 1990. Identify those problems that will be the easiest to resolve.

NOTES

1. ***Growth in German Industrial Productivity, 1871–1914***

Industrial Sector	*1871*	*1914*
Kilometers of railroad track	19,500	61,000
Coal output, in metric tons	29,400,000	191,500,500
Pig iron output, in metric tons	2,729,000	14,794,000
Steel output, in metric tons	1,548,000	3,149,000
Total mercantile tonnage of freight	982,000	3,000,000

These data are taken from: J.H. Clapham, *The Economic Development of France and Germany 1815–1914* (Cambridge: Cambridge University Press, 1966), 338, 281, 235, 356. Although the figures do not always specifically reflect data produced in 1871 and 1914, they show the changes in productivity that occurred during this period.

2. ***Occupations, Persons Engaged in Them, and Their Dependents, 1882–1907***

Occupation Sector	*1882*	*1907*
Agriculture and Forestry	19,225,000	17,681,000
Industry	16,058,000	26,387,000
Public Service and Professions	4,531,000	8,278,000
Nondomestic Service and Casual Labor	939,000	793,000
Independent Means	2,246,000	5,175,00

Ibid., 365

3. Dietrich Orlow, *A History of Modern Germany* (Englewood Cliffs, N.J.: Prentice Hall, 1995), 46.

4. ***Key Economic Indicators for the Weimar Republic***

Year	*Foreign Trade Imports*	*Exports (Mil. RM)*	*Foreign Loans to Germany (Mil. RM)*	*Unemployment (Mil RM)*
1900	5,766	4,612		
1913	10,770	10,097		
1925	12,362	9,290	1,265	0.636
1928	14,001	12,276	1,465	1.368
1929	13,447	13,483	349	1.899
1930	10,393	12,036	0	3.076
1932	4,667	5,739	0	5.575

These data are from the *Statistisches Jahrbuch des Deutschen Reichs* for the years 1932 and 1939–40, and from *Zahlen nach Bevölkerung und Wirtschaft 1872–1972* as reprinted on the following Web sites: http://www.dhm.de/lemo/objekte/statistik/epauhand/index.html; http://dhm.de/lemo/objekte/statistik/kredite1/index.html; and http://dhm.de/lemo/objekte/statistik/arbeits11a/index.html.

5. ***Index of German Economic Decline after the Depression of 1929***

Year	*Manufactured Goods*	*Investments*	*Employment*	*Standard of Living*	*Real Wages*
1928	100	100	100	100	100
1929	100	103	99	102	101
1930	86	84	92	98	97
1931	61	54	80	90	93
1932	46	35	71	80	87
1933	54	45	74	78	91
1934	77	75	85	80	95

1928 = 100[5]

These data are taken from the *Sozialgeschichtliches Arbeitsbuch,* reprinted on: http://dhm.de/lemo/objekte/statistik/wewikr;index.html.

6. Raul Hilberg, *The Destruction of the European Jews,* student ed. (New York and London: Holms and Meier, 1985), 84.

7. Currency of measurement is East German Marks, identified as GDRs. *The German Democratic Republic* (Berlin: Grafischer Grossbetrieb Völkerfreundschaft, 1984), 153–54, 158–59.

8. Ibid., 159.

9. *Library of Congress Country Studies—East Germany,* chapter 3, "The Economy," http://lcweb2.loc.gov.frd/cs/gxxtoc.html.

10. Press and Information Office of the Federal Government, *The Unification of Germany in 1990: Documentation* (Bonn: Press and Information Office, 1991), 13.

11. Ibid., 35.

12. *Statistical Office Germany, 2002,* "National Accounts—Per Capita Data and per Hour Data," http://www.destatis.de/basis/e/vgr/vgrtab1.htm.

13. Otto Singer, "Constructing the Economic Spectacle: The Role of Currency Union in the German Unification Process," *Journal of Economic Issues* 26, no. 4 (December 1992), 1095 ff.

14. "10th Anniversary of German Unification—A Review of the Progress Made in Bringing Living Standards in the Eastern Section of the Country into Line with Those in the West," 1, http://www.bundesregierung.de/dokumente/Artikel/ix_16830.htm.

15. *The German Democratic Republic,* 158.

16. "Europe's Sleeping Giant," *The Economist Global Agenda,* November 22, 2001, http://www.economist.com/agenda.

17. Ulrich Rippert, "Germany's Tax Reform: The End of the 'Social Market Economy,'" *World Socialist Web Site,* July 27, 2000, http://www.wsws.org.

18. "Eastern Germany's Slow Revival," *The Economist* (U.S.) 355, no. 8172 (May 27, 2000), 51.

19. Charles P. Wallace, "Germany Faces Reality," *Time Atlantic* 158, no. 26 (December 24, 2001), 43. "It's the Economy, Dummkoph [*sic*]!" *The Economist* 362, no. 5256 (January 19, 2002), 41 ff.

SUGGESTED READINGS

Readings on the economy are of two types: those that offer background information and those that cover recent developments. The classic history texts give good historical information on the German economy to World War II. See Hajo Holborn's *History of Modern Germany* (Princeton, N.J.: Princeton University Press, 1982) and Koppel S. Pinson's *Modern Germany, Its History and Civilization,* 2nd ed. (Prospect Heights, Ill.: Waveland Press, 1989). Dietrich Orlow's *A History of Modern Germany: 1871 to Present,* 4th ed. (Englewood Cliffs, N.J.: Prentice Hall, 1998), and Eleanor L. Turk, *The History of Germany* (Westport, Conn.: Greenwood Press, 1999) carry the discussion through unification and more recent events for the BRD.

There are fewer basic texts on the economy of the DDR, and those that are available tend to be of a somewhat scholarly nature. See Wolfgang Stolper, *The Structure of the East German Economy* (Cambridge, Mass.: Harvard University Press, 1960), and Arthur W. McCardle and A. Bruch Boernau, *East Germany: A New German National under Socialism?* (Lanham, Md.: University Press of America, 1984).

Good statistical information is available on both the BRD and the DDR from the Library of Congress Country Studies (http://lcweb.loc.gov/). The German Statistical Office also provides good economic data, offering many by state or by the two formerly separate regions (http://www.destatis.de).

When the Christian Democrats were in power, the government published annually an informative handbook titled *Facts about Germany.* The Schröder government makes much of this same information available on the Web site of its Press and Information Office (http://www.deutschland.de, "Das Deutschland Portal"). This site has helpful links to all aspects of current government and provides the opportunity for individuals to subscribe to the service, which offers up-to-date press releases from the government.

Excellent publications such as *The Economist, Business Week,* and the *Wall Street Journal* pay specific attention to the global economy. Researchers can also check http://www.world-newspapers.com/germany.html for current news, including links to government sites, the *Frankfurter Allgemeine Zeitung,* and the *Deutsche Welle.* There are both German- and English-language versions.

3

GERMANY, ANTI-SEMITISM, AND THE HOLOCAUST

BACKGROUND

What Is Anti-Semitism?

Anti-Semitism is a term that means "hatred of the Jews." The term has its basis in linguistics. Semites are those who speak the Semitic languages of southwestern Asia. Those languages historically included Babylonian, Assyrian, Phoenician, and Aramaic (the language of Jesus). Today the most widely spoken Semitic language is Arabic. Hebrew is also a Semitic tongue. For a long time it served mainly as the medium for Jewish religious activities. Many Jews spoke the language of the area in which they lived. Many eastern European (Ashkenazi) Jews spoke Yiddish (a combination of German and Polish), and Spanish (Sephardic) Jews spoke Ladino (a Spanish-based language) instead of Hebrew. Hebrew was revived as a spoken national language with the foundation of Israel in 1949.

What Was the Holocaust?

The word *Holocaust* stands for the deliberate mobilization of European society by Adolf Hitler's dictatorship in Germany between 1933 and 1945 to support and carry out a policy of genocide. It is a specialized historical case of ethnic cleansing. No issue troubles recent German history more than the Holocaust. The word stands for the deaths of millions of European Jews, Roma (Gypsies), Jehovah's Witnesses, homosexuals, and the mentally and physically disabled. This genocide was a significant part of Hitler's goal to impose German rule on all of Europe. It was also coldly developed, like an industry, utilizing great masses of manpower and materials, even during wartime.

Although Hitler's dictatorship was the driving force behind this terrible extermination, most of its victims were not Germans. Most were individuals rounded up in other eastern and western European countries and then sent to specially constructed death camps, located mainly in Poland. The majority of the estimated 6 million victims were Jews. The numbers are staggering (see Table 3.1).

History of Anti-Semitism

Hitler had a pathological hatred of Jews, but his fanaticism alone could not have caused the Holocaust. He built his policy on the historical, deeply rooted religious anti-Semitism of Christian Europe. With the Christianization of the Roman Empire in the fourth century, the Roman Catholic Church condemned the Jews as the killers of Christ. Roman Catholic canon law added many regulations over the centuries discriminating against Jews in marriage, legal actions, and commerce. The First Crusade targeted Jews in Europe as well as the Muslims and Jews in the Holy Land. Jews were expelled

Table 3.1
Jewish Victims of the Holocaust, by Country of Origin

Country (1937 Borders)	Number of Deaths
Poland	up to 3,000,000
USSR (Soviet Union)	over 700,000
Romania	270,000
Czechoslovakia	260,000
Hungary	over 180,000
Lithuania	up to 130,000
Germany	over 120,000
Netherlands	over 100,000
France	75,000
Latvia	70,000
Yugoslavia	60,000
Greece	60,000
Austria	over 50,000
Belgium	24,000
Italy (Including Rhodes)	9,000
Estonia	2,000
Norway	under 1,000
Luxembourg	under 1,000
Danzig	under 1,000
Total	**5,100,000**

Source: Raul Hilberg, *The Destruction of the European Jews,* student ed. (New York and London: Holmes and Meier, 1985), 339.

from England in 1290, from France in 1306, and from Spain in 1492. They were blamed for the Black Death (1348–50), which killed up to one-third of Europe's population, and were burned as witches and sorcerers. In the feudal monarchies of Europe, where political power was based on land grants from the monarch to the military aristocracy, Jews were usually forbidden to own land. There they were crowded into urban ghettos where they were useful in commerce because they did not accept the Catholic Church's bans on lending money at interest and on making profit in trade.

As European commerce grew during the Middle Ages, resentment against Jewish bankers and merchants gave anti-Semitism a new economic dimension. Jews were targeted for special taxes and fees, and they received little help if criminals attacked them. The Protestants of the Reformation were no less anti-Semitic. Martin Luther, the leader of the Reformation in Germany, called Jews "disgusting vermin." In 1543, near the end of his life, he wrote a vicious pamphlet titled *Von den Jüden und iren* [*sic*] *Lügen* (About the Jews and their lies). Luther recommended expelling Jews from the German states, confiscating their possessions, and burning their synagogues.

The Enlightenment and the French Revolution of the seventeenth and eighteenth centuries gave new political and philosophical concepts to Europe. These concepts recognized talent and intellect, and they lessened anti-Semitic antagonisms somewhat in western Europe. With the rise of the urban middle classes, Jews began to assimilate into urban society, as merchants, bankers, and even financial advisors to the kings. Many benefited from private education and tutors to become scholars, physicians, and lawyers, although their professional practice was often limited by prejudice. Modern philosophy and more democratic politics gave Jews a more active role in most European countries.

The New Anti-Semitism of the Nazis

After the disastrous defeat of Germany in World War I and the punitive Treaty of Versailles, German fanatics began to blame the woes of the nation on the Marxists (Social Democrats and Communists) and on Jewish financiers. But they went well beyond blaming the Jews for the death of Christ and resenting their wealth. They now identified Jews as a tainted race and as mortal enemies of Aryan Germans. One of these fanatics, Alfred Rosenberg, picked up on this theme and later expanded on it in a number of unscientific and racist works vilifying the Jews. He joined Hitler's Nationalsozialistische Deutsche Arbeiterpartei (National Socialist German Workers Party, the Nazi Party) in 1920 and became the editor of its major paper, the *Völkischer Beobachter* (Popular Observer) in 1923. His major work, *Der Mythus des zwanzigsten Jahrhunderts* (The myth of the twentieth century), first published in 1930, is a bitter primer of racial anti-Semitism. It is considered to be the second most important statement of Nazi ideas after Hitler's *Mein Kampf.*

Hitler also associated with Julius Streicher, whose newspaper *Der Stürmer* (The Stormer) attacked Jews with every issue. Also established in 1923, it was distinguished by its disgusting and stereotyped cartoons. With a relatively small circulation in the 1920s, *Der Stürmer*'s readership grew from 47,000 in 1934 to 473,000 in 1938.[1]

These two colleagues helped Hitler distill his hate, which he expressed in the savage language of his autobiography, *Mein Kampf*:

> Wherever I went, I began to see Jews, and the more I saw the more sharply they became distinguished in my eyes from the rest of humanity.... a people which even outwardly had lost all resemblance to Germans.... [I]t became positively repulsive when, in addition to their physical uncleanliness, you discovered the moral stains on the "chosen people."... Was there any form of filth or profligacy, particularly in cultural life, without at least one Jew involved in it? If you cut even cautiously into such an abscess, you found, like a maggot in a rotting body, often dazzled by the sudden light—a kike [derogatory name for a Jew]!... Gradually I began to hate them.[2]

Hitler's Program against the Jews

The political program of the Nazi Party clearly targeted Jews and Germans with new racial identities:

> 4. Only a racial comrade can be a citizen. Only a person of German blood, irrespective of religious denomination, can be a racial comrade. No Jew, therefore, can be a racial comrade....
>
> ...6. We therefore demand that every public office, no matter of what kind, and no matter whether it be national, state, or local office, be held by none but citizens.
>
> ...The party, as such, stands for positive Christianity, without, however, allying itself to any particular denomination. It combats the Jewish-materialistic spirit within and around us, and is convinced that a permanent recovery of our people can be achieved only from within.[3]

Anti-Semitism soon came methodically into law in Nazi Germany. On 1 April 1933 Hitler, now the chancellor of Germany, called for a one-day boycott of Jewish businesses, using the slogan "German people, defend yourselves! Do not buy from Jews!" On 7 April Hitler issued a decree: "non-Aryans" were to leave government service. An 11 April decree clarified that the term *non-Aryan* applied to all Jews, defined as those who had a parent or grandparent who practiced the Jewish religion. Those with only one Jewish grandparent or who had left the Jewish faith were known as Mischlinge (of mixed blood) but were still subject to discrimination under the decrees.

The Nuremberg Laws

This racist Arierparagraph (Aryan Paragraph) became the basis for the Nuremberg Laws, which began with the Law for the Protection of German Blood and Honor and the Reich Citizenship Law, both of 15 September

1935. The first outlawed marriage and sexual contact between Jews and Germans, as well as employment of German women by Jews. The second stipulated that a citizen "is that subject only who is of German or kindred blood." Only they were entitled to "full political rights in accordance with the provision of the laws." In November the First Regulation under the Reich Citizenship Law further stipulated that a Jew could not be a citizen or vote or hold public office.[4] Because Hitler had banned the sale of all Jewish newspapers on 6 September, the Jews were unable to offer much protest.

In 1938 the government's campaign against the Jews strengthened. They were required to carry a special identity card, and their passports and ration cards were stamped with a "J" for "Jude" (Jew). On 9 November the government instigated the Kristallnacht (Night of Broken Glass), a violent rampage throughout Germany to vandalize Jewish stores and synagogues. It then blamed the Jews and required them to pay a fine of one billion Reichsmarks to pay for the damage. This violent episode was used as an excuse for intensifying Germany's anti-Semitic laws.

The strategy behind Hitler's persecution of the Jews was diabolical. First, propaganda vilified them and isolated them from German society. Then the economic measures deprived them of income and accumulated wealth. Because many of the urban Jewish communities had welfare funds, there was a gradual concentration of Jews from all over Germany in these communities as they sought help. Although Hitler's administrators might not have foreseen this migration, they took advantage of it as they began to round up Jews to put into ghettoes and to deport them to the concentration camps.

Many Jews began to emigrate from Germany to escape the persecution. The authorities made wealthy Jews pay for the emigration of poorer Jews by a high tax on income in order to be sure that no impoverished minority remained. Jews were not allowed to take any foreign currency with them because the Reich needed it for trade. By the end of October 1941, when emigration was no longer possible, German Jews had provided $9.5 million to the German government.[5]

The Extension of Anti-Semitic Laws to Occupied Europe

With the incorporation of Austria (1938) and the conquest of Poland (1939) Hitler expanded his anti-Semitic campaign. German and Austrian Jews were deported to Poland; Polish Jews were required to wear a yellow Star of David badge on their clothing and were forced into ghettoes in cities such as Warsaw, Łodź, and Lublin. When Germany invaded the Soviet Union in June 1941, Einsatzgruppen (Mobile Killing Units) accompanied the frontline troops to capture and kill Jews and resistors. More than 35,000 Jews in the Ukrainian city of Kiev were herded into a ravine at Babi Yar outside the city and murdered. As German forces conquered throughout Europe, the surviving Jews from those lands were rounded up and deported to Poland.

The "Final Solution"

The "Final Solution" of the "Jewish question," decided upon at the Wannsee Conference in January 1942, was to eliminate European Jewry. Fifteen top Nazi officials agreed to annihilate the estimated 11 million Jews of Europe, using an industrial efficiency to round them up, transport them to the death camps, and put them to death. The minutes of the top secret conference, written by Adolf Eichmann, chief of the Gestapo's Jewish section, stated the process:

> Under proper guidance, in the course of the final solution the Jews are to be allocated for appropriate labor in the East. Able-bodied Jews, separated according to sex, will be taken in large work columns to these areas for work on roads, in the course of which a large portion will be eliminated by natural causes ["natural causes" was the terminology for overwork and starvation]. . . .
>
> Another possible solution of the problem has now taken the place of Emigration, i.e. the evacuation of the Jews to the East ["to the East" meant to the death camps], provided that the Führer gives the appropriate approval in advance.[6]

In 1942 the six infamous Polish concentration camps—Auschwitz, Bełżec, Chelmo, Maidanek, Sobibor, and Treblinka—turned into death camps. The extermination of their prisoners continued into 1944, until the Russian forces pushed in to liberate them. In Germany concentration camps such as Buchenwald, Sachsenhausen, and Dachau, which had been built to house Communists and other political opponents, became death camps for Jews as the German forces took them west on their retreat from the Russians. Author Elie Wiesel, an Auschwitz survivor, tells of that death march in his haunting autobiographical novel *Night*. Those German camps were liberated by the Americans and British.

ISSUES

The Holocaust Is Over: Germany Accepted Punishment for the Nazi Crimes and Has Worked to Compensate the Survivors. Modern Germany Should Not Still Be Blamed for These Crimes

Agree:

After the defeat of Germany in World War II, the victorious Allies conducted the Nuremberg War Crimes Trials. Hitler, who had conceived and commanded the process of extermination, committed suicide near the end of the war rather than be judged for his actions. The trials dealt with 22 of his major accomplices. On the basis of the evidence 7 of them were sentenced to death by hanging for "crimes against humanity" related to the Holocaust. They were: Hans Frank, who governed Poland (1939–45) during the deportation, exploitation, and extermination of the Jews; Wilhelm Frick, who helped frame the Nuremberg Laws and the takeover of Jewish assets; Julius

Streicher, the editor of the venomous *Der Stürmer;* Martin Bormann, Hitler's secretary, never captured but tried in absentia for his work to expel Jews to Poland; Ernst Kaltenbrunner, chief of the Reich Security Main Office, which was responsible for the Einsatzgruppen, who murdered Jews in the Soviet Union; Alfred Rosenberg, Hitler's chief anti-Semitic propagandist; Arthur Seyss-Inquart, the Austrian minister for public safety, who, after the Anschluss (annexation of Austria), helped plan the deportation of Jews from Germany, and, as Reich commissioner of the Netherlands, helped send Dutch Jews to the death camps and then confiscated their property. The de-Nazification programs of the U.S., British, Russian, and French occupation authorities also identified Nazis and Nazi sympathizers in their zones of occupation, then tried and punished them.

There are three clear proofs that Germany has overcome the terrible legacy of the Holocaust: the first is in the growth and development of the Jewish community in Germany; the second is in the progress of German relations with the new Jewish state of Israel; the third is its effort to reach out to Holocaust victims worldwide.

After the Bundesrepublik Deutschland (BRD, Federal Republic of Germany) was established in the west in 1949, its government enacted laws that made anti-Semitism subject to severe penalties. Recognizing the responsibility of the German people for the Holocaust, the BRD also enacted laws to compensate the 30,000 remaining German Jews for their suffering and losses at the hands of the Nazis. From the immediate postwar remnant population of 30,000, the Jewish population in Germany rose to 80,000 in 2000. The BRD has the largest-growing Jewish community in Europe and is the destination for thousands of Jews emigrating from the former Soviet Union. Only France and England have larger Jewish populations in Europe.[7]

Both the BRD and Israel came into being in 1949. In 1951 the BRD reached an agreement with the new Jewish state that set a schedule of reparations payments on behalf of the Holocaust victims. This treaty, signed in September 1952, obligated the BRD to pay 345 billion marks to the state of Israel during the following 12 years. Programs of student exchange began in the 1950s, as well as numerous other cultural, political, and scientific projects between the two countries. Sister city agreements between the two nations began in 1975, and now there are more than 100 pairs. Since German unification the momentum has increased. In 1994 Israel was given "privileged status" with the European Union (EU) through a German-sponsored initiative. A further agreement on scientific and technical cooperation came into force in 1999 during the German presidency of the EU.

Beyond the reparations to Israel, an additional 100 billion marks were paid to individuals worldwide as indemnities for their losses and suffering (some 40 billion of this to Israelis). During the 1980s the government implemented a policy of reaching out to German Jews who had immigrated abroad because of the Nuremberg Laws instituted in the 1930s. By the thousands they were invited to return, at German expense, to visit Germany and begin the process of reconciliation. The program planners made special efforts to reunite scattered family members and friends and to learn from the emigrants how to improve the country's efforts to end anti-Semitism.[8]

Thus, Germany has worked successfully to overcome its dark legacy of anti-Semitism, and this effort has been acknowledged by world Jewry. Symbolic of this acknowledgment, in 1998 the American Jewish Community, which previously had offices only in the United States and Israel, opened an office in Berlin. There it works with resident Germans to provide educational programs and to assist European Jews immigrating to Israel.

Disagree:

The Nuremberg Tribunal's judgment to execute seven men for Holocaust crimes did not begin to account for the extensive German operations against the Jews. Thus, the question has been raised: To what extent was the general German public accountable for the Holocaust? Why are many participants still unpunished today? Why have they been able to share Germany's prosperity with their family and heirs?

The allied occupying forces in the western zones relaxed de-Nazification once it became apparent that they needed local leaders to help with German recovery. The United States ordered General Lucius Clay, commander of its occupation forces, to cease de-Nazification. It has been estimated that some 40 percent of the BRD's upper-level civil servants and 30 percent of the owners of private industry in 1947 were former Nazis. In 1950, moreover, 65 percent of its teachers had also been Nazis.[9] Konrad Adenauer, the BRD's first chancellor, had several men in his government with a "brown (Nazi) past." This inclusion encouraged Germans to deny any complicity with the Holocaust. For a long time many said that the very secret and intimidating nature of the Nazi dictatorship kept such matters from them. But in the decades since the war much information has come to light. American historian Christopher Browning has proved in a number of important studies that the Foreign Office, the Wehrmacht (army), and a broad spectrum of government administrators were deeply involved in carrying out genocidal orders, even if they did not design or issue them. Raul Hilberg has identified nearly 30 agencies linked to various stages of implementation. Many Germans, even non-Nazis, clearly enforced the anti-Semitic laws, participated in the boycotts and violence, built the railroads and death camp facilities, and helped transport and murder the victims, or simply stood by and let it happen. The failure to eliminate the breadth of Naziism made it possible for racist anti-Semitism to survive and provide roots to continuing extremism. The emergence of the Nazi-style Sozialistische Reichspartei in the early 1950s, and, more recently, the extreme right Nationaldemokratische Partei Deutschlands, the Freiheitlichen Arbeiter Partei, and the Nationale Liste demonstrate the residual

Nazi attitudes among the Germans. The actions taken by the government to ban these parties cannot correct the problem.

Moreover, the Deutsche Demokratische Republik (DDR, German Democratic Republic), unlike the BRD, never took responsibility for the Holocaust. The Communists and Socialists were among the first victims of the Nazi political purge of the Reichstag. Their successors after World War II maintained that they had been unable to participate in the Holocaust actions because they themselves were prisoners in the German concentration camps. Their ideology identified fascism as an outgrowth of capitalism, not Marxism; therefore, it was fitting that the West Germans, not the East Germans, bear blame for the genocide. However, in 1996 Daniel J. Goldhagen, using documents from the East German Stasi (State Secret Police) files, argued that ordinary Germans were "Hitler's willing executioners," in both their attitudes and their activities. Thus, the whole German people must be constantly reminded of the historic dangers in their political past and be held accountable for the extremism evident today.

Europe and, to Some Extent, the United States Bear Responsibility, along with Germany, for the Holocaust

Agree:

Hilberg calculates that of the 5.1 million Jewish victims of the Holocaust only approximately 120,000 were German. The overwhelming majority were Jews from eastern Europe, more than 3 million from Poland alone. There is historical evidence that other countries offered little or no resistance to Hitler's genocide. Some even enacted anti-Semitic measures on their own. For example, in May 1939 the government of Hungary passed its own law to deport 300,000 Jews. The Poles made no significant effort to save their 3.25 million Jewish citizens or to prevent the setting up of the many ghettos and death camps in their country during the war. After the Germans conquered northern France in 1940, the French Vichy government of unoccupied France sent 5,000 Jews from Paris into labor camps and later 12,000 more into concentration camps. In 1939 Cardinal Eugenio Pacelli, who was overtly pro-German, became Pope Pius XII. In office he failed to condemn Hitler's actions against the Jews. He told U.S. envoys in 1942 that he was unable to verify the reports of these actions but would do what he could "to mitigate the suffering of *non-Aryans*."[10] Finally, the organization and transportation of Jews from all over German-occupied Europe could not have been accomplished without the compliance of their home governments and fellow citizens. Germany was fighting a war and had to force foreign laborers to work in their military industries.

Polish participation was particularly incriminating. The Poles turned over their Jews, then took over Jewish buildings and property:

The real estate owned by Jewish communities before the war included 228 Synagogues (seven currently in use), 70 prayer houses, 25 mikvahs (baths for ritual Purification), 28 funeral homes, 27 schools and four hospitals (including Warsaw's Kasprzaka Street Hospital)—a total of around 350 buildings. This number doesn't include 1,020 cemeteries, of which fewer than half are in good condition, and a Third of which have been destroyed.[11]

The city of Kraców, familiar to many as the setting for the novel and film *Schindler's List,* went from 65,000 Jews in residence before the war to only approximately 200 today. After the war the Socialist government took over the property of the Holocaust victims and nationalized much other private property. The *Warsaw Voice—Society* reports that 200 of the 270 apartment buildings in the Jewish quarter of Kazimierz were once owned by Jews. After the end of the socialist government in the 1990s, they, like other Poles, began filing suits for restitution of some 50 buildings formerly owned by Jewish organizations and communities. Polish legislation says only this communal (not private) property can be reclaimed by the Jews, and only if it is not being used by a public institution or has not been purchased by others "in good faith." In those cases the successful claimant can receive compensation, but that compensation can be used only in Poland to restore or maintain "Jewish Cultural landmarks."[12]

The removal of the European Jews and confiscation of their wealth and property actually benefited some Europeans. Claims are being filed throughout Europe for restitution. The process of settling these claims is ongoing. In Austria, for example, there have been many acts of restitution since World War II, but claims continue. In January 2001 a treaty was signed in Washington, D.C., by Austria, the Conference on Jewish Material Claims, the Austrian Jewish Community, the United States, and attorneys for the victims. It requires the Austrian government and Austrian companies to establish a general settlement fund totaling some $380 million to resolve property interests (approximately $7,000 per claimant), plus $25 million for insurance. Another $112 million is earmarked for pensions and benefits for survivors.[13] The Swiss banks are also working to settle claims (see chapter 10).

The United States, too, stood by while the atrocities were occurring. In 1942 the World Jewish Committee of Switzerland notified contacts in New York and Washington of the atrocities. The U.S. government, busy rounding up and interning its Japanese citizens, did not respond to this information about these anti-Semitic crimes. It also refused to relax U.S. immigration quotas for European Jews, thus condemning tens of thousands of them to remain in Europe, where they were rounded up and murdered.

There is one significant omission from the list of European countries that are guilty by association, however: only the Danish government refused to carry out the anti-Semitic regulations of the German occupying forces. Indeed, Danes helped escaped Jews flee to neutral Sweden, where they would be safe. Few Danes became Holocaust victims. What might have happened if the other Europeans had been as courageous and principled?

Disagree:

The evidence clearly shows that the Germans were the originators and administrators of all of the Holocaust activities. The minutes of the Wannsee Conference, taken by Adolf Eichmann, clearly show the intent and process. No non-Germans were part of that inner circle. With German armies and secret police in total control of Europe, the people of the conquered lands had little choice but to comply with their orders. These people had a moral obligation to protect their own families. Risking death by defying orders had no purpose. Although a small number of non-German individuals have been tried and sentenced for serving as brutal guards in the death camps or for assisting with the deportations, there has been no significant proof of widespread non-German collaboration with the Holocaust. The Jews who once lived outside of Germany were casualties of the war, not of local anti-Semitism.

The Holocaust Did Occur

Disagree:

Some deniers evince an angry Germanic nationalism, claiming that the Holocaust is a myth in the vindictive tradition of the Versailles Treaty, blaming Germany for the problems of European society. These deniers tend to see Germany as the victim of history. They are called "revisionists." Even as early as the 1920s and 1930s, deniers such as Sidney B. Fay, a diplomatic historian, used evidence to show that Germany was not the sole cause of World War I. After World War II this approach reappeared in the work of Harry Elmer Barnes, who wrote a pamphlet called *The Struggle against Historical Blackout,* claiming that the Allies were responsible for the war. Early revisionists did not deny the Holocaust, but they opened the door to denial. In 1977 David Irving, a British historian, published *Hitler's War,* a very controversial and often factually incorrect work that claimed that Hitler had nothing to do with the actual policy. He offered $1,000 to anyone who could prove that Hitler knew about Auschwitz. Two years later Willis Carto founded the Institute for Historical Review and held the first Revisionist Conference in Los Angeles. The institute director offered a $50,000 prize to prove that the Nazis actually used gas chambers to kill Jews during the war. The institute's *Journal of Historical Review* purchased the mailing list of the prestigious Organization of American Historians and tried to solicit readers and contributors.

Some deniers are blatant anti-Semites. One is Ernst Zündel, a German resident in Canada, whom the German government claimed is a major provider

British author and historian David Irving arrives at the London High Court January 2000 to attend his libel case against U.S. academic Deborah Lipstadt, professor of modern Jewish and Holocaust studies at Emory University (Atlanta, Georgia), and her publisher Penguin Books for claiming he is a Hitler partisan. (AP/Wide Worlds Photo)

of neo-Nazi materials. He and other overt anti-Semites try to prove that it was technically impossible to have carried out the genocide. Zündel has produced a series of videos in this vein. In addition to denying the Holocaust, he claims that Auschwitz was a recreational facility, that Jews were sent there for their protection during the chaotic war years, and that those who were missing after the war went to the United States and changed their names.

Agree:

There is so much evidence on the Holocaust—from the masses of captured German documents and photographs, from the testimony of the survivors, from the archeology of the ghettos and camps—that it seems incredible that some deny that it ever took place. Yet they do. Some Holocaust historians and survivors say that this denial should not be acknowledged or dignified by discussion. They miss the point, however. Discussion does not dignify the Holocaust deniers; it exposes their manipulation of history for what it is. Once their reasons and tactics are recognized, there is ample logic and fact to refute them.

The deniers have not fared well once confronted with factual evidence and logical argument. In 1993 Deborah Lipstadt published one of the finest exposures of the deniers and denial phenomenon: *Denying the Holocaust: The Growing Assault on Truth and Memory.* In 2000 David Irving, one of the deniers, sued Lipstadt and her publisher, Penguin Press, for libel in stating that he denied the Holocaust. Testimony in the case centered on Irving's use and interpretation of factual evidence. The court ruled against him.

In 1984 Ernst Zündel was tried in Canada for "willfully and knowingly publish[ing]...false news or tale whereby injury or mischief is or likely to be occasioned to any public interest." At issue was his pamphlet *Did Six Million Really Die?* Zündel was found guilty on the evidence but appealed on constitutional issues. In 1988 he was again tried and convicted and thereafter was sentenced to nine months in jail.[14] In 1993 his application for Canadian citizenship was denied, as was his reapplication in 2000. The Canadian minister of citizenship labeled him "a threat to the security of Canada."

In 1986 Mel Mermelstein, an Auschwitz survivor, sued the Institute of Historical Review and its principal officers because they had refused to respond when he submitted a notarized statement with evidence about the gas chambers in Auschwitz. In 1986 Mermelstein won $5.25 million in damages from the *Jewish Information Bulletin,* a denial publication that had attacked him and ridiculed the stories of the Jews in Auschwitz.

QUESTIONS AND ACTIVITIES

1. Using the Web, contact the United States Holocaust Memorial Museum (http://www.ushmm.org/), the Simon Wiesenthal Center (http://wiesenthal.org), and the Holocaust History Project (http://www.holocaust-history.org) to identify, download, and print materials for a classroom reference collection on the Holocaust.

2. Prepare a map to identify the European countries affected by the Holocaust. Use color to help point out those countries that lost the greatest numbers of Jews in this genocide.

3. Using the Web, contact the Nizkor Project (http://www.nizkor.org) to identify, download, and print materials for a classroom reference collection that exposes the deniers of the Holocaust.

4. Find out if there are any Holocaust survivors in your community who are willing to come to your classroom to speak about their experiences. With their permission plan a program that is open to others in the school.

5. As a class, read Elie Wiesel's *Night* or view the French video *Night and Fog* ("Nuit et brouillard," Alan Resnais, director, co-produced by Como-Films, Argos Films, Cocinor, 1983). Discuss what you have learned from it about the experience of the Holocaust.

6. Ask your teacher to rent or purchase the video *America and the Holocaust* (Shanachia Home Video, 1994). After viewing it, hold a classroom discussion on the

policies of the United States at the time and on what our government and people might have done to aid those threatened with genocide.

7. Write a short paper explaining what you think the world has learned from this terrible episode. Have we developed ways to prevent genocide from recurring?

8. Assume that you are a teacher who has to explain the Holocaust to young students. Write an outline of the lesson you would give. What insights and values do you want these students to learn from your class?

NOTES

1. Randal Bytwerk, "*Der Stürmer:* 'A Fierce and Filthy Rag,' " *Calvin: Minds in the Making,* http://www.calvin.edu/academic/cas/faculty. Select Bytwerk and search "Julius Streicher." (This is an on-line publication of Calvin College, Grand Rapids, Michigan.)

2. Quotation from *Mein Kampf* cited in Joachim C. Fest, *Hitler,* trans. Richard and Clara Winston, Vintage Books ed. (New York: Random House, 1975), 39.

3. Quoted in Joachim Remak, ed., *The Nazi Years: A Documentary History* (Prospect Heights, Ill.: Waveland Press, 1969), 28, 30. The program cited was written by Gottfried Feder in 1932.

4. Quoted from Jeremy Noakes and Geoffrey Pridham, *Documents on Nazism 1919–1945* (New York: Viking Press, 1974), 463–67. The quote is also available at:. http://www.us-israel.org. See also *The Nizkor Project* on the Web (http://www.nizkor.org).

5. *Jewish Emigration from Germany 1933–1939*

Between April 1933 and May 1939, 304,500 Jews emigrated from Germany (including areas occupied by Germany in May 1939. They emigrated to:

U.S.	63,000
Palestine	55,000
Great Britain	40,000
France	30,000
Argentina	25,000
Brazil	13,000
South Africa	5,500
Italy	5,000
Other European countries	25,000
Other South American countries	15,000
Other	8,000
Total	**304,500**

Source: "Statistics of the Holocaust," http://faculty.ucc.edu/egh-damerow/Statistics.htm. [Author's note: many of the Jewish emigrants to France, Italy, and other European countries were also rounded up and deported to ghettoes and concentration camps once the Third Reich established control in Europe.]

6. The transcript of the Wannsee Conference is available in English at "The Wannsee Conference," *The History Place: World War II in Europe,* http://www.historyplace.com/worldwar2/timeline/wannsee2.htm. Raul Hilberg, *The Destruction of the European Jews,* student ed. (New York and London: Holmes and Meier, 1985), 793 n. 55. "The Wannsee Conference."

7. "German-Israeli Relations," 200/05/15, http://www.bundesregierung.de.

8. Ibid.

9. Alexander Cockburn, "Austria—Pariah among Nations," *Nation* 270, no. 8 (28 February 2000), 8.

10. Cardinal Pacelli quoted in Joseph R. Mitchell and Helen Buss Mitchell, *The Holocaust: Readings and Interpretations* (New York: McGraw-Hill/Dushkin, 2001), 298. The emphasis is mine.

11. "50 Years and Counting," *The Warsaw Voice—Society Voice* 4, no. 31 (26 January 1997), 1–2, http://www.warsawvoice.pl/old/v831.Soc00.html.

12. Ibid.

13. Austrian Press and Information Service, Washington, D.C., 19 January 2001, http://www.austria.org/press/.

14. "Supreme Court of Canada: 1992 Zündel Judgement," *The Nizkor Project*. http://www.nizkor.org.

SUGGESTED READINGS

So much has been written about the Holocaust that it is difficult to narrow the selection. A good procedure would be to consult the written works listed here as a starting place, then to use their notes and bibliographies as references for more intensive study. The Web sites listed can be used the same way. By combining these sources, the reader can learn about the policies, administrative structures, procedures, results, impacts, and judgments of this terrible historical episode.

Anti-Semitism

It is important to understand the deep hold that anti-Semitism had in Europe. Robert S. Wistrich's *Antisemitism: The Longest Hatred* (New York: Pantheon Books, 1991) is one of the most readable explanations of historical anti-Semitism. There is also a film of this name, produced by Films for the Humanities and Sciences in 1991. Raul Hilberg's *The Destruction of the European Jews,* student ed. (New York and London: Holmes and Meier, 1985), is an abridgement of his longer, three-volume study. Its eight chapters provide background, analysis, and documents on each stage of the process. It also has a superb annotated bibliography to guide those seeking more information. Joseph R. Mitchell and Helen Buss Mitchell's *The Holocaust: Readings and Interpretations* (New York: McGraw-Hill/Dushkin, 2001) also offers documents and interpretations by issue. Each chapter also has recommended readings and the URLs of recommended Web sites (especially http://www.holocaust-history.org/ and http://www.ushmm.org/, the site of the United States Holocaust Memorial Museum).

The Holocaust

There are good starting points for obtaining an understanding of the human tragedy of the Holocaust. *The Diary of Anne Frank,* available in many versions, conveys the terror of the Jews as the Nazis began their sweep. Elie Wiesel's *Night* (New York: Bantam, 1982) details the agony of existence in Auschwitz. Aaron Hass's *The Aftermath: Living with the Holocaust* (Cambridge: Cambridge University Press, 1996) provides Holocaust survivors' first-person accounts of their lives. Many survivors felt guilt for their happy fate: some tried to atone, others tried to forget. Similarly, Helen Epstein's *Children of the Holocaust:*

Conversations with Sons and Daughters of Survivors (New York: Penguin, 1998) demonstrates that the children of survivors are also affected by the horror their parents experienced.

Who Was Accountable?

Christopher R. Browning has pursued the question of accountability intensely and has proved that a large number of ordinary men and women, well outside the Nazi inner circle, knowingly carried out the Nazi extermination policies. See *The Final Solution and the German Foreign Office* (New York: Holmes and Meier, 1978); *The Path to Genocide: Essays on Launching the Final Solution* (Cambridge: Cambridge University Press, 1992); *Ordinary Men: Reserve Police Battalion 101 and the Final Solution in Poland* (New York: Harper Collins, 1992); and *Nazi Policy, Jewish Workers, German Killers* (Cambridge: Cambridge University Press, 2000). Daniel J. Holdhagen's controversial *Hitler's Willing Executioners: Ordinary Germans and the Holocaust* (New York: Random House, 1996) argues that Germany had a uniquely "eliminationist anti-Semitism" that carried them to the extremes.

More than 3 million Polish Jews died in the Holocaust, the overwhelming majority. Yet no body of literature studying the complicity of the Poles in these actions is available in English. Angelika Konigseder's *Waiting for Hope: Jewish Displaced Persons in Post–World War II Germany* (Chicago: Northwestern University Press, 2001) details how hundreds of thousands of Jewish concentration camp survivors returned to eastern Europe and found it dangerous and often impossible to resettle there. Instead they migrated to the British and American zones of Germany and stayed in the refugee camps between 1947 and 1949 until they emigrated to Israel. As the archives of the former Soviet bloc states open up to researchers, more data on eastern European collaboration in the Holocaust will undoubtedly come to light.

Regarding the many international bystanders, David S. Wyman's *The Abandonment of the Jews: America and the Holocaust 1941–1945* (New York: Pantheon Books, 1984) is a good starting point for a review of the U.S. government's failure to take action when it was first informed of the threat to Europe's Jews.

Denial of the Holocaust

Deborah Lipstadt's *Denying the Holocaust: The Growing Assault on Truth and Memory* (New York: Free Press, 1993) is the most comprehensive and insightful study of this phenomenon. Michael Shermer and Alex Rappoport's *Denying History: Who Says the Holocaust Never Happened and Why Do They Say That?* (Berkeley: University of California Press, 2000) analyzes the varieties of denial and exposes the fallacies of their arguments.

The World Wide Web is rich with the documentary evidence and analysis of the denial phenomenon. The most comprehensive site is the Nizkor Project site (http://www.nizkor.org), which provides links by subject. The transcripts of the Zündel and Irving trials can be found through Nizkor. The excellent "Holocaust Denial Timeline" can be found at the site http://www.holocaustdenialontrial.org/timelinedenial.asp.

4

THE *SONDERWEG* AND THE *HISTORIKERSTREIT:* THE BATTLE OVER GERMAN HISTORY

BACKGROUND

What Is the Historikerstreit?

German historians are having difficulty interpreting the nation's history, and the battle among them has reached epic proportions. This is not surprising because Germany has transformed itself in just about every generation in its brief 130-plus years as a modern nation. Much of its history has been very authoritarian and warlike, yet today, despite that troubling past, it is a peaceful, prosperous, and democratic leader in Europe. What is the real essence of German history? That is the focus of the controversy.

The term Historikerstreit refers to the particularly heated warfare of articles about Germany that began in June 1986. Its initial theme was the place of the Holocaust in German history: Was it typically German or a terrible exception to national development? This question led scholars to analyze Germany's unique path to modernization through top-down authoritarianism, in contrast with most other European nations in which the aristocratic elites gradually opened their political systems to the middle and working classes. These other nations had matured into representative constitutional states. Many felt that Germany's authoritarian, antidemocratic past represented a Sonderweg (unique path) in European history.

Why Have the Historians Divided?

At the opening of an exhibit at Haus der Geschichte (House of the History of the Bundesrepublik Deutschland, or Federal Republic of Germany) in

Bonn on 7 July 2001, Chancellor Gerhard Schröder observed, *"Politik ohne Geschichte gibt es nicht"* (There are no politics without history).[1] The chancellor might easily have completed that statement with the observation that "there is no history without politics." History is the art of *interpreting* the facts, and there are often many points of view. Like politics, history has extremist, conservative, liberal, and radical points of view. History is always written "now," and what was considered the final interpretation just a short time ago can be significantly changed by new information, new events, and new questions. Politicians often use history to argue issues. Regarding U.S. history, for example, they debate issues such as the New Deal or the leadership of Richard Nixon or the causes and outcome of the Vietnam War and can usually find credible historians on all sides of the discussion. Given the complexity of German history in the twentieth century, it is not surprising that its historians are in turmoil.

The Historical Controversies in German History

The first controversy of modern German history concerns the meaning of the term Germany. Before Germany became the name of a modern political nation, it was basically a cultural conception. At best, Germany was a region of small independent dynastic states where the people shared a common language and cultural past. Most of them belonged to the Holy Roman Empire, actually a federation of principalities established in the Middle Ages. By 1800 the empire included 300 of these states and was headed by an Austrian dynasty, the Habsburgs. But Habsburg Austria also included Hungary and many Slavic peoples, non-Germans all. The two largest states in the Holy Roman Empire were German Prussia in northern Europe and multicultural Austria in the south. They competed for the allegiance of the smaller German states in the middle. Napoleon used this rivalry to carve up the German states to suit his own political plans. He reduced their number to 39 by combining many of the smallest of them. After he was defeated in 1815, the victors established the Deutsches Bund (German Confederation) of 35 German states, with Austria once again at its head.

During the Revolutions of 1848, some of the Germans fought to adopt the liberal principles of the Enlightenment that had taken hold in England and France. A popular movement forced the German monarchies to accede to a constitution-writing assembly in Frankfurt. Its middle-class leaders composed the basis for German unity through a constitutional monarchy. However, the members of the Frankfurt Parliament could not agree whether the historical Germany was Grossdeutsch (Great Germany, including Austria with its non-German population) or Kleindeutsch (Little Germany, which meant the German states excluding Austria's non-German populations). As a result, this collection of lawyers, academics, and journalists simply argued the revolution to death. Austria was not about to give up the power and prestige of its massive multicultural empire; the other rulers of the German states regained their confidence and power and then prosecuted the revolution's ringleaders (although a number of them fled to the United States). The Bund resumed its role, and Austria continued to control it. Historians have called the collapse of the Frankfurt Parliament "the turning point that failed to turn." It meant that the authority of the German monarchies and aristocracy continued without significant dilution, and "Germany" was still a concept waiting to take hold.

That first great historical controversy was overtaken in the 1860s by the second: *Which state should lead the Germans?* Prussia, under the leadership of King William I and Minister-President Otto von Bismarck, decided to challenge Austria for the leadership of the Germans. Prussia used politics within the Bund to force a confrontation with Austria. There were two short, tightly controlled wars (in 1864 and 1866), and in the second war Prussia, with its superbly trained army, defeated Austria in just a few weeks. The price of defeat for Austria was its agreement to end its political control over the German states. Bismarck then designed the Norddeutsches Bund (North German Confederation) in 1867, which included its German allies in the wars and the pro-Austrian opponents that it had conquered. Three southern German states, Baden, Bayern (Bavaria), and Württemburg, remained outside the Bund, but agreed to an alliance to defend it when it was attacked. When Bismarck provoked France to attack the Bund in 1870, these states came to its defense. On 18 January 1871, with France preparing to surrender to the armies of the Norddeutsches Bund, the rulers of all the Bund states and the three southern German rulers inked a treaty establishing the Deutsches Reich (German Empire), giving King William I of Prussia a second crown as Deutscher Kaiser (German emperor). Germany had become a unified modern national state, the last to take its place in Europe. The historians noted that the state was unified by the army and by agreement among the dynastic rulers. There was no popular participation in its design. This was, indeed, the Sonderweg, but look how much it had achieved. Why criticize? Did not the end justify the means?

The Second Empire

The third historical controversy was over domestic politics: Who really controlled the Empire? Prussian leader Otto von Bismarck had given the empire the most liberal voting laws in Europe. Suddenly every German adult male in every state could join a political party, could vote, and could discuss national issues. It certainly looked like democracy. But Bismarck's system gave authoritarian Prussia the upper hand: all legislation passed by the Reichstag (Legislative) had also to be passed by the Bundesrat (Federal Council), the "upper house" of delegates appointed by the state rulers. Bismarck made sure that Prussia had enough delegates to veto any measure it did not want. Finally, all legislation had be signed by the imperial chancellor (Bismarck modestly gave himself that position while remaining as the chief minister in Prussia) and the by the Kaiser. Thus, Bismarck left little chance for the Reichstag to force legislation on the administration. He even outlawed the popular Social Democrat Party for 12 years, then created Europe's first system of social insurance in order to try to wean away the party's working-class support. This top-down system was meant to preempt popular pressure and keep the conservative elite in power. It worked. Moreover, the Industrial Revolution blossomed in Germany after unification: new industries, new work opportunities, and a growing economy began to benefit the middle and lower classes. Why criticize? Was not paternalism working well?

William II and His "Personal Regime"

After William I died (1888) and Bismarck resigned (1890), the nature of politics changed. William II (1888–1918) was erratic and sought political popularity at home by reinstating the Social Democrats and by building a navy and colonial system to gain international prestige abroad. He made rash decisions and questionable compromises, often embarrassing ones. He believed he ruled by divine right and became infuriated with the popular criticism of his actions. He fired a number of chancellors who did not defend him from that criticism. The importance and influence of the Reichstag increased as it learned to manipulate public opinion and use its power over the national budgets to obtain leverage. Yet the Social Democrat Party, the working-class party that had the largest Reichstag voting constituency in the empire between 1890 and 1918, was prevented by constitutional constraints from wielding real power. The Sonderweg was faltering, and there seemed to be no way to correct it. It could be productive only with expert leadership.

World War I and the German Republic

William II's diplomatic bungling plunged Germany into World War I and to humiliating collapse.[2] The threat of defeat led, in turn, to his abdication on 9 November 1918 and to the proclamation of the German (Weimar) Republic by the Social Democrats. The republic and the Social Democrats later had to bear the brunt of the penalties imposed by the victorious Allies through the Treaty of Versailles, 1919: acceptance of full blame for starting the war, with the resultant reparations payments to the Allies for their expenses and losses; demilitarization; loss of territory to surrounding states; and occupation by Allied military forces. Germany was also stripped of its overseas colonies, which were not freed, but instead were turned over to the new League of Nations and then to the victorious powers. It was a terrible humiliation of the once proud empire, especially to the military elite and conservatives who had been in power for so long. (Because the Kaiser had abdicated *before* the treaty was signed, however, they absolved themselves of any blame for the postwar consequences.) But to the victors the penalties seemed appropriate. Germany had to be punished. Historians began to wonder why Germany had taken such a different and disruptive path in its national development.

The Weimar Republic[3]

Nonetheless, with the old regime gone, the German liberals began to write a constitution that was one of the most liberal in the world. They used western models to create a British-style cabinet form of government, in which the government leaders would be elected representatives from the largest party in the Reichstag. The republic now had universal, free, and secret adult suffrage—for men and women—and a system of proportional representation in which every party received seats in the Reichstag according to the percentage of votes it had obtained in the elections. This type of representation resulted in many political parties, which gave voice to all points of view and required open debate to construct a majority for proposed legislation. The president was elected separately and given emergency power to rule by decree in the event that the Reichstag was unable to reach consensus. Out-of-power conservatives and extreme nationalists, however, blamed the defeat in World War I and the Treaty of Versailles on the pacifistic socialists and the Jews. They rejected the republic on principle and began to work against it. The economy was in shambles, having been bankrupted by war and shackled with reparations. These elements led to protests and street violence. There were Putsch (overthrow) attempts by militarists and radicals and rebellions within some of the states for the next five years. Despite its ultrademocratic constitution, Germany was having no success trying to adopt and learn the western political model as an alternative to the old Sonderweg. On several occasions the republic had to ask the army to defend it.

The Depression, World War II, and a Second Defeat

Thanks to U.S. loans and a renegotiation of the World War I reparations payment schedule, Germany experienced a brief period of stability from 1925 to 1929. The constitutional republic seemed to work. But the 1929 U.S. stock market crash rippled across the Atlantic and sent the German economy and the government into a tailspin by 1931. The chaos facilitated the rise of the Nationalsozialistische Deutsche Arbeiterpartei (National Socialist German Workers' Party, the Nazi Party) and the Drittes Reich (Third Reich) with Adolf Hitler's dictatorship. It ironically was a mass movement until it created a dictatorship. Then, once again, general participation in government was stifled and the Nazi Party ruled alone, from the top down. This was the *Sonderweg* at its worst. Hitler's two goals were aggressive German expansionism to control Europe and the extermination of Jews. World War II and the Holocaust were the direct results of his deadly regime, and there was no question about who was to blame. Germany's surrender in May 1945 was total and unconditional. The Sonderweg had finally failed completely.

The Allies Teach Germany a Lesson

The victorious Allies agreed that Germany needed to change, needed to learn how to govern itself democratically and peacefully, without the authoritarianism and aggression that had characterized its first 70 years of existence. So after the surrender Germany was returned to its 1937 frontiers, divided into U.S., British, French, and Soviet occupation zones; demilitarized; and de-Nazified through a series of war crimes trials. Part of Germany was also democratized under the tutelage of three of the occupying powers, which helped establish representative local and zonal government.

Germany's second crushing defeat in less than 30 years was clear evidence, to many, that its historically antidemocratic Sonderweg was the real problem of its political maturation. The Nazi dictatorship seemed to be the inevitable outcome of Germany's inability to internalize the constitutional and democratic outlook that characterized western civilization. The Nuremberg War Crimes Trials laid the evidence bare and confirmed the accusations made by the victors after World War I. But as the Cold War distanced the Soviet Union from the western powers, democracy took two forms in divided Germany. The three western zones joined together in a capitalist society, but the eastern zone conformed to Soviet socialism. These two systems took concrete form when the two new German republics came into being in 1949.

The West German Historians

History serves politics, and nowhere was this more apparent than in the two German republics established in 1949. During the 1950s scholars mainly described and discussed Germany's decline in the first half of the century and the evils of the Third Reich. But in the 1960s West German historians' examinations turned to the root causes for the Third Reich. They looked not only at the Third Reich, but also at Bismarck's Deutsches Reich for the answers: they began to analyze the Sonderweg.

Implicit in their research was a condemnation of the Sonderweg and of the German state it generated. Scholars today point particularly to a work by Ralf Dahrendorf, *Society and Democracy in Germany* (1968), as the launching point of the discussion in the 1960s. He basically asked why the German monarchy did not develop the way the British monarchy did. In *The German Conception of History: The National Tradition of Historical Thought from Herder to the Present* (1968), George Iggers compared historical eras in Germany rather than comparing it with another country. Many other scholars began to pursue these issues.[4]

Liberal West German historians, such as Erich Eyck (*A History of the Weimar Republic,* 2 volumes, 1952), came to the conclusion that the German Republic established after World War I *could* have brought Germany into the mainstream of liberal constitutional government. Germans really did build a more liberal, constitutional form of government. But its potential was blocked from the outset by the vindictive Versailles Treaty, the German reactionaries, and the depression. Clearly, the new Bundesrepublik Deutschland (BRD, founded in 1949) was overcoming its past.

These scholars were shocked and angered, therefore, by the extraordinarily well-researched work by Fritz Fischer, *Germany's Aims in the First World War* (1961, trans. 1967), which blamed that war on the basically aggressive nature of the Germans themselves. If this were true, then Hitler was a natural product of German society, not just a terrible deviation from it.[5] The Fischer controversy turned the discussion away from political structure and focused a cold light on the German people instead. This process paved the way for the Historikerstreit. What was the true nature of the German culture? What responsibility did Germans themselves bear for Hitler's dictatorship and especially for the Holocaust?

A subtle but very important aspect of this controversy is that it occurred in the West German BRD and not in the East German Deutsche Demokratische Republik (DDR). The West Germans assumed that they had the only legitimate German state. Therefore, they had inherited the legacy of Germany's continuous history, including Bismarck's empire, the failures of the German Republic, and Hitler. They had also inherited its guilt, especially for the Holocaust. This awful history motivated government policy. From the outset the BRD had established laws against anti-Semitism and fascism. It designed ways to compensate the survivors and to support Israel, which was also founded in 1949. Indeed, this continuity and the acceptance of responsibility for it were major aspects of the BRD's political legitimacy.

The East German Historians

The East Germans, by contrast, found their legitimacy by denying any legacy of Germany's terrible past. They considered themselves to have formed, with Soviet help, an entirely new type of German state that utterly repudiated the Sonderweg; it was a people's democracy. It arose from the heritage of the Social Democrat and Communist Parties that had been suppressed by Bismarck, hamstrung by the Allies and the depression during the Weimar era, then attacked by the Nazis. Many members of these parties had been persecuted and executed by the Nazis. Their representatives had been expelled from the Reichstag, and those remaining were imprisoned in the Sachsenhausen and Dachau concentration camps before the war and the Holocaust ever took place. Those few who escaped Nazi persecution had fled to exile in the Soviet Union, which sheltered them. There they learned how to break the shackles of the old aristocratic and authoritarian Sonderweg and how to implement a socialist state to fulfill the needs of the working class. Following Germany's surrender they had returned to their homeland with the Soviets to help found and govern the new DDR. Thus, they assumed no responsibility for the atrocities of the Third Reich, which they blamed entirely on the West Germans. The West Germans were the ones who had supported fascism, which is the inevitable consequence of industrial capitalism. The West Germans had participated in the war and the Holocaust. East German scholars devoted much of their time to proving the merits and legitimacy of Soviet-style socialism.

Ernst Nolte and the Opening Shot of the *Historikerstreit*

The Historikerstreit (Historians' Conflict) intensified in June 1986 with the publication of an article by the well-regarded senior historian Ernst Nolte of Berlin. It was published in a widely circulated newspaper, the *Frankfurter Allgemeine Zeitung,* instead of in one of the academic journals usually favored by scholars. In his article "Vergangenheit, die nicht vergehen will" (The past that refuses to go away), Nolte did the unthinkable. He suggested that the actual model for Hitler's concentration camps were Stalin's "gulags," the terrible labor camps to which Stalin sentenced his political opponents. In other words, Nolte broke the uniform practice of assigning to the German culture the guilt for Hitler. He wondered whether Germany's fascism should instead be considered within a broader European historical context. Although he acknowledged that the political climate in Germany had made him fearful of taking this direction, he criticized his colleagues for failing to address it as well.[6]

Andreas Hillgruber Gave the Debate Substance

Later that year Andreas Hillgruber published a slim volume, *Zweierlei Untergang—Die Zerschlagung des Deutschen Reiches und das Ende des europaischen Judentums* (Two downfalls—The destruction of the German Reich and the end of the European Jews). With this work he, too, challenged his colleagues to overcome the taboo of taking a wider view. Anti-Semitism was found all over Europe, yet German historians had avoided placing it in a European context. The western Allies and eastern Europeans had been diligent in focusing the accusation of anti-Semitism on Germany, using it long after the surrender to divide and weaken Germany. He went even further into revisionism. He defended the German eastern front forces. They fought to protect Germans in the historical core settlement regions of Prussia from the viciousness of the Russians, well known for their "arbitrary murder and countless deportations." He pointed to the Soviet murders of Polish officers at the Katyn Forest as an example. The *Frankfurter Allegemine Zeitung* published a review of Hillgruber's book on 8 July 1987, pronouncing it "relatively factual and objective."[7]

These two publications unleashed an editorial battle of the scholars. It opened the door to revision of the unrelieved "history of guilt" and challenged the public use of history that had been standard since the BRD's earliest days. This Historikerstreit was unique in that it was carried out almost entirely in the pages of the daily press, not in obscure and stuffy academic journals. The public could read and even participate through letters and, of course, through personal conversations within their own circles. Karl Dietrich Erdmann, the founder and editor of *Geschichte in Wissenschaft und Unterricht* (History in science and instruction), observed that German scholars had heretofore been too uniform in their analyses, which he felt was a dangerous trend.[8] But this process of Vergangenheitsbewältigung (conquering the past) had another, uglier aspect. It involved unprecedented personal attacks among the scholars and attempts to discredit one another.

The Reaction of the German Foreign Office

The German Foreign Office worried about the impression all this very public controversy was making abroad. It sent a very detailed position paper to its embassies on 6 November 1986. The explanation in its cover letter is significant because it, too, incorporates a wider context, well beyond academic squabbling:

> This controversy shows how our public sphere, against the backdrop of the Nazi period, is struggling for the meaning of history and an understanding of history in the Federal Republic. In part the debate links the fortieth anniversary of the end of the war and President Reagan's visit to the military cemetery at Bitburg in 1985. The discussion is also related to the preparation of a plan for two museum projects, the House of the History of the Federal Republic of Germany in Bonn and the German Historical Museum in Berlin.

The letter continued by raising some of the major points of the initial debate:

- Should history provide meaning, be a bearer of national identity, and if so, how?
- Is history being misused as an instrument of political debate?...
- Are the crimes of the Nazi period unique, or are they comparable to other mass annihilations of history, such as those in the Soviet Union?...
- Is the destruction of the Third Reich a response to the crimes of the Third Reich?[9]

The unification of the two German republics in 1990 prolonged the debate. Germany became the largest and most powerful state in western Europe, which worried some of its neighbors. They were concerned that the revisionist attitude might foreshadow a whole new period of aggression, especially because there was no longer a Soviet Union in the east to help restrain it. In a February 2000 book review for *The New Republic,* Jeffrey Hert showed that their worst fears did not seem to be warranted. He called this change in viewpoint "the twentieth century's last surprise," explaining that "a unified Germany has not become a menacing Fourth Reich, and Russia, despite a collapse of its economy and the spectacular loss of the Cold War, did not turn in bitterness and frustration to the alliance of nationalists and communists who were seeking to reverse the humiliations of a decade ago."[10]

The Historikerstreit continues today, albeit in a milder tone. The questions it raises are important to an understanding of both the nature of history and its use by contemporary government and society. For the BRD these questions are especially important as the nation reflects on the implications of unification and the meaning of the past.

Historians cannot use all available evidence in their works. They always select the facts they wish to emphasize in order to construct their interpretations. A basic history of Europe in the twentieth century may be helpful in contextualizing the issues raised in the next section.

ISSUES

Germany Is the Only European "Rogue" Nation in the Twentieth Century

Agree:

Fritz Fischer was right. The Germans were not satisfied with simple unification; they wanted expansion and empire as well. William II kept talking about Germany's "place in the sun" as he sought overseas colonies. His plans for a new modern German navy set up an arms race across Europe, and he used that navy to threaten intervention in Latin America and North Africa. He exploited the German Industrial Revolution to build a massive and threatening military force. His diplomacy was provocative. He supported the Dutch rebels against the British authorities during the Boer War in South Africa. When the heir to the Austrian throne was assassinated by a Slavic terrorist in June 1914, he agreed to help Austria retaliate without even considering the consequences. In fact, he launched German forces into France, which was about as far away from the Slavic front as you can get in Europe. Moreover, that attack went through neutral Belgium, a flagrant violation of international law. Although supposedly pacifist Social Democrats had a majority in the Reichstag, they voted overwhelmingly to fund the "Kaiser's War." They certainly were not trying to oppose authoritarianism and militarism, as they long claimed.

The Weimar Republic was a farce and facade. The so-called liberal Constitution gave extraordinary emergency authority to the president, and it was certainly no coincidence that the first president elected was Paul von Hindenburg, a Prussian aristocrat and the former commanding general of the

German World War I armies. While seeming to try to fulfill the requirements of the Treaty of Versailles, the Germans were actually breaking it by secretly training military pilots in the Soviet Union. When the depression destroyed what little stability existed, the true nature of the Germans emerged through the vicious street battles conducted by the paramilitary forces of the political parties. Hitler fit naturally into this climate of deceit and aggression. His powerful Third Reich came into being legally by the vote of the populace and by Hitler's appointment to office by President Hindenburg. Germans had full knowledge of his intentions, fully disclosed in his book *Mein Kampf*.

Germans must acknowledge that the aggressions of World Wars I and II and the cold-blooded, industrial-style atrocities of the Holocaust are entirely of their own making. They tried to conquer and control Europe and to destroy the liberal, constitutional, and Christian values that characterize it. No other nation has such crime and blood on its hands and history.

Disagree:

Nolte, Hillgruber, and Erdmann are right to point out that German history has not been examined from the full range of perspectives. With exclusive focus on the Sonderweg, many of the positive aspects of this history are ignored. Although Germany was the youngest nation in Europe at the beginning of the twentieth century, it led the way in providing universal and equal suffrage to adult men and women. It led the way in designing social security for the working classes. It had one of the best-educated populations in the world; its research universities and technical institutes led the way in developing the new materials and processes that characterized the modern industrial revolution. Although Kaiser William II talked a militaristic game, Germany was basically a nation at peace from 1871 to 1914. The Weimar Republic was a positive expression of German aspirations for constitutional democracy. Despite all the obstacles put in its way, it lasted far longer than most of the so-called new democracies of the Baltic states and Poland in eastern Europe, which the Allies carved out of Germany, Austria, and Russia. These aspirations survived even through the Hitler years and were realized in the foundation of the BRD. The post–World War II occupying powers like to think they taught Germans how to be democratic. That is not the case at all: they only made it possible for basic political principles of peace and democracy to emerge at last.

Examine the history of Great Britain and the United States, which claimed the moral high ground at the beginning of the twentieth century. They were considered to be models of democracy, yet both still had voting laws that excluded women. Native Americans, already stripped of their lands and confined to reservations, were denied the vote, and African Americans had to endure literacy tests and poll taxes even to try to cast a ballot. England went to war anywhere for any reason: to fight Russia in the Crimea (1854–55), to suppress a rebellion in India against an overbearing colonial regime (Sepoy Mutiny 1857), to suppress the indigenous Dutch population in the British South African colony (1880–81 and 1899–1902). It hardly gained the world's largest overseas empire by extending invitations. The United States was not far behind: it fought the Spanish-American War in 1898 to gain Cuba, Guam, and the Philippines. It intervened brutally in the affairs of the small Central American republics in order to protect its commercial interests, including Santo Domingo in 1904 and Nicaragua in 1912. It bullied those countries throughout the twentieth century and often supported dictators so long as they protected U.S. interests.

Joining these nations in making the world safe for democracy was their World War I ally, the Russian Empire. It was the most expansionist land power in the world, conquering and subordinating hundreds of indigenous populations across 11 time zones into Siberia. This record is tougher than that produced by the U.S. "manifest destiny." The empire's collapse in World War I and the 1917 revolutions led to disintegration and civil wars of uncommon brutality. The Bolshevik Soviet dictatorship, the continent's first one-party state, exterminated a whole class of its own independent farmers (kulaks) for resisting collectivization. The toll has been estimated at more than 10 million, although the regime closed the records that could verify that estimate. Stalin did indeed establish the system of gulags, penal labor camps, after massive purges and executions failed to eliminate the opposition to Communist Party ideology and control. They were in full operation long before the Nazi concentration camps.

Another of Britain's World War I allies, Italy, designed and refined fascism. Benito Mussolini began to install his fascist dictatorship in 1922, well before Hitler appeared on the German horizon. In defiance of the League of Nations Mussolini launched attacks in Africa to obtain colonies, and the Western powers did nothing to stop him. Moreover, almost all of the new "successor" states succumbed to similar dictatorships by the end of the 1920s. Despite the arrogant propaganda of Woodrow Wilson and his World War I allies, they had not "made the world safe for democracy." They had fought only to protect their own trade and colonies. In the process they unleashed the worst forms of virulent nationalism and political extremism. The tensions they produced in the Balkan states have continued to trouble Europe up to the present.

Thus, many outside pressures on Germany helped shape its fate. One extraordinary but overlooked consideration is that Germany held out against these pressures for so long. Recognizing the full dimensions of twentieth-century history is not a denial of the bad parts of Germany's past. It is merely a recognition that nations do not act in a vacuum. Other nations must examine their own history with the same rigorous criteria they have applied to Germany and its history. If balance rather than guilt is made the operating standard, the twentieth century will be better understood.

The Unification of the Two German Republics in 1990 Has Brought about Final Closure of World War II

Agree:

Between 1949 and 1990 the BRD showed that Germany was working hard to eliminate anti-Semitism and fascism and to make reparations for the evils committed by the Third Reich. It has been welcomed back into the community of nations, into the United Nations, the North Atlantic Treaty Organization, and the European Union. Its social market economy, which provides security for the workers while providing a climate for capitalist development, is stable and productive. Its democracy is genuine and stable. It remained at peace throughout those four decades, despite the many conflicts going on around it. It has opened its doors to refugees and asylum seekers in unprecedented numbers and has treated them with compassion.

Most recently it has absorbed the much smaller East German DDR without firing a shot and without compromising the principles of constitution and economy that have made it such a strong and welcome world partner. With this reconciliation of the two parts of Germany, the last outstanding issue of World War II has been resolved. The newly expanded German nation will continue the BRD's policies and peaceful conduct.

The one issue that keeps cropping up is the German responsibility for the Holocaust, but Germany's record of taking responsibility for those past horrors is commendable. We must seriously ask, What more is expected of it? Imposing constant requirements for admissions of guilt, especially admissions by generations born long after the deeds were committed, is hardly the way to reduce anti-Semitism. These demands come primarily from the Jewish community in the United States and from Israel. But it must be remembered that the United States did little to ease the plight of German Jews trapped under Hitler and that Israel hardly offers a model for equitable handling of a minority population. Perhaps that memory of the German Holocaust helps them ease their own consciences.

Why has Germany been singled out for this type of treatment? The world community, which still wants Germans to feel guilty for the Holocaust, did little to intervene to prevent it. It has paid scant attention to genocide in Asia and Africa. Europe only reluctantly agreed to intervene in the ethnic-cleansing campaigns of the Yugoslav Serbs and had to work hard to persuade the United States to help. Although they may have been quicker to act against Sadaam Hussein in Iraq, it might also be observed that his nation has the second-largest known oil reserves in the world. "To the victor goes the spoils" is an appropriate adage to keep in mind. Is it correct or honest to choose one particular genocide to be condemned or combated, but let other instances of it go on unobstructed? One must ask, What is to be gained by this continuing accusation against the Germans? Both the war and the Holocaust are long over. It is time move on.

Disagree:

Some acts are so inhumane, so criminal, that there must be a constant reminder to be on guard against them. Hitler's deliberate launching of World War II and the Holocaust are such acts. It is precisely because they occurred in the heart of western Europe, not in some small backward and out-of-the way country, that the vigilance must be maintained. Modern, industrialized countries such as Germany—with a highly educated population, advanced technology, skilled political leadership, and highly mobile, well-equipped military forces—are the most dangerous to world peace and stability, for if their leadership, like Hitler, has the power to launch such a war and mass slaughter like the Holocaust, then no one is safe anywhere.

Hitler's Germany exhibited all of the evil elements of dictatorship: extremist ideology; racial stereotyping; provocative and expansionist diplomacy; and overwhelming military force.

He marshaled these elements in a country that had been resoundingly punished for aggression less than two decades earlier. Clearly, that defeat could not eliminate the cultural and national tendencies that induced the Germans to start two devastating wars and the Holocaust all within 50 years. Germany needs to be reminded constantly of its past if any possibility of its making similar attempts again in the future is to be eliminated.

Finally, it should be remembered that the Holocaust was the product of a so-called civilized country. By keeping the German example constantly in view, people everywhere can become sensitive to their own tendencies to persecute minorities. It is true that the wide majority of the contemporary German population have no personal responsibility for the Holocaust. Perhaps this is a case of the sins of the fathers being passed on to the next generations. But given Germany's history as a modern nation, it seems a small price to pay in the present.

QUESTIONS AND ACTIVITIES

1. Consider the ways that historical periods change the identity of nations by examining U.S. history. Identify the major characteristics of the United States in some of the following eras, for example: the colonial period, the revolutionary period, the era of expansion toward the Pacific, the Civil War, World War I, the New Deal, the Cold War, and the post–Cold War era. Are there positive and negative aspects in all the eras of U.S. history? Which "history" do you think most represents the country's national identity?

2. Make a list of the major characteristics of the eras of German history. Can you find elements of continuity in them, or are there some significant differences? Write a

short paper explaining which era you think had the most influence on German self-identity. Use historical facts to prove your point.

3. The DDR made its own history for 50 years, longer than some of the new states of Africa or Asia. In a role-playing exercise assume you have been born and brought up in the former DDR. Do some research to find out more about its history. Explain to some of your classmates how German history should remember the state of your birth.

4. Write a short paper explaining whether or not you believe Germany's history must be evaluated using different perspectives. Explain your point of view and prove it using historical information. Try to persuade your classmates to join your school of thought.

5. Select one of the historians mentioned in this chapter and learn more about him. In a short report provide information on his background, education, politics, and employment. What other works did he publish? What events in his life may have influenced his viewpoint in the *Historikerstreit*?

6. Discuss the influence of the Holocaust on the problem of German national identity. Why did it occur? Was there anything in German history that could have prevented it? Will it always color our attitude toward the Germans?

7. Using the Web and other sources, prepare a display of pictures representing twentieth-century German history. Where possible, include pictures that represent some of the events that reflect both sides of the *Sonderweg* debate.

NOTES

1. Gerhard Schröder, "Keine Politik ohne Geschichte," *Die Zeit,* 29/2001, http://www.zeit.de/reden/Geschichte/pring_200129_schroeder.html.

2. Germany and its allies, the Central Powers, did not actually lose the military conflict in World War I. Germany was never invaded along the important western front; the war stayed mired in the battlefields of France. Yet all sides were exhausted after four years of stalemate and trench warfare. They concluded an armistice: an agreement to cease firing at 11:00 A.M. on 11 November 1918 and to resolve the issues at a peace conference. But England, France, Italy, and the United States agreed among themselves how to treat Germany and its allies. If the Central Powers refused their terms, they would renew the war. Thus, Germany lost through diplomatic, not military, action.

3. Because of the lawlessness in Berlin after the war, the writers of the Constitution took refuge in the city of Weimar. The republic is often designated the Weimar Republic for that reason.

4. My purpose here is only to identify the starting point of this debate. For the broad scope of this type of analysis and the works that arose through it, see David Blackbourn and Goeff Eley, *The Pecularities of German History: Bourgeois Society and Politics in Nineteenth-Century Germany* (Oxford: Oxford University Press: 1984).

5. Fritz Fischer, *Germany's Aims in the First World War* (New York: W.W. Norton, 1967). The German-language version is *Griff nach der Weltmacht* (Düsseldorf: Droste Verlag, 1961).

6. Dr. Rolf Kosiek, "Der westdeutsche Historikerstreit: Ein Schritt zum Revisionismus," *Deutschland in Geschichte und Gegenwart* 35, no. 2 (1987): 6–11, reprinted at http://www.vho.org/D/Dgg/Kosiek35_2.html., (6 pp.), 1.

7. Ibid., 1–2.

8. Ibid., 4.

9. Quoted in Siobhan Kattago, *Ambiguous Memory: The Nazi Past and German National Identity* (Westport, Conn.: Praeger, 2001), 57–58.

10. Jeffrey Herf, "The Twentieth Century's Last Surprise," *New Republic* 222, no. 6 (2 July 2000), 43 ff. Herf reviewed Angela Stent's *Russia and Germany Reborn: Unification, the Soviet Collapse, and the New Europe* (Princeton, N.J.: Princeton University Press, 1998).

SUGGESTED READINGS

The best preparation for a discussion of these issues would be a general history of the twentieth century. The goal should be to understand German history in the larger European or world context. Eleanor L. Turk, *The History of Germany* (Westport, Conn.: Greenwood Press, 1999) provides an overview of German history from the founding of the Empire to the present. There are several varieties of general histories, and it is important to consult the latest edition possible. One type is a handbook of history, which lists historical fact chronologically or thematically, without much interpretation, such as Peter N. Stearns, gen. ed., *The Encyclopedia of World History,* 6th ed. (Boston: Houghton Mifflin, 2001). Close to it is Michael Howard and William Roger Lewis, *The Oxford History of the Twentieth Century* (Oxford: Oxford University Press, 1998). Robert Paxton's *Europe in the Twentieth Century,* 4th ed. (Belmont, Calif.: Wadsworth, 2001), is a well-researched but densely packed college textbook. Carter Findley and John Rothney's *Twentieth-Century World,* 5th ed. (Boston: Houghton Mifflin, 2001), broadens the perspective even further and encourages the reader to consider history from a comparative perspective.

Dr. Rolf Kosiek's article "Der westdeutsche Historikerstreit: Ein Schritt zum Revisionismus," *Deutschland in Geschichte und Gegenwart* 35, no. 2 (1987): 6–11 (reprinted at http://www.vho.org/D/DGG/Kosiek35_2.html), is written with clarity and style. It is an excellent introduction to the *Historikerstreit.*

The debates over the *Sonderweg* and the new German identity are summarized and discussed in Jan-Werner Müller, *Another Country: German Intellectuals, Unification, and National Identity* (New Haven, Conn.: Yale University Press, 2000), and in David Blackbourn and Geoff Eley, *The Peculiarities of German History: Bourgeois Society and Politics in Nineteenth-Century Germany* (Oxford: Oxford University Press, 1984). Both are academic studies, but each has an excellent introduction to the breadth of the *Historikerstreit* and its participants, and a bibliography that can direct interested readers to a number of important works in both German and English.

5

GERMANY'S IMMIGRATION DILEMMA: NATIONALITY STATE OR MULTI-ETHNIC SOCIETY?

BACKGROUND

The struggle of the German peoples in the nineteenth century, to transform the German cultural heritage into a German national state, is well known. The conflicts that this state created within the continent of Europe during the twentieth century are equally well documented, the two terrible wars that smashed its economy and stripped its political sovereignty. But the German identity remained. In the last half of the twentieth century, the German identity remained strong, although divided in territory, ideology, and economic orientation. In 1990 it was powerful enough to bring about the peaceful unification of the two German states created after World War II. This appeared to resolve, at last, the nature of the German national state. The Bundesrepublik Deutschland (BRD) set about the enormous task of integrating the 17 million East Germans into its economy and society.

It is not surprising, therefore, that Germans are perplexed and bewildered by the wholly new population phenomena that occurred at the same time. There was an immediate rush of people from eastern Europe asking to live and work in Germany. But Germany was not a country built by immigration. Its nationality law, first written in 1913, was reflected in Article 116 of the 1949 Grundgesetz (Constitution). It identified a German as an individual born of German parents. Germans were a "Volk" (people), not just a political or territorial construct. Being born in Germany or taking up residence there did not automatically qualify one to be a citizen. The Grundgesetz assures everyone equality before the law, personal and religious freedom, and freedom of expression. But some very important rights seem to pertain only to Germans: *"Alle Deutschen haben das Recht"* (all Germans have the right).

A member of the Committee for Problems of Foreigners holds a Turkish passport *(left)* and a German passport in front of a committee office poster promoting tolerance and understanding, Munich, January 1999. The German government announced details of its controversial bill to allow dual nationality under which foreigners obtaining German nationality could keep their old passports. (AP/Wide Worlds Photo)

They have the right to associate, to assemble, to travel freely within the country, to choose their own livelihood, and to become permanent citizens.

That language was still in effect in 1990. It facilitated the integration of the East Germans and of the Aussensiedler, residents of other countries who could prove their German heritage. But all others could be excluded from citizenship. In fact, Germany had more than one million Turkish permanent residents, some who were even second- or third-generation residents but were not citizens. Application for naturalization and citizenship required the completion of a difficult 50-page form, demonstrated knowledge of the German language and cultural practices, a hefty fee, and a 15-year waiting period. Yet because of Germany's terrible heritage of anti-Semitism, the German government was reluctant to bar foreigners after 1990. The question of what to do with them was, and is, Germany's immigration dilemma.

The immigrants came to Germany for basic economic, political, and cultural reasons. Of the three, the hope for better economic opportunity was probably most compelling.

The Fall of the Berlin Wall

The collapse of the Soviet system in eastern Europe signaled an end to state policies that blocked the free travel and migration of their peoples. Thus, the fall of the Berlin Wall on 9 November 1989 symbolized more than opening the gate between eastern and western Germany: it opened the doors of the other eastern European nations as well. This opening has led to a westward surge of peoples, most in search of better jobs and economic opportunities. Almost half of these people went to Germany, which had the strongest economy on the continent.

The Balkan Refugees

At the same time, long-smoldering ethnic and religious conflicts in Yugoslavia resumed with more deadly force. This Balkan state was home to a number of small, intensely self-conscious Slavic ethnic groups and their three competing monotheistic religions: Eastern Orthodox Christianity, Latin Catholicism/Protestantism, and Islam. Yugoslavia spoke and wrote in four official languages. Put together at the end of World War I by the victorious powers, it demonstrated all of the problems and conflicts of a multicultural state. Throughout much of its existence it had been controlled by dictators. In World War II it went into the Soviet orbit. When that collapsed, so did the socialist ideology that had restrained the ethnic conflicts. The Slovenes and Croatians broke away to form independent states. In the remaining state the majority Serbs, who are Orthodox and Slavic, began a brutal campaign of ethnic cleansing to gain control over the lands and wealth of the non-Serb, non-Orthodox minority populations.

Those who could escape fled to northern and western Europe to ask for asylum. They aimed for Germany because its Grundgesetz (Article 16.2) stipulated: "Persons persecuted for political reasons enjoy the right of asylum." This article was originally designed to entice dissidents in the Deutsche Demokratische Republik (DDR) to escape. Its authors never foresaw that it might become a magnet for non-Germans as well.

The *Aussensiedler*

Of all the easterners, the eastern Europeans of German *volkish* descent could claim the constitutional right to German citizenship and residence. Most were the descendants of ancestors who had settled in the East many generations earlier. For example, there were Crimean and Volga Germans whose forefathers had accepted the invitation of Russia's Catherine the Great, in the 1760s, to accept free land and cultural autonomy in return for settling and building the Russian frontier. Large numbers of ethnic Germans had been expelled from eastern European lands following World War II. But others, whose families were perhaps better assimilated or more loyal to the regime, had remained. As the economies of the eastern European states crumbled around them, the prospect of relocating in Germany became very attractive.

The European Scope of Migration

In July 1993 the United Nations Population Fund issued a report that estimated that 15 million migrants entered western Europe between 1980 and 1992, and that as many as 10 million more were planning to move there from eastern European countries in the years ahead. Probably half of those would head for Germany. The European Union (EU), formed among the western European states, had agreed upon policies to allow the free movement of EU member citizens among the member states. It had not fully dealt with the problem of migration from outside the union. Many of the migrants coming for economic reasons were claiming political asylum in order to get favorable treatment. Germany was not alone in trying to curb migration. France's interior minister stated that he wanted to move his country toward a policy of "zero immigration." Sweden and Denmark both imposed immigration restrictions, and Denmark, Greece, Austria, and Spain made plans to return migrants who did not meet the strict requirements.[1]

How Could Germany Handle the Immense New Population Problem?

Before 1990 Germany had a substantial resident foreign population, initially contract workers who had settled there permanently and "asylum seekers." That population of under 4.5 million was relatively stable and economically helpful. They did not, in German eyes, require a set of immigration laws. But then the sudden unification of the two German republics totally changed the social and economic circumstances. The DDR economy crashed. Thousands of businesses and industries closed down; the actual unemployment rate in the DDR in the early 1990s (including individuals temporarily in state-subsidized projects and retraining programs) probably exceeded 25 percent. Once unification was in effect, East Germans began competing with the West Germans for work and housing in the western states. Moreover, they could vote, which put considerable pressure on the government. Germany's first concern was, therefore, to integrate the 17 million East Germans into the West German society and economy. The addition of the new migration of eastern Europeans only compounded the stress on the limited resources of the economy and social services. Some statistics help illustrate the magnitude of the dilemma (see Table 5.1).

Foreigners made up 8.8 percent of the unified BRD's population by 31 December 2000. However, there was not much economic opportunity for the newcomers in its newly incorporated eastern Länder (states), where

Table 5.1
Growth of Foreign Population in Germany, 1980–2001*

1980	4,453,300
1985	4,489,100
1990	5,342,500
1995	7,173,500
2000	7,296,800
2001	7,318,600

*These figures are summarized from: Statistisches Bundesamt Deutschland, "Ausländische Bevölkerung 1980 bis 2001," http://www.dstatis.de/basis/d/bevoe/bevoetab7.htm. These data and others dealing with population sometimes differ because of the date or means of data collection. For the purposes of this chapter, however, these differences are not significant.

before unification they had usually made up less than 2 percent of the population (2.4 percent in Brandenburg). They impacted the western Länder the most. They formed 12.2 percent of the population in Baden-Württemburg, 11.1 percent in Nordrhein-Westfalen, and 9.3 percent in Bayern (Bavaria). The largest cities were especially affected. Foreigners made up nearly 25 percent of the population in Frankfurt, 15.5 percent in Hamburg, 12.8 percent in Berlin, 11.9 percent in Bremen. In the western part of the country, where the citizens were already paying new taxes to support the East Germans, the increased competition from the immigrants for housing and for jobs and the increased welfare payments for those without these essentials raised understandable concern and resentment.[2]

Thus, it became necessary for Germany to reconsider some issues that it had taken for granted. What is the relationship between ethnic heritage and citizenship? How can Germany incorporate Aussensiedler who have the right to citizenship, but no knowledge of the German language or culture? How can it attract the type of skilled worker necessary to develop the economy, and how should that worker be handled through immigration laws? How can it prevent foreigners from overloading the resources of the society and economy?

The key to answering these questions was to develop a workable immigration policy. This was quite a departure. Although Germany had long had foreign residents, it had never wanted to be an immigration state. Germany was not like Britain or France, with their former international empires and their consequent multicultural outlook. Germany had a narrower perspective: "Anything outside of Europe for them is close to Mars," observed Erwin Scheuch, a sociologist at the University of Cologne.[3]

The Turks: Foreign Residents without Citizenship

Immigration was not a new experience for Germany in the 1990s. In the 1950s the BRD economy took off. To keep labor costs in line, manufacturers could either move their industries offshore or import labor that would work for lower wages. That policy was being recommended at the time by the Organization for Economic Cooperation and Development (OECD). The government and industry opted to recruit Gastarbeiter (guest workers), mainly from Greece, Turkey, and Yugoslavia. Beginning in 1960 these workers were brought in on short-term contracts to move into the unskilled, low-paying jobs. They freed German workers for more skilled employment. The basic premise of the Gastarbeiter system was that contracts were short term; the labor force could remain at the necessary level without having to make major commitments of security or benefits to the foreign worker. The workforce rotated in and out of Germany. It was a successful strategy. Industry kept production costs under control; the Gastarbeiter benefited from wages higher than he could receive at home.

But as some of the foreign workers proved to be especially valuable, their contracts were extended, and they were allowed to bring their wives and children to join them. The greatest number, approximately 1.7 million, came from Turkey, and many of them filled the gaps in the urban workforce, especially in Berlin. As a result, permanent communities of Turkish Gastarbeiter developed. They started families and established their own schools, religious and cultural centers, and media. They raised generations of children. They did all of this without assimilating and without the benefit of German citizenship. They were, after all, not ethnic Germans. By 1988, when the population of the BRD was slightly more than 61 million, its foreign population of almost 4.5 million was approximately 7.3 percent of the total. But because the Turks were the predominant minority, the BRD did not have a noticeably diversified society.

The New Wave of Foreigners

One major difference in the contemporary wave of immigration is the rate at which it has grown. Germany's foreign-born population currently is 8.9 percent of the total population, a number that does not seem alarmingly higher than the 7.3 percent prior to 1990. But if the percentage were calculated on the basis of the 1988 territory and population of western Germany (which, indeed, has received the majority of the immigrants), it would be almost 12 percent, or an increase of nearly 30 percent in only a decade.

The other major difference, of course, is the incredible ethnic diversity of the new wave of immigrants. Although Turks remain the largest component, their numbers have grown only slightly in comparison to the number of immigrants from eastern Europe. There were 7,267,600 foreigners in Germany in 2000, with a wide range of national origins (see Table 5.2).

Table 5.2
The National Origin of German Immigrants, 1999–2001*

	1999	2000	2001
Germans	74,827,400	74,992,000	—
Foreigners (total)	7,336,100	7,267,600	—
Including:			
- Turkey	2,053,600	1,998,500	1 947,900
- Yugoslavia (Serbia/Montenegro)	737,200	662,500	627,500
- Italy	615,900	619,100	616,300
- Greece	364,400	365,400	362,700
- Bosnia and Herzegovina	167,700	156,300	159,000
- Poland	291,700	301,400	310,400
- Croatia	214,000	216,800	223,800
- Austria	186,100	187,700	189,000
- United States	112,000	113,600	113,500
- Macedonia	49,400	51,800	56,000
- Slovenia	18,600	18,800	19,400

*"Bevölkerung nach Geschlecht und Staatsangehörigkeit," http://www.destatis.de/basis/d/bevoe/bevoetab4.htm.

Not only was Germany receiving more immigrants than the rest of western Europe, and receiving them at a faster rate, it also was quickly becoming the most culturally diverse state in the region. This was a phenomenal change for a nation that, long before Hitler, had perceived itself as *ein Volk* (one people).

The Antiforeigner Backlash

Germany accepted more than 885,000 asylum seekers between 1989 and 1992. The initial proofing of their claim took an average of 13 months. If their claim was denied, the appeal process could last several more years. Meanwhile, the so-called refugees were maintained at the expense of the state. In the end, very few of them were found to have verifiable claims of the need for asylum, and the expensive process was under considerable criticism.

The German response to this surge of humanity occurred on two levels, from the population at large and from the government. Regrettably, some of the first reactions were violent ones. Some Germans in the eastern Länder resented that funds went to immigrants instead of being used to invest in new enterprises in the eastern regions. In 1990, 246 attacks against foreigners were reported, a serious enough record, but by 1991 the incidence of that type of crime rose to 2,462. By October 1992 the applications for political asylum in Germany were coming in at a rate of 50,000 per month, for a total of 438,191 that year. That was a 71 percent increase over the number received in 1991 and the highest in all of Europe. The number of attacks against foreigners skyrocketed to 4,587 in 1992. Most of these attacks seemed to originate in political movements of the skinheads on the far right. Some crimes were individual; others, such as the days-long siege of a hostel for asylum seekers in Rostock, seemed to be a more organized event.[4] Some feared that the antiforeigner agitation was fueling neo-Nazi movements.

Resolving the Refugee Crisis

The international community sharply criticized the Helmut Kohl government in October 1992 for letting the situation get out of hand:

> [The federal government] disregarded warnings that East Germany was too burdened by its own problems to take on responsibility for asylum seekers and assigned asylum seekers to the East long before the necessary infrastructure had been created. In their eagerness to reduce the strain on West Germany by transferring asylum seekers to the East, the German government failed to make a realistic assessment of the ability of local authorities to protect foreigners.[5]

The initial proposal of Kohl's Christian Democrat government was to ban four extremist political groups in November: the Nationalist Front, the German Alternative, the Alliance of German Comrades, and the National Offensive; observation of the right extremist Republican Party was added in December. The authorities also launched a campaign to prosecute hate crimes, resulting in the sentencing of some 1,500 individuals for antiforeigner activities. In many localities public and private groups initiated campaigns to reduce tensions. In Potsdam during the summer of 1992, for example, the municipal government organized a very successful free street fair for the foreign residents to showcase their culture, crafts, and food.

The government's next proposal was to amend the Grundgesetz to remove the unrestricted right of asylum. The Social Democrats and the parties of the left fought this measure fiercely, denouncing it as superficial. They wanted Germany to formulate an immigration policy; without one, they argued, the claim of asylum was the only way for foreigners to enter as legal immigrants. Chancellor Kohl continued to insist that Germany was not an immigration country, but his government did agree to a compromise. In December 1992, in an effort to control the flow, the German government adopted guidelines that stipulated that any migrants claiming asylum had to do so in the first "safe country" they reached. This stipulation took advantage of EU policy (Dublin Agreement of 1990) that limited refugees to applying to only one country for asylum. Significantly, Germany identified as "safe countries" most of its neighbors to the east: Bulgaria, the Czech Republic, Hungary, Poland, Romania, and Slovakia.

In May 1993 the language of the Grundgesetz was amended to read: "Those politically persecuted enjoy the right to asylum." This means that applicants for asylum must immediately show proof of the threats against them. Although criticized by some human rights groups, this legislation had the effect of slowing the influx after it went into effect in July 1993.

In addition, through a series of bilateral agreements in 1993, Romania agreed to the return of 21,000 of its citizens and the Czechs to the return of 18,000. Bulgaria and Poland accepted similar arrangements, especially because all were sweetened with cash payments to help those countries reabsorb the migrants. From a high of 322,599 applications for asylum in the BRD in 1993, the number of applications fell to 127,210 in 1994, to 98,644 in 1998, and to 88,000 in 2001. The combination of the new guidelines and the bilateral treaties seems to be having the desired effect.[6]

Immigration Benefits for the Turks and Other Long-Term Foreign Residents

The crisis of the asylum seekers called attention to the circumstances of the large resident population of Turks. They, too, had been subject to the antiforeigner violence even though their communities were decades old. The numbers are revealing. As of 31 December 1999 almost one-third of them (31.9 percent) had lived in Germany for 20 years or more, and 20.2 percent had been there from 10 to 20 years. Only 19.6 percent had resided in Germany for 4 years or less.[7] Responding to political pressure and criticism, Kohl pushed a bill through the Bundestag (Legislature) in 1990 that authorized naturalization for German-born children of resident aliens. As of January 2000, the German-born child of any foreigner who had lived in Germany for at least eight years was automatically considered a German citizen. There were approximately 700,000 children eligible when the bill passed, and they had until 31 December 2000 to submit applications. If they qualify, they have until they are 23 years of age to renounce the citizenship of their parents' homeland, or they will lose their German citizenship. (Approximately 100,000 babies are born in Germany each year to resident aliens.) This bill also resolved some of the outstanding issues of residence and the right to work. It was the first step away from Germany's traditional *volkish* definition of a German citizen.

This apparent resolution of the Turkish problem did not respond to the demand raised by the Social Democrats and parties of the left for the establishment of an immigration law and a process for immigrants to obtain citizenship. These steps seemed all the more necessary in light of research completed in 1994 by the Institute of German Business in Cologne. The study concluded that Germany would need 12.5 million immigrants by 2020 to compensate for the decline in the birthrate that was depleting the labor force.[8]

The Social Democrat Immigration Policy

Without having taken further steps on the immigration issue, Chancellor Kohl went down to defeat in the elections of September 1998. After a 12-year term in office, during which he oversaw the unification of the German republics, he was the first BRD chancellor to be voted out of office. He was succeeded by Gerhardt Schröder, a Social Democrat, who campaigned on a platform of creating more jobs and providing more flexibility in the labor market.

Once in office, the Social Democrats and their coalition partners, the Greens, appointed a commission to study immigration issues. While the government was deliberating, it introduced a green card program to admit 20,000 foreign professionals. On 4 July 2001 the commission recommended that Germany admit 50,000 immigrants a year, to include 20,000 professionals as settlers (with their family), 20,000 with work permits for a five-year stay, and 10,000 trainees on two-year permits. Under certain circumstances, the individuals on the five-year and two-year work permits might also be granted the right to settle in Germany. These recommendations were written into legislation that stated specifically that "Germany is an immigration country." The bill went to the Bundestag in August 2001. After considerable debate it was passed in the lower house (320 to 255) on 1 March 2002 and narrowly (35 to 34) by the Bundesrat (Federal Council) on 22 March 2002. President Johannes Rau signed the BRD's first immigration bill into law on 20 June 2002. Chancellor Schröder concluded that this policy properly placed the employment of German workers first, ahead of the employment of immigrants: "In the area of work-related immigration, it was important that we meet a demand voiced by employers, a demand we also consider to be proper, namely that clear priority be given our domestic labor force."[9]

In a mirror image of the Gastarbeiter program, which had recruited unskilled workers in the 1960s, Germany's new immigration policy will reserve entry primarily to skilled professionals. This was yet another step away from Germany's traditional *volkish* definition of citizenship.

The *Aussensiedlers*

The final category of immigrants are those descended from Germans who at some point settled in eastern Europe and who experienced hardships and discrimination in their homeland because of their German heritage. Article 16.2 of the Grundgesetz gave them automatic citizenship. Before the collapse of the Soviet system, very few of them gained travel permits in order to take advantage of this opportunity. Prior to 1987 approximately 37,000 of them entered per year. But 2.4 million eastern ethnic Germans claimed citizenship between 1989 and 1997, 1.5 million of them former Russians. Their rate of immigration leveled off to about 100,000 per year after 1998.[10]

Despite their German heritage, most of them have little if any ability to speak German and are unfamiliar with German customs. Many have been prevented from gaining the advanced work skills necessary to succeed in the contemporary German economy. If they are unemployed, they apply for government assistance, which runs about $1,500 a month for a family of four. Because of the difficulties in integrating the Aussensiedler into German society, the government began to offer payments to help them improve their life at home. For example, by 2000 it had expended nearly $50 million to provide basic necessities to ethnic Germans in Kazakhstan and to help them establish small businesses.[11] As part of the new immigration policy, the foreign-born ethnic Germans will lose their automatic admission into the BRD as citizens in 2010.

ISSUES

Germany's New Immigration System Is Discriminatory and Uses Ethnic Profiling to Prevent Eastern Europeans from Entering

Agree:

Germany has virtually locked its doors to migrants who do not fit very narrow and elitist specifications. The new green card law does not really permit immigration; it is a disguise for an economic recruiting plan, a brain drain of skilled information technology professionals at the expense of other nations. The refugees from eastern Europe are trapped in the bordering "safe nations" unless they can afford airfare from their homelands to Germany. Those nations cannot offer them the same level of opportunity to recover from their losses that Germany can. Eastern Europeans who wish to enter Germany legally under migrant status are therefore at an enormous disadvantage. Because their countries have not caught up to western technologies, their workers have not developed the skills or experienced the training to meet the qualifications of the three new types of German green cards. Even the ethnic Germans in the east will lose their opportunity for German citizenship with this new orientation. It is shameful that Germany is paying them to stay away.

But even more alarming is the program to deport eastern Europeans already residing in Germany. The most ominous example was its agreement with Romania to deport 43,000 Roma (Gypsies) from Germany, a move with a disturbing resemblance to the racial policies of the Third Reich. In 2000 approximately 650,000 foreign nationals entered Germany for stays of 90 days or more, but 562,000 left. Included in that number were 23,459 deported by air for the first time, including 3,500 individuals repatriated to Turkey, 2,800 to Yugoslavia, and 2,000 to Ukraine. In proportion to their total in residence in Germany, the eastern Europeans were expelled in far larger numbers. That action was purely discriminatory.[12]

Disagree:

Germany has accepted more refugees and immigrants than any other European country since the early 1990s. But it has reached the limits of its resources and must consider the needs of its own citizens. First among them are the East Germans, whose economic well-being and political education were for so long hostage to the socialist state. They made enormous sacrifices to bring about the peaceful unification of the German republics. Every mark or Euro spent on supporting foreign workers reduces the government's ability to bring the new eastern states up to the level of the western states. The world economy is changing owing to new technologies; it requires skilled workers, not untrained refugees, for Germany to keep up with the pace of the competition from the advanced countries. Large numbers of German skilled professionals are being attracted by higher salaries in the United States and elsewhere. Germany has every right to focus immigration policy to help strengthen its national economy. The new green card system does just that. It does not discriminate against any particular nationality; it simply makes technical knowledge and ability the prime criteria. Qualified eastern Europeans can apply.

Moreover, those immigrants who have been in Germany for a longer term, eight years or more, have paved the way for the naturalization of their children to be German citizens. That amounts to more than 30 percent of the present number of foreigners currently in residence. That policy establishes no discrimination by nationality.

So Many of the Foreigners in Germany Are Unemployed and Unemployable That They Are a Drain on the Economy

Agree:

There were already 625,000 foreign immigrants unemployed in Germany in 1999, with some additional 3,579,000 of them outside the workforce as dependents.[13] Given the high cost of welfare to support them, estimated at $1,500 per month for a family of four, Germany has to prevent further immigration of persons without verifiable employment potential. It has raised taxes and welfare payments to the maximum amount that is prudent and affordable. The new selective green card system is far more effective than a system of quotas by nationality, as in the United States. It is similarly far more cost-effective to help prospective eastern European immigrants to remain in their homelands in order to build their own economies. It is the very lack of opportunity in those nations that induces emigration. This crisis-induced migration further reduces the available workforce and tax revenue in those countries. Germany's aid to them, which helps meet the basic daily needs of the ethnic German population and trains them for the local economy, is an investment for both nations.

Disagree:

It is untrue that immigrants are unemployable and a drain on German society. In 2000 a report of the OECD estimated that there were more than 273,000 self-employed immigrants in Germany, more than double the number in Great Britain and France. A German government report in 2002 indicated that there were 870,000 salaried foreign workers and 1,752,000 in other forms of employment in Germany.[14] Germany offers immigrants the best economic climate for success. Immigrants should be allowed to participate in the same types of training programs as German nationals and to compete with them for jobs on an equal footing. They can also attain the levels of professional skill that the German economy requires. After having twice destroyed much of the economy of eastern Europe in the twentieth century, Germany has a moral obligation to assist its peoples in the present century.

Germany Violates EU Policy through Its Decisions to Restrict Asylum, to Regulate Immigration by Profession, and to End the Rights of Ethnic Germans to Claim Citizenship

Agree:

If this is not the case now, it certainly will be once the 10 applicants from eastern Europe—Poland, Hungary, the Czech Republic, Slovakia, Slovenia, Estonia, Latvia, Lithuania, Malta and Cyprus—are admitted to the EU. The "General provisions for the right of residence," passed by the EU in 1990, stipulate:

> Member States will grant the right of residence to nationals of Member States who do not enjoy this right under other provisions of Community law[,] provided that they themselves and the members of their family (spouse, dependent descendants and dependent relatives in the ascending line of the person concerned or his or her spouse) are covered by sickness insurance in respect of all risks in the host Member State and have sufficient resources to avoid becoming a burden on the social security system of the host Member State during their period of residence.[15]

Basing immigration on specific employment qualifications and regulating it through the green card system will bar immigrants with independent means from entering Germany. So long as the immigrants were from western Europe, Germany had no such policy in place. However, as soon as eastern Europeans began applying for EU membership, the government felt it was necessary to have this new policy in place.

Disagree:

It is important to recognize that citizens of EU member nations already have the right to reside and work in any other member nation. Germany has fully complied with those regulations. Germany is not the only country concerned about the explosive migration from eastern Europe in the 1990s. Virtually all of the western European countries limited such immigration long before Germany did. The EU countries discussed immigration policy at their June 2002 summit meeting in Seville. They expect to establish uniform standards for immigration and asylum by the end of 2003. Doing so is particularly important because negotiations are currently under way with Poland, Hungary, the Czech Republic, Slovakia, Slovenia, Estonia, Latvia, Lithuania, Malta, and Cyprus to enlarge the EU. These applicants certainly will need to take more responsibility for their own citizens. Germany's current aid to these countries to retain their would-be migrants will assist them in meeting the requirements for EU membership. With judicious policy and patience the eastern European migration crisis can be resolved on a regional basis. It is unreasonable to expect Germany alone to bear half the weight of it.

QUESTIONS AND ACTIVITIES

1. Prepare a classroom exhibit using the map of Europe to show the countries that are sending emigrants to Germany. Use different colors to show the volume of migration to Germany.

2. Prepare a classroom exhibit showing the number of foreign immigrants residing in the various German states. Use different colors to show the volume of migration into the individual states. Population data are available on the Web site of the BRD Federal Statistical Office.

3. Select one of the eastern European states and do some basic research on its economy since the end of the Soviet system. Prepare a short report explaining how that economy contributed to the emigration of its citizens to Germany.

4. Using the Web and other sources, write a short paper on the history of the resident Turkish community in Germany. Find out how the new naturalization law is affecting them.

5. Assume you are an eastern European who wishes to emigrate to Germany. Prepare an application essay to prove that you deserve to be admitted. Explain why your case is urgent and why you are more qualified than others from your home country.

6. Assume that you are a German representative in the Bundestag. What arguments did you make to help write the new immigration law? What were the major arguments of those who opposed the new law? Prepare a mock legislative debate of this issue for the class and hold a vote at the conclusion of the discussion.

7. Assume you are the administrator of a local school system in Germany. Brainstorm with your classmates about the education adjustments necessary to integrate the immigrants and the Aussensiedler into the local community and economy. Be sure to consider both the traditional and trade school curricula.

NOTES

1. Cited in Bruce W. Nelan and Bruce Crumley, "Europe Slams the Door," *Time* 142, no. 3 (17 July 1993), 38 ff.

2. Daniel Cohn-Bendit, "Heimat Babylon: The Challenge of Multicultural Democracy," *NPQ: New Perspectives Quarterly* 10, no. 1 (winter 1993), 4. Cohn-Bendit, known as "Danny the Red," was a leader of the radical student movement in France in 1968. See also: http://www.destatis.de/jahrbuch/jahrtab2.htm.

3. Quoted in Andrew Nagorski and Theresa Waldrop, "The Laws of Blood," *Newsweek* 121, no. 24 (14 June 1993), 38 ff.

4. "Recent Changes in German Refugee Law," *From the 'Lectric Law Library Stacks,* http://leclaw.com/files/into7.htm. (This is a summary of an article by Sam Play and Andreas Zimmerman, "Recent Changes in German Refugee Law," *American Journal of International Law* no. 4 (1994)). Commission on Security and Cooperation in Europe (CSCE), *Implementation of the Helsinki Accords: Human Rights and Democratization in Unified Germany* (Washington, D.C.: Government Printing Office, December 1993), 17, http://wpxx02.toxi.uni-wuerzburg.de/~drasel/CoS/germany/csce.html.

5. CSCE, *Implementation of the Helsinki Accords,* 17. The statement was issued by the Helsinki Watch group.

6. Nelan and Crumley, "Europe Slams the Door," 38 ff. The German Embassy Home Page, "Foreigners in Germany and Europe Compared," *Facts about Germany,* http://www.german-embassy.org.uk/foreign.html.

7. German Embassy, "Foreigners in the Federal Republic of Germany."

8. Summarized in "Immigrants Are Important," *Presidents and Prime Ministers* 3, no. 2 (March–April 1994), 29 ff.

9. German Press and Information Office, "Bundesrat Approves Immigration Bill," 17 March 2002, http://eng.bundesregierung.de/.

10. Anthony Richter, " 'Blood and Soil': What It Means to Be German," *World Policy Journal* 15, no. 4 (winter 1998–99), 1 ff. "Germany: New Immigration Law," *Migration News* 7, no. 7 (July 2000), http://migration.ucdais.edu/mn/archive_mn/jl_2000–09.html.

11. "Auf Wiedersehen," *The Economist* 355, no. 8166 (15 April 2000), 37–38.

12. Cohn-Bendit, "Heimat Babylon," 7. "Germany: New Immigration Law," *Migration News* 9, no. 4 (April 2002), http://migration.ucdavis.edu/mn/Archive_MN/apr_2002–08mn.html.

13. William Echikson, Schmidt, Katherine A., Dawly, Heidi, and Bawden, Anna, "Unsung Heroes," *Business Week* 3671 (3 June 2000), 92 ff. German Embassy, "Foreigners in Germany," 2.

14. German Embassy, "Foreigners in Germany," 2.

15. "General Provisions for the Right of Residence," *Activities of the European Union: Summaries of Legislation,* http://europa.eu.int/scadplus/leg/en/lvg/123003.htm.

SUGGESTED READINGS

The United States prides itself on being a multicultural immigration country, so it is often difficult for American students to understand the different attitudes of other countries whose history is based on a single national heritage. Peter Schuck and Rainer Münz's *Paths to Inclusion: The Integration of Migrants in the United States and Germany* (New York: Berghahn Books, 1998) is a collection of essays by contemporary scholars that offers comparative perspective on several important issues. It is good for background reading in preparation for dealing with the current issues. It also contains a useful bibliography of works in both German and English.

Statistical data offer important insight into the magnitude of the immigration problems. The scholarly study by Steinman, Gunter, and Ulrich, Ralf E., eds., *The Economic Consequence of Immigration to Germany* (New York: Springer Verlag, 1994), offers essays with excellent tables and charts. The Web site of the German Statistical Office (http://www.destatis.de) provides a wide range of the most recent data and links to other sites with useful information. Explanations are available in both German and English.

A wealth of information from the press and periodicals discussing Germany's immigration issues is available on the Web. Some good ones are cited in the Notes for this chapter. The *Migration Newsletter* at the University of California at Davis Web site (http://migration.ucdavis.edu/mn/) provides both statistical data and analytical commentary in a clear, concise format.

6

IS GERMANY REALLY UNITED?

BACKGROUND

Die Mauer im Kopf

Unification was a constitutional process. Unity, however, is a state of mind. Despite all the treaties and solemn statements, there is still *die Mauer im Kopf* (a "wall in the mind") of the German people. An early (December 1993) report of the Helsinki Commission summed up the problem succinctly: "As long as unification is perceived as humiliating and heartless by easterners, and costly and thankless by westerners, national unity will elude all Germans and political instability will be one uncomfortable result."[1] Do these concerns still exist a decade after unification?

Eastern Germany

Eastern Germany has always been different from western Germany. In the nineteenth century, when much of Germany was industrializing, becoming more urban and middle class, the German lands east of the Elbe River lagged far behind. This was the region of the Junkers, the aristocratic holders of large commercial farms known as Latifundia, who retained legal control over their peasantry well into the nineteenth century. It was a predominantly agrarian economy, with income based on the production and export of grain. The peasantry consisted mainly of tenant farmers who had little voice in public affairs. Much of the eastern land was in Prussia, where a three-class voting system kept the peasantry and much of the middle class politically powerless until World War I. (The total tax revenues collected from a district were divided into three equal parts, each part becoming a "class" of payers. Each of these classes had one vote for a district electoral candidate. The first class, the wealthy landowners, might consist of just one individual, whereas the third class could represent hundreds of peasants.) This was a region barely penetrated by the progressive political and social ideas of the French Revolution. It learned little about these ideas from the brief chaos of the Weimar Republic (1918–33). Then, for the next 57 years, more than half of the twentieth century, the East German people lived in a one-party authoritarian state.

The Deutsche Demokratische Republik

For 45 of those years the East Germans resided in the socialist Deutsche Demokratische Republik (DDR, German Democratic Republic). This one-party state was the showpiece of the Soviet socialist bloc in eastern Europe. Despite the destruction of World War II, despite the absence of major industrial resources (other than brown coal) and urban complexes, despite the western policies that barred its trade, this nation of only 17 million people was counted among the top 20 economies in the world for much of its existence. Unlike the Bundesrepublik Deutschland (BRD, German Federal Republic) on the western side, the DDR had received no infusions of Marshall Plan aid and Western trade to help produce a Wirtschaftswunder (economic miracle). It built its economic foundations on doctrinaire centralized planning, cooperative agriculture, programmed full employment, and generous state-supported benefits for housing, health, recreation, and child care. It was a productive economy, but a labor-dependent one, technologically well behind the west. Although the wealth of the East German citizen did not begin to approach that of the West German worker, she or he had security and equality with other citizens of the state. The DDR also had a position of high status within the Soviet sphere.

Only one political party functioned in the DDR: the Sozialistische Einheitspartei Deustchland (SED, Socialist Unity Party). In 1945 Soviet occupation forces combined the eastern zone's existing political parties into this coalition, which the Communist Party soon dominated. Only token political opposition to this state of affairs was offered throughout the existence of the DDR, until the 1989 reform movement that led to the collapse of the government. The proliferation of political parties in 1989 and 1990 represented a wide spectrum of opinions, but the enthusiasm was naive. None had any experience in open elections or with government responsibility. Thus, the electoral process in March 1990 was captured by the BRD's political parties and by the unprecedented campaigning of BRD chancellor Helmut Kohl in the parliamentary elections of what was still at that time a separate sovereign nation.

Unification became the dominant issue in those elections. Yet only 57 percent of the East German voters cast ballots for candidates who supported it. Many East Germans believed their state could be reformed and preferred to keep their separate national identity. As Stefan Heym, an East German writer, put it: "Those who wanted a better [DDR] carried out the revolution, but those who did not want a [DDR] at all are the ones who won the election."[2]

The Bundesrepublik Deutschland

More than 62 million Germans lived in the BRD on the eve of unification. This predominantly urban industrial and commercial land had been tightly incorporated into the U.S. orbit since the end of World War II. Its government was structured around a parliamentary democracy. Its social market economy had been built with Marshall Plan aid and capitalist investment. In principle the government used financial and taxation policies to support a favorable climate for competitive business and, at the same time, made sure that law and policy offered security for the working classes. But, unlike the DDR, the BRD did not program full employment or other social benefits. In the BRD both business and individuals could fail and did if they were not competitive.

But the West Germans were nonetheless extremely successful. By 1990 they boasted of the world's third-largest economy and of a fiercely outspoken democratic process.

Unification in 1990

The first German unification in 1871 had brought together separate states with similar cultures: most of these states were monarchial, and most had synchronized their economy to Prussia's Zollverein (customs union). The monarchs signed on behalf of their subjects, who accepted the process because it fulfilled their feelings of German nationalism. But the second German unification in 1990 brought together separate states with by this point quite different cultures, different political systems, and different economies. The hurried unification process once again was carried out by treaties accepted by the heads of the two states, but two competing nationalisms were involved this time. As a result of the total westernization of the often reluctant East Germans, unification has not been harmonious. For 45 years each country had used the other as the example of what was wrong in the world. Treaties could not wipe away such attitudes. A number of more concrete issues also have troubled German affairs in the past decade. In April 1990 Dietrich Dettke of the West German Friedrich Ebert Foundation (affiliated with the Social Democratic Party) reflected the tone of the West when he warned:

> Unification is bound to make the values, life styles and work habits of the [BRD] prevail. There are not many [DDR] achievements worth standing up for in the unification process. It is a psychological problem for the [DDR] population to deal with a situation of temporary inferiority. It calls for a lot of understanding on the part of West Germany—business, government, and others, the media for instance—to strike the proper balance.[3]

But that "balance" was determined exclusively by the West Germans.

Law and Justice

Article 19 of the Unification Treaty stipulated that "Administrative acts of the German Democratic Republic performed before the accession took effect shall remain valid." But the BRD had long refused to recognize the DDR as a legitimate state. Many German politicians and jurists argued that the West German Basic Law and legal system had always applied to all of Germany. Therefore, even though East German leaders and civil servants had acted according to the law of their own sovereign country, many in the west believed that the DDR leaders were criminals for violating basic laws and civil liberties identified in the West German Grundgesetz (Basic Law). It was not enough for them that the East Germans had used their own political and judicial processes to unseat their repressive rulers. Despite the treaty terms, the West Germans decided to put the East Germans on trial.

Trial of the DDR Leadership

The proceedings against the DDR leadership, which began on 12 November 1992, resembled the Nuremberg War Crimes Trials of 1945. Instead of "de-Nazification," the goal appeared to be "de-Communization." The former DDR head of state, Erich Honecker, together with five other high officials of his Communist Party regime, were charged with exceeding their authority and with violating human rights and civil liberties. In particular, Honecker was charged on 49 counts of manslaughter and 25 counts of attempted manslaughter for ordering East German border guards to fire on those attempting to flee to the west. Although firing on civilians was a violation of human rights, prosecutors could produce little evidence that proved that Honecker himself had ordered the shootings. The German Constitutional Court dropped this charge in January 1993. Honecker and two of the other defendants were critically ill at the time, and their trials were suspended. Polls taken that January show that more than 60 percent of East Germans regarded the whole process as a political show trial and that 39 percent of them had opposed the Honecker indictment altogether.[4]

Screening East German "Collaborators"

These trials represented only a beginning to a deliberate process of "lustration," or the examination of all DDR public officials, civil servants, educators, and others for their fitness to continue their work under the BRD. Each of the targeted individuals was required to fill out a long and detailed questionnaire to reveal his or her political affiliations and activities under the DDR. Those with any connection with the top administrative and enforcement offices of the former government, especially with the activities of the Ministerium für Staatssicherheit (Stasi, for short), the dreaded State Secret Police, were immediately dropped from consideration. Others who were still suspect had to appear before a panel of local reviewers for further demeaning questioning. Many were accused, sometimes anonymously, of "collaborating" with the Stasi. Others paid the penalty of growing up under the socialist system and of representing it in education and policymaking decisions. This scrutiny was particularly hard on the younger generations of teachers who had been born and educated in the DDR. Even if they had done well in their preparatory education, they found themselves out of work that they loved and needed because their socialist views were not to be taught in the schools. In Sachsen (Saxony), for example, 12,000 of the 65,000–75,000 teachers were fired by the citizens' committees.[5] Those who made it through the process were required to be "retrained" to offer the West German curriculum in the eastern schools, although they had few opportunities to retrain. In most instances the positions of the "unfit" were quickly filled by West Germans, causing even further resentment.

Trials of the East German Border Guards

In August 1961 the DDR began building the Berlin Wall and zonal barricades that physically defined its borders. The government later passed the Grenzgesetz (Border Statute) on 25 March 1982, which, among other things, stipulated that trying to cross over the zonal wall by using a ladder was a major crime. An estimated 5,000 East Germans at that time managed to escape over the wall into West Berlin. But some 940 died in the attempt to escape; almost one-third (270) of these were shot and killed by East German border guards. Thirty years later, after unification, there was little disagreement that those soldiers should be prosecuted, although some people had doubts over the legality of the process.

The guards mounted a defense claiming exemption, under the Unification Treaty Article 19, for carrying out the laws in effect prior to unification. The issue was put to the German Constitutional Court, which ruled in 1995 that the Grenzgesetz violated sections of the International Covenant on Civil and Political Rights of 19 December 1966. Because the DDR had signed that covenant on 23 March 1976, charges were filed against some 375 former guards: 24 generals, 134 officers, and 179 soldiers in other ranks. As of December 2000, there were 259 convictions, 78 acquittals, and 15 cases that were dismissed.[6]

The Stasi Files

The least-controversial decision was to open the secret files of the East German Secret Police, the Stasi. There were some 200 kilometers of files, 10 percent of which were actually the records of Stasi agents and of individuals they had accused. The Stasi had collected and stored information on more than 6 million of the DDR's 17 million citizens through a network of 90,000 employees and 170,000 informers. By comparison, Hitler's Gestapo had 43,000 employees. Did that indicate that the Communists of the DDR were far less confident of their popular support than the Nazis had been? (But who knows how large the Gestapo would have become if the Nazis had remained in power for 45 years instead of 12.) If BRD estimates can be believed, more than 1,000 East Germans were in prison based on Stasi indictments.

The East Germans hated the Stasi as the symbol of the worst kind of authoritarian police state. In addition to spying, wiretapping, intercepting mail, censoring, and committing other offenses,

> The rule of law was not upheld. Persons could be arrested without warrants and held in continued detention without judicial review. According to the U.S. State Department, in most political cases it took weeks before interested parties were informed of an individual's arrest, and contacts between a defense attorney and his or her client could be monitored and restricted by the prosecutor.[7]

The East Germans themselves had taken the first steps against the Stasi when a large mob stormed its Berlin headquarters at Normannenstrasse on 15 January 1990 and gained control of the records. There was considerable debate, however, over what to do with these records. Some argued that all those victimized by the Stasi should have immediate access to their own records. Others feared the harm this access would do. Lothar de Maizière, the DDR prime minister and former lawyer for some of the accused, feared that "murder and manslaughter" would result when individuals learned the identity of informers who had betrayed them. Some feared that journalists would turn the records into a circus of scandal; others feared that foreign intelligence agencies would use them unscrupulously. Although retaining the hard copy files, the DDR destroyed the electronic index in February 1990.

Whatever the procedural disagreements were, all agreed that East Germans, not West Germans, should make the decision about the Stasi records. When it was rumored that the Kohl government wanted to move the files to the Federal Archives in Koblenz, one German dissident protested: "This is our dirty laundry and our stink, and it is up to us alone to clean it up." One example of how the East Germans handled the files reflects back on the examination of the teachers in Sachsen, as mentioned earlier. Each teacher was given his or her personal file before the process began, so they were not used in that instance. Other examples were not so comfortable, as a number of individuals were exposed as Stasi collaborators. Individuals were anguished to learn that their own family members or friends had spied on them. The most shocking revelation was about Lothar de Maizière. He was Chancellor Kohl's hand-picked candidate for prime minister in the DDR's only free election before unification. The records, however, showed that he had informed for the Stasi from 1981 to 1989.[8]

After unification, the government passed legislation on 15 November 1991 that let citizens review their own files and prohibited journalists from using any information from the files that they received unofficially. The government, however, had the right to do background checks on potential employees. The files were turned over to a commission that began accepting applications to review them in January 1992. Although the records revealed often shocking activities, there was virtually no way to punish the Stasi agents for spying on their fellow East Germans or to compensate those victims.

Property Issues

Property claims caused real problems in the new Länder (states) because of the arbitrary actions of the two successive dictatorships. The Nazis had confiscated virtually all of Jewish-owned properties, and the DDR had nationalized both land and enterprises. On 7 March 1990, just 10 days before the elections, the Hans Modrow government in the DDR decreed that by paying a nominal fee individuals could reclaim the property rights to more than 11,000 firms that had been nationalized in 1972. This process was well under way at unification. The BRD (the name under which the two governments unified) chose to continue it, but that decision opened up the whole property issue to tremendous uncertainty.

Before unification the government in the west had already established a precedent for restoring property that the Nazis had taken from the Jews. When the property could not be returned, the government compensated the Jews. This had not occurred in the DDR, which maintained that the Communists were the first to be imprisoned by Hitler and were therefore not responsible for the Holocaust. Although the Modrow decree recognized the rights of owners in the 1970s, it had no provision for owners of land nationalized by the DDR, much less land taken from the Jews by the Nazis.

In September 1990 the BRD passed the Vermögensgesetz (Statute for the Regulation of Open Property Questions) to facilitate the restitution of property illegally seized by the Nazis or nationalized by the DDR. It set a deadline of 31 December 1992 for claims asking the return of real estate or enterprises and a deadline of 30 June 1993 for claims involving other types of property. Detailed forms required specific information about the property and the basis for the ownership or inheritance of it. The statute required special permits for the new sale of property in the eastern states, but no permit would be issued if there was an outstanding claim filed against it.

Chaos resulted. By the end of 1992 more than one million claims had been filed on more than 2.5 million different properties. Because the land had been confiscated by different regimes at different times, many claims could be filed for the same piece of property. Over the course of the decades of war and divisions, families had been divided and lost track of each other. In many instances multiple heirs filed claim to a property, which ran into the barrier of a BRD law that required all heirs to act together to file a single claim. A claim filed by a property owner from the socialist state could run counter to the claim of a Jew whose parents had lost the property during the Nazi era. Many claims arising out of the Holocaust had been previously dealt with by the U.S. Foreign Claims Settlement Program, which had used frozen Nazi assets. Recipients of those compensations had to decide by 31 December 1992 whether to retain that settlement or to return it and compete for the property through the German process. Many gave up their U.S. award because the value of the property was considerably more than the amount they had received in compensation. That decision, of course, simply added to the number of claims filed.[9]

Many of these claims are still under litigation. Many of them come from individuals who never lived in the DDR, and they compete with the claims of the most recent owners. They have had a chilling effect on the economic development of the eastern states because investors are unwilling to invest in properties that might later be taken away from them. Tension between the BRD policies and the East Germans will continue until these issues have been resolved, and probably long afterward as well.

Wages and Salaries

The comparative statistics plainly tell the story of the economic differences between the old and new regions of the BRD. In 1991 East German productivity and per capita gross domestic product were only 31 percent of that in the West. The typical East German weekly wage was 435 marks, the equivalent of only 50 percent of the average West German weekly wage. By 1998, after the billions of marks in subsidies and investments, the average weekly wage in the East German states was 782 marks. On the surface, this was a significant improvement, but it still amounted to only 75 percent of the West German weekly wage at that time. East German productivity had increased to 59 percent of that in the West, but still only 56 percent of the West German contribution to the gross domestic product. The eastern states constantly surpassed the western states in only one statistic: unemployment. After unification, unemployment in the new Länder was at least double that of the western states and equivalent to 17 to 20 percent of the workforce.[10]

What makes that situation especially difficult to analyze is the movement of people between the eastern and western states during the same period (see Table 6.1).

The migration data suggest that in 1991, after a full year of unification, West Germans scrambled to get to the east. Their migration was more than 32 times the number of those who had headed east in 1988, two years prior to actual unification. This number undoubtedly reflects the individuals who came to replace the officials, civil servants, teachers, and others disqualified from working owing to their supposedly questionable activities for the DDR. And there seems to be little success in creating other types of employment opportunities in the eastern states, where approximately 250,000 jobs have

Table 6.1
Internal Migration in Germany 1987–1998*

Year	Population Flow East to West	Population Flow West to East	Cumulated East Germans in West Germany
1987	22,800	2,400	20,400
1988	43,300	2,500	61,200
1989	388,400	5,100	444,500
1990	395,343	36,217	803,626
1991	249,743	80,267	973,102
1992	199,170	111,345	1,060,927
1993	172,386	119,100	1,114,213
1994	163,034	135,774	1,141,473
1995	168,336	143,063	1,166,746
1996	166,007	151,973	1,180,780
1997	167,789	157,348	1,191,221
1998	182,478	151,750	1,221,949

*Adapted from Michael C. Burda, "East-West German Wage Convergence after Unification: Migration or Institutions?" Table 4.

been lost since 1998. In July 2002 the number of unemployed in the eastern states reached 1.4 million. As a result, a significant migration of East Germans, especially younger workers, continues to the western states.[11]

All Germans, in both the west and the east, have been paying the Solidarity Tax to provide funds to invest in the economic development of the eastern states, so they are understandably frustrated by the lack of significant results in new jobs and employment there. The West Germans resent the complaining of the *"Jammerossies"* (whining easterners) and the East Germans resent the arrogance of the self-proclaimed *"Besserwessies"* (superior westerners).

ISSUES

East Germany Is Making Good Progress toward Building Its Economy and Productivity

Agree:

The eastern states of Germany are making good progress in overcoming 45 years of socialist manipulation of their economy. By 1990 that economy was well on the way to collapse. DDR leaders concealed the magnitude of the problems from their own people, and the BRD was so anxious to complete the unification process that it made no serious analysis of the crisis. In fact, Chancellor Kohl naively announced that it would not cost the BRD much to carry the unification through. The plan was to sell eastern enterprises to private investors, which would help pay any costs of the conversion from socialism to capitalism.

Thus, everyone's expectations were that the eastern states would simply convert to capitalism, and all would be well. Even before the final actions of unification the DDR established the Treuhandanstalt (Trust Agency) to begin privatization of the state-owned enterprises. Only at that point did the depth of the problem begin to emerge. The plants and their equipment were generally worn out and their products obsolete in the competitive western markets. Thousands of these enterprises found no buyers and had to be shut down. Investors hesitated because of the property disputes and because of the possible staggering costs to modernize existing plants or to clean up the pollution they had caused.

The only way to overcome that problem was for the BRD to subsidize the economy in the East. The Aufbau Ost (Rebuilding the East) program began with the Solidarity Tax of 7.5 percent on all German wages for 1991. The amount proved insufficient, and the tax was extended through 1995. Since then it has been extended indefinitely, although the rate is now 5 percent. The government began spending 6.6 billion marks annually on the economy of the eastern states and plans to continue at that level to 2005. Much of this aid was used to help support the unemployed. Many easterners had been put out of work when the factories shut down; many others were put out of work by the "lustration" process that declared them unfit for their previous work because of their political background.

One recent study, however, asserts that "[t]he market economy has taken firm root in the eastern states," pointing to the hundreds of thousands of new businesses.

> In 1998 the eastern states were home of 20,000 small and medium sized businesses most of them founded since unification with a total of 3.2 million employees on their payrolls. The number of self-employed easterners has also grown rapidly jumping from 30,000 shortly before unification to 240,000 in 1998.

According to a *Business Week* report, East German women have founded 150,000 new businesses. This is particularly encouraging because the implementation of unification policies put 94 percent of them out of work.[12]

Unemployment remains high, but it is not simply an East German phenomenon. The BRD has troubling unemployment across the land. There were 4.1 million Germans out of work in 1999 and still 3.9 million at the beginning of 2002, a rate higher than 10 percent. Although the rate in the eastern states is more than double that in the western states, it is necessary to remember how many West Germans migrated east in order to take over the government and management jobs there. It seems like a double standard: the Wessies shut down the factories and displaced the civil servants, but then criticized the Ossies for being out of work.

Disagree:

The statistics do not lie. Even with billions of marks poured into the eastern states for more than a decade, they lag far behind the productivity of the western states. They are dragging the whole economy down. The German economy is hardly growing at all, estimated by the European Commission to be only 0.7 percent in 2002. And although one can argue that the United States, Japan, and other countries are facing problems because of the world recession, Germany has mainly itself to blame for its economic problems.

At first the West Germans thought of the eastern states simply as new markets and so flooded them with consumer goods. They drained the east of the funds that could have been invested locally to maintain jobs and build productivity. The exchange of currencies at a one-to-one ratio meant that the prices of goods from the east shot up overnight, and its traditional export markets in eastern Europe could not afford them. The East Germans preferred to buy western products as well. So the process completed the destruction of the East German economy.

As a result, the government has spent 1.2 trillion marks in the eastern states over the past 10 years. These funds could have been invested nationally in new technology and competitive industry. Too much emphasis has been placed on bringing East German wages and pensions up to the level of those in the west. Until their productivity and contribution to the gross domestic product reach similar levels, the government should scale back its support. These payments are creating such a large budget deficit that Germany may exceed the 3 percent (of gross domestic product) limit set by the European Community.

The modest increase in productivity of the eastern states would disappear if it were not for the flow of billions of marks annually, roughly $65 billion, the equivalent of 5 percent of the output from the western states. It has been noted that "Every third D-mark spent in the east comes from outside, mainly western Germany, either in the form of public transfers or private capital investment." The East Germans make up approximately 20 percent of the population but contribute only 8 percent of the tax revenues, and the six eastern Länder collect 80 percent of the tax equalization funds that the federal government distributes to all the states. The one economic sector that shows real increase is construction, but this has resulted in a great deal of office and mall space, built on speculation, that remains unleased.[13]

The East Germans simply have not learned how to manage a modern capitalist economy. They still expect the state to bail them out, and, unfortunately, both the conservative Kohl government after unification and the socialist Gerhardt Schröder government since 1998 have been doing that for political reasons. There may be praise for all the small companies created since unification, but their markets are almost all strictly local. Moreover, they are unstable. Some 250,000 jobs have been eliminated since 1998. In

2000 the government extended the Solidarity Tax collection to 2019, which shows that it does not think that the East Germans have even begun to contribute to the economy or will do so in the near future.

Unification Has Led to Political Instability in the BRD

Agree:

Unification has disrupted the traditional politics of the BRD. In 1990 the coalition between the Christian Democratic Union (CDU) and the Christian Socialist Union (CSU), headed by Chancellor Kohl, seemed firmly in place. The voters returned him and his coalition to power in 1994 with 41.5 percent of the vote. In 1998, however, the poorly performing postunification economy cost him their allegiance and 49 seats in the Bundestag (legislature). The Social Democrats gained 46 seats. After leading Germany for 16 years, Kohl became the first BRD chancellor to be voted out of office in a national election.

One of the ominous aspects of the 1998 election was the number of votes cast for the new right extremist parties, some of which might be designated as neofascist. Three, in particular, were on the ballot in all 16 states: the Republikaner Partei (REP), self-identified as a "patriotic law and order" party; the Deutsche Volksunion (DVU), strongly nationalist and vehemently opposed to immigration; and the Nationaldemokratische Partei Deutschlands (NPD), which calls itself the only true opposition. The NPD's program language is so reminiscent of the Nazis that the government is considering whether to outlaw the party. In the 1998 federal election the REP polled 1,115,664 votes, and the DVU polled 906,383. Although neither party amassed the 5 percent of the vote necessary to be seated in the Bundestag, they continue to worry electoral officials.

The importance of these numbers becomes clearer at the state level.[14] In the five new Länder (excluding Berlin), the DVU, with its nationalist and anti-immigrant stance, attracted the largest vote, ranging from 2.6 percent in Sachsen to 3.2 percent in Sachsen-Anhalt. Altogether, 245,398 ballots were cast for the DVU. The REP garnered another 121,216 votes, and the NPD 52,118. In Sachsen some 5.7 percent of the voters favored the extreme right. In Berlin, which has both old and new voters, these far right parties gained 4.9 percent of the votes.

In the western states the votes for the extremist parties total far more, although the percentages are lower. This region favored the REP with 624,057 votes. Baden-Württemburg alone cast 240,402 votes for that party. The DVU gained another 355,835, and the NPD 64,453. More than one million western voters selected extreme right parties as well. These trends may well reflect the unresolved issues of unification, especially controversies over the economy and foreign immigrants. On 1 August 2002, when the government published the list of 24 political parties that would be on the ballot in all states for the 22 September 2002 federal elections, the REP and NPD were on it, but the DVU was not.

Moreover, since the 1998 federal elections, which ousted Kohl and the CDU/CSU leadership, state elections have reflected further discontent with Schröder and the Social Democrat/Green coalition. They lost in Hesse in 1999, in Baden-Württemburg in 2001, and in Sachsen-Anhalt in 2002. The September 2002 election campaign issues were once again the economy and immigration, which probably benefited the parties of the right.

Disagree:

Germany's democracy is one of the strongest and safest in the world today. Although having 24 parties on the federal ballot may seem like chaos to an American, it is a quite traditional pattern in Germany. It is one of the characteristics that strengthens the political process there, rather than weakens it. In 1998, in an election that represented an enormously broad spectrum of programs, 82.2 percent of the voters cast their vote, 49,308,512 of them. This is more than 30 percent higher than voter participation rates in the United States, where two umbrella parties distill a wide range of issues into two campaign platforms. In the United States third parties weaken the prospects of the Republicans and Democrats. In Germany the vast number of smaller parties are mainly competing with each other. Only six parties share the actual Bundestag political area, the CDU/CSU partnership, the Social Democrat Party (SDP), the Greens, the Free Democratic Party (FDP), and the Party of Democratic Socialism (PDS, which is the successor to the DDR's Social Unity Party). The others have not surpassed the 5 percent of the vote barrier to gain a seat in the legislature. (In the September 2002 elections the PDS did not achieve the 5 percent mandate to continue to seat delegates in the Bundestag.) The campaigning of small parties provides the majority politicians with an excellent barometer of the political climate. It also provides a more peaceful outlet for protest and a more productive one for democracy than the election boycotts favored by the disaffected electorate in the United States.

Observers should not be surprised at a trend toward the right by the German electorate. The CDU/CSU has led the government in the majority of the BRD's history. What is noteworthy is that Germany has not swung further to the right. Neofascist parties have already won their way into the governments of Austria and Italy. A right extremist was a run-off finalist for the presidency of France. Even with all its problems, Germany has demonstrated greater stability and support for the moderate parties than have its nearest neighbors.

QUESTIONS AND ACTIVITIES

1. As a group, brainstorm and list the benefits resulting from unification and the problems remaining because of unification. Rank each list from the most important

items to the least important. Analyze why some results of unification were more positive than others.

2. Using the Web and printed sources, find opinions that the Germans expressed about unification over the past decade. Try to identify the source of these opinions as either East German or West German. Write a short report on how these opinions have changed during the years.

3. Divide into two role-playing groups, a "Wessie" group and an "Ossie" group. In a role-playing exercise, identify the major impact your group has experienced as a result of unification. Identify both positive and negative aspects. Examine how unification has affected your attitudes toward the other group.

4. Select one of the German Länder as your subject. Prepare a short report on how its economy, population, and politics have changed since unification.

5. On the Web find and examine the statements of one of the local extremist parties identified in this chapter. Analyze how unification has influenced their statements.

6. Imagine that you are an advisor to the German chancellor. Based on what you have learned about the continuing concerns over unification, recommend some legislation that might reduce tensions. Be sure you include a statement about the origins of the problem and a consideration of the impacts your proposal would have, both positive and negative.

NOTES

1. Commission on Security and Cooperation in Europe (CSCE), *Implementation of the Helsinki Accords: Human Rights and Democratization in Unified Germany* (Washington, D.C.: Government Printing Office, December 1993), 21. This commission is an agency of the U.S. government. It consists of 18 members of the Congress and 1 member each from the Departments of Commerce, Defense, and State. More information about the commission can be found at http://scn.martinobrien.com;ABUSE/KRASEL/COS/GERMANY/CSCE.htm?FACTNet.

2. Ibid., 4.

3. Ibid., 6.

4. Ibid., 12.

5. Project on Justice in Times of Transition, *Truth and Justice: The Delicate Balance. Documentation on Prior Regimes and Individual Rights* (Budapest, Hungary: Project on Justice in Times of Transition, 20 October–1 November 1992), http://www.ksg.harvard.edu/justiceproject/budapestreport.htm.

6. "The German Border Guard Cases and International Human Rights," *European Journal of International Law*, http://www.ejil.org/journal/Vol9/No3/art6–02.html. "Memory of Berlin Wall Casualties Haunts Germany," *CNN.com* (6 November 1999), http://www.cnn.com/WORLD/europe/9911/06/wall.death.strup/index.html. "Grenzer Justice," http://www.grenzer.com/justice.

7. CSCE, *Implementation of the Helsinki Accords*, 8.

8. Jolyon Naegele, "Germany: Historian Culls Stasi Archives," in *Ten Years After: The Fall of Communism in East/Central Europe* (Radio Free Europe, n.d.), http://www.rferl.org/nca/special/10years/germany4.html. A. James McAdams, "Reappraising the Conditions of Transitional Justice in Unified Germany," *East Euro-*

pean Constitutional Review 10, no. 1 (winter 2001), 3, http://www.law.nyu.edu/eecr/vol10num1/special/mcadams.html. Project on Justice, *Truth and Justice: The Delicate Balance.* Commission on Security, *Implementation of the Helsinki Accords,* 10.

9. McAdams, "Reappraising the Conditions of Transitional Justice," 3. A summary of this legislation can be found in David J. Rowland, "Deadlines Affecting Property Claims in East Germany," *New York Law Journal* (23 December 1992), http://www.german-claims.com/articlelj2.htm.

10. Rudi Dornbusch, "East Germany: 10 Years of Unification with a Vengeance," http://web.mit/edu/rudi/www/media/PDFs/Germany.pdf. Michael C. Burda, "East-West German Wage Convergence after Unification: Migration or Institutions?" table 1, paper presented at "Conference on Migration: Political Economy Aspects," New Orleans, 24–25 March 2000, http://www.tulane.edu/~dnelson/PEMigConf/Burda.pdf.

11. Michael Finn, "East's Stalled Recovery Becomes Election Campaign Issue," *International Herald Tribune: The IHT Online,* 29 July 2002, http://www.iht.com/articles/66016.html.

12. Quote about the market economy from "Reunification," in *Technology and Its Dislocating Effects in East Germany,* http://www.csua.berkeley.edu/~erickyo/isf/html/a05.html. "Women Lead the Pack in East German Startups," *Business Week Archives,* http://www.businessweek.com/1996/23/b347875.htm.

13. "Eastern Germany's Slow Revival," *The Economist* (U.S.) 355, no. 8 (27 May 2000), 51.

14. The election data given here are the author's unofficial calculations, based on statistics from "Endgultiges Ergebniss Bundestabswahl 1998—Bundgesgebiet," http://www.bündeswahlleiter.de/wahlen/ergeb98/d/t/lan912_20, and from sites linked to this one.

SUGGESTED READINGS

The background and problems of German unification are discussed in more detail in chapters 1 and 2 of this volume. See their Suggested Readings. Also see Dieter Brosser, ed., *Uniting Germany: The Unexpected Challenge* (Providence, R.I.: Berg, 1992), and Konrad Jarausch, *The Rush to German Unity* (New York: Oxford University Press, 1994).

The 1993 report of the Helsinki Committee is the U.S. government's analysis of the problems of unification. Commission on Security and Cooperation in Europe, *Implementation of the Helsinki Accords: Human Rights and Democratization in Unified Germany* (Washington, D.C.: Government Printing Office, December 1993). It is accessible on the Web by setting the browser to the report title.

The best source of economic statistics is the Statistisches Bundesamt, or Federal Statistical Office (http://www.detatis.de). This site is available in English and German; its links are clearly marked.

The American Institute for Contemporary German Studies (http://www.aicgs.org) publishes excellent analyses of German state elections and their impact on national politics. These analyses are available for past elections and for state as well as national elections.

The party programs of the three major right-extremist parties are also available on the Web in German. See: the REP at www.rep.de/programm; the DVU at http://dvu.de; and the NPD at http://npd.net. The materials on these parties need to be read carefully, and sometimes between the lines, to understand the nature of each party's appeal to the discontented.

As indicated in the Notes, many press commentaries regarding German political and economic affairs are available on the Web.

AUSTRIA

7

THE KURT WALDHEIM CONTROVERSY

BACKGROUND

What Is the Waldheim Controversy?

Kurt Waldheim (1918–) served as an Austrian career diplomat for 40 years. He also served two terms as secretary-general of the United Nations (1972–82) and was president of Austria from 1986 to 1992. But during the 1986 presidential election campaign, accusations emerged that he had participated in atrocities during World War II.

Who Is Kurt Waldheim?

Waldheim was born on 21 December 1918 in St. Andrä-Wörden, Austria.[1] His father was a civil servant, and Waldheim prepared for a similar career by studying at the Vienna Consular Academy after completing his basic education. He volunteered for one year of service in the Austrian army in 1936 and was assigned to a cavalry unit. At the end of the year he was placed on the army reserve list. He began to study law at the University of Vienna in 1937 and was there when the Anschluss (Nazi Germany's annexation of Austria) occurred. Army records list his name as a member of the National Socialist German Students League.

Waldheim's Acknowledged Military Service

The Nazis incorporated Waldheim's reserve unit into their army, and he was made a noncommissioned officer. After the dismemberment of Czecho-

Kurt Waldheim, former secretary-general of the United Nations, after his inauguration as president of Austria in Vienna, July 1986. (AP/Wide Worlds Photo)

slovakia in September 1938, Waldheim's unit was sent as part of the forces occupying the Czech Sudetenland, an area that formerly was part of Germany. It was a short tour of duty, and by late October he was back at his studies in Vienna. He was also a reserve officer candidate. In early November, following Kristallnacht (a night of Nazi attacks on Jewish synagogues and businesses), according to his military record, he was a member of the Nazi Party Sturmabteilung (Storm Trooper militia). Waldheim finished his studies at the Vienna Consular Academy in the 1939 spring term. The army then sent him to an officers' training academy in Berlin. When the Germans attacked Poland in September 1939, Waldheim was assigned to a reconnaissance unit but stayed in officer training. In March 1940 his unit was stationed in Hesse, Germany, ready for the new campaign against the west.[2]

Following his graduation from the Consular Academy, Waldheim studied for his law exams. He passed them in March 1940. In April his unit was ordered up, and he moved with the forces invading France as a senior noncommissioned officer. His ability to speak French and thus to negotiate with the locals facilitated the peaceful arrangements for his unit in the Pas-de-Calais region. In December he received his promotion as a lieutenant in the reserve. When Hitler then turned his forces toward Russia in June 1941, Waldheim's unit invaded with the Forty-fifth Infantry Division, which took Brest-Litovsk. Waldheim received the Iron Cross, Second Class, for his part in the battle. As the army pushed forward toward Moscow, he received a second decoration, the Cavalry Assault Badge, and later the Eastern Badge. He was wounded in December 1941 during the Russian counteroffensive and sent back to a field hospital in Minsk. From there he was flown to a hospital in Vienna, where he spent the next three months recuperating.

In Waldheim's memoir, *In the Eye of the Storm,* published in 1986 as he embarked on his campaign for the presidency of Austria, he discusses his military service only briefly:

> I was serving in Reconnaissance Section 45 of the Upper Austrian Division. In the spring of 1941 we were ordered to the eastern front. Serving in the German army was hard to bear, but it was almost a relief to get away from the strains and suspicions that surrounded us at home....
>
> By December we had reached the area south-west of Orel, where our division was surrounded by Russian forces.
>
> I was wounded in the leg by a grenade splinter. It was not a serious wound, but in the days before other German forces could fight their way through the encirclement to join us it had turned septic. They got me out to a field hospital, where by happy chance I was treated by a Viennese surgeon. 'Mein lieber Freund [my dear friend],' he said, 'another day and your leg would have gone.'
>
> I was evacuated home, but it took several months in a sanatorium in the mountains before my leg started to heal properly. I walked with a bad limp, and to my undisguised relief was discharged from further service at the front. I made a formal request to be permitted to resume my law studies and take my Master's degree and rather to my surprise, this was granted. I still had my pay as lieutenant and this helped to see me through.[3]

Waldheim's Diplomatic Career

According to the general published biographies, Waldheim served in the German army for four years, then returned to law school and completed his degree in 1944. Shortly after that he was appointed to the reestablished Austrian Foreign Service and began his diplomatic career. Waldheim was part of the team that negotiated the Austrian State Treaty (1955). Between 1948 and 1955 he served in various posts in Paris and Vienna, and then briefly as a permanent observer to the United Nations (1955–56). For the next four years he was the Austrian representative and ambassador in Canada, then returned home to serve as director-general of political affairs in the Austrian government (1960–64). In 1964 he went again to the United Nations as a permanent representative. In 1968 he was appointed minister of foreign affairs in the government coalition headed by Chancellor Josef Klaus of the

Österreiche Volkspartei (ÖVP, Austrian People's Party, the Christian-conservative faction in the "grand coalition"). When Bruno Kreisky's Sozialistische Partei Österreichs (SPÖ, Austrian Socialist Party) won the 1970 legislative elections, Waldheim lost that post and returned to the United Nations. In 1971 he campaigned unsuccessfully as the ÖVP candidate for the presidency of the republic.

But his career in diplomacy resumed when he was elected for a five-year term as secretary-general of the United Nations in 1972. He held that post for the next 10 years, confronted with issues such as the Iran-Iraq conflict, the China-Vietnam conflict, the American hostages in Vietnam, and the Arab-Israeli conflict. Although there was some Third World resistance to his candidacy, he was reelected in 1976. When a Chinese veto blocked his reelection to a third term as secretary-general at the United Nations, he accepted the post of research professor of diplomacy at the prestigious Georgetown University in Washington, D.C.

The Accusations

In 1986 Waldheim ran again as the ÖVP candidate in the presidential election. That is when his image began to shatter. His accusers pointed out that his short account of his military service was incomplete. Waldheim was charged with serving in the German forces that committed atrocities in Greece and the Balkans and with deliberately covering it up. He won the election nevertheless and was installed for a five-year term as president of Austria. World reaction to his success despite the accusations was mixed: for example, on 28 April 1987 the Reagan government in the United States put him on the Watch List of individuals prohibited from entering the United States; the next month, however, Pope John Paul II received him in the Vatican and awarded him a papal knighthood.

Waldheim has always asserted that he had no direct influence on any of the events identified as atrocities and has maintained he is innocent of the charges laid against him. But, as a result of continuing accusations and investigations he announced on 21 June 1991 that he would not seek a second term as president of Austria.

The Documented Record of Waldheim's Additional Military Service in Southeastern Europe

The records clearly show that Waldheim was not discharged from the army after his recuperation leave in 1942, as his memoir indicates. When he returned to active status in April 1942, he was transferred to the German Twelfth Army in Belgrade, Yugoslavia. This is the tour of duty that he failed to disclose.

Owing to his knowledge of basic Italian, his initial assignment was to serve as a liaison with the Italian armies also operating in Yugoslavia. As the Germans moved into Banja Luka, Bosnia, he was next assigned to mainly clerical duties in the quartermaster department of the battle group. In July he received the King Zvonimir Medal with Oak Leaves from the Yugoslav regime "for bravery under fire." In August 1942 he joined the headquarters staff of the High Command of Army Group Twelve in Arsakli, northern Greece. There he worked as an interpreter for the intelligence office. After a furlough (19 November 1942 to 31 March 1943) to complete his law degree, during which he received promotion to first lieutenant, he returned to active duty. Again he served as an interpreter and liaison with the Italian forces, then stationed in Tirana, Albania. From July to October 1943 he was in Athens, Greece, as liaison with the Italian Eleventh Army. From October 1943 to April 1945 he was back in Arsakli, with occasional leaves home to receive his law degree, marry, and recuperate from a thyroid condition. In April 1945 he joined the German army forces in retreat from the Russians, during which he was reassigned to an infantry group (although there is no record that he actually joined it). He was demobilized 9 May 1945 in the state of Styria, Austria. On 18 May he was sent to a U.S. prisoner-of-war camp at Bad Toelz, Bayern (Bavaria), from which he was released in June 1945 after debriefing by U.S. intelligence officers.[4] In 1948 the Yugoslav government denounced Waldheim to the United Nations War Crimes Commission, but the documentary evidence had been falsified, so the charges were dismissed.

The Investigations of Waldheim's Military Record

The investigations of Kurt Waldheim were of three types: those initiated and supported by the World Jewish Congress (WJC), headquartered in New York City; those that were "official" or commissioned by government authorities; and those that capitalized on the controversy for political or other purposes. These categories are explained in the following sections. Waldheim gave a number of interviews to the investigators.

The WJC Investigation

The WJC had an important role in the discovery of Waldheim's military service record.[5] In January 1986 the organization's secretary-general, Israel Singer, met with Eli Rosenbaum, who had just taken the position as the WJC's general counsel. Earlier in his career Rosenbaum had served as a trial attorney with the U.S. Justice Department in the Office of Special Investigations, which had been charged with seeking out and prosecuting Nazi war criminals. Singer instructed Rosenbaum to go to Vienna to meet with Leon Zelman, director of the Jewish Welcome Service and a Holocaust survivor. Zelman had evidence that Waldheim was a Nazi.[6]

In March 1986, after meeting with Zelman, Rosenbaum contacted Robert Edwin Herzstein, a historian of the Nazi era and professor at the University of South Carolina. He told Herzstein that the WJC was looking for "a reputable, German-speaking historian experienced in working with captured German military records" to conduct research on Waldheim. Herzstein agreed to the assignment as a paid consultant, and his first results were announced at a WJC press conference in New York City on 25 March.[7] Both Rosenbaum and Herzstein continued their research after that initial shocking denunciation of Waldheim's war record.

Official or Authorized Inquiries

In 1986, following the WJC's announcements about Waldheim's previously undisclosed military service, the British Ministry of Defence conducted an inquiry into Waldheim's involvement in the fate of British soldiers captured by the Germans in Greece and the Greek islands. The findings of the initial inquiry were reviewed, and the inquiry was expanded for publication in 1989.[8]

In May 1987, as the president of Austria, Waldheim sent a request to the Austrian federal government for the appointment of an independent investigatory commission. He wanted the commission to carry out "the further examination and evaluation of the entire body of material in light of the allegations made against the President." In response to a resolution passed on 18 May the Austrian Foreign Office persuaded a Swiss legal and military historian, Dr. Hans Rudolf Kurz, to chair the commission and to select its other members. This International Commission of Historians (ICH) included experts from Belgium, Great Britain, the Bundesrepublik Deutschland, Greece, Israel, and the United States. Its charge was:

> to determine the facts concerning the wartime service of Waldheim and of his participation in the National Socialist organizations. The political content of his doctoral dissertation will be examined.
>
> The Commission may interview witnesses and examine documentary evidence in national and private archives without restraint.
>
> The Austrian Foreign Ministry, while defraying the expenses of the Commission, has no power to alter the final report of the Commission.[9]

Other Investigations

The accusations of Nazi war crimes against a sitting head of state and former secretary-general of the United Nations created a phenomenal reaction, most directly evident in a spate of publications motivated by the authors' particular viewpoints, often their political viewpoints. Most of these publications are based on information produced by the authorized ICH investigation, which was then supplemented by comments from others who had experienced the war in the Balkans and Greece. These works often have pictures of Waldheim in his military uniform, together with German army officials, but they also include pictures of various events associated with the battles or the Holocaust that do not show Waldheim. Many of them support the accusations, probably both out of conviction and because the accusations are what attracted the reading public.

ISSUES

Waldheim Improperly Covered Up His Full Military Record

Agree:

In the section of his memoir that discusses his war record Waldheim avoids any mention of his appointments to the headquarters staffs of the German armies operating in Yugoslavia and Greece between 1942 and 1945. Moreover, his responsibilities undoubtedly made him aware of activities against civilians in those regions, actions contrary to the Geneva Convention on the conduct of war. This omission was deliberate and was framed to imply that his active military service ended when he returned to Vienna to study for his law degree.

The documents and photos cited in the authorized reports clearly demonstrate that Waldheim was appointed to the German army headquarters in both Yugoslavia and Greece between 1942 and 1945. The ICH used files from the German Bundesarchive-Militärarchiv (Federal Military Archives); the Österreiches Staatsarchiv (Austrian State Archives); the Allgemeines Verwaltungsarchiv (General Administrative Archive in Vienna); the National Archives and Records Service of the United States; the United Nations War Crimes Commission; the WJC files in New York (some were also in U.S. and German files); Yugoslavia, including some from the Military Archives in Belgrade, the Yugoslav State Archives, official archives from Croatia, Zagreb, Banja Luka, and the Kozara Museum; and Greece, including Salonika, Macedonia, and Chania. It also used materials from the State Prosecutor's Office in Bremen and private materials. The ICH clearly made an exhaustive search.

For their 1986 study of British servicemen captured in Yugoslavia and Greece, the British made use of the German military archives, the U.S. National Archives, British government archives, and the records of British war crimes investigations. Their 1989 review of findings also consulted the ICH report, the WJC studies, and the research done for a British documentary by Thames Television. The British investigators also sought out testimony of survivors of both sides of the conflicts.

Many independent authors have reviewed and corroborated this material. In failing to confess to his deeds Waldheim has deceived his fellow Austrians and all of the member nations of the United Nations.

Disagree:

Waldheim's military service was scrutinized long before 1986. Records recently released by the U.S. Central Intelligence Agency (CIA) show that both British and U.S. intelligence forces had information on his service in 1945.[10] If he had committed war crimes, it certainly would have come out in their investigations and prosecutions at that time. Nor was he among the some 137,000 Austrians indicted under its Kriegsverbrechergesetz (War Crimes Law) of 1945. In 1948 the Yugoslavs fabricated some documents and filed charges against him with the United Nations. At that time Waldheim was in the Foreign Service of occupied Austria. As a former intelligence officer he had extensive information about the Communist partisans of Yugoslavia, and their action was probably motivated by the desire to have him removed from his position.[11]

Thanks to the Moscow Declaration of 1943, which identified Austria as a victim of Nazi aggression, there has been no widespread stigmatization of World War II military service in that country. Austrian military forces were commandeered by the Germans, and Waldheim served with them. Austrian veterans' organizations have developed their own "official myth of victimhood."[12] They "did their duty." Most were granted amnesty by the government in 1947. In that climate it was acceptable not to amplify military assignments forced by the German command. In writing his memoir, Waldheim did discuss the periods in which he had soldiers under his direct control and in which he led them in battle. When he was in Yugoslavia and Greece, he had no authority to shape policy or direct any military actions of the units to which he was attached. He did not care to discuss them, especially after the embarrassing episode of the bogus Yugoslav "war crimes" files.

However, there is also evidence that the United States may have encouraged Waldheim to downplay his work on the eastern front, probably because of the value of his information on the Communist resistance groups there. On 14 July 1998 Professor Herzstein, who helped break the first allegations against Waldheim, talked about this connection in a statement to the House of Representatives committee that was holding hearings on the Freedom of Information laws. He made the following statements:

> For almost ten years, I have been told that national security concerns prevent me and the public from learning more about the involvement of this government in Kurt Waldheim's postwar career and cover-up. But I can tell you this: For at least twenty-eight years, individuals working for at least two agencies protected Waldheim and propagated false information about him....
>
> The CIA, in one of the few documents it has released on this case, admits that Waldheim was "particularly effective in confidentially working out Austrian formulations acceptable to the United States." Had there been a tradeoff, silence about his activities during the war, in return for cooperation?...
>
> The CIA's 1980 report to a Congressman who had inquired into Waldheim's biography, cleared Waldheim. Its letter contained inaccurate information which to my knowledge did not then or now exist in what the agency calls "open source materials." The CIA collaborated with Waldheim in the production of parallel alibis. How do we obtain the full truth, hidden somewhere in agency files?[13]

Herzstein clearly was frustrated by the lack of access to presumed information in support of his allegations against Waldheim. But if Waldheim had not been charged with war crimes and did, in fact, collaborate with the U.S. government during the war, why were these charges raised against him in 1986, some 42 years later? The charges were first made in the reports initiated and sponsored by the WJC. They were made specifically to coincide with Waldheim's campaign for the presidency of Austria and with the extraordinary rise of the Freiheitliche Partei Österreichs (FPÖ, Austrian Freedom Party). Many feared that the FPÖ was neo-Nazi. Waldheim's military record is really just a convenient ploy. In a recent analysis of Austrian history Hella Pick helps answer this question with a quote from Edgar Bronfman, president of the WJC: "The issue is not Kurt Waldheim. He is a mirror of Austria. His lies are of secondary importance. The real issue is that Austria has lied for decades about its own involvement in the atrocities Mr. Waldheim was involved in."[14]

Herzstein also acknowledges this motivation, although he attributes it to "Austrian Socialists and other domestic opponents" who wanted "his [Waldheim's] past to be exposed by foreign organizations."[15] In a 1988 book about the Waldheim files Michael Palumbo goes even further: "In America he [Waldheim] is useful to the powerful Zionist lobby not only in exposing Austria's Nazi past but, more important, in discrediting the UN—which made many anti-Israeli resolutions while Waldheim was Secretary General, including the 1975 declaration equating Zionism with racism."[16]

Thus, the controversy included many agendas besides Waldheim's own. How many soldiers come away with clean hands? In trying to evade his past, Waldheim did nothing more improper than any other veteran from any other country has done in coping with his wartime experiences: he closed the book on activities that bothered him. The apparent cover-up by the United States, in addition to prevailing attitudes in Austria, made that possible.

Waldheim Was a War Criminal

Agree:

The case against Waldheim is made by the WJC-sponsored reports and by the British Ministry of Defence. In summary, they are:

1. He lied when he said he was never a Nazi.
2. In April and May 1942 the Bader Combat Group, to which Waldheim was assigned as liaison with the Italian Fifth Mountain Division, . . . carried out a very brutal campaign against the partisans.
3. From the end of May to the end of August 1942 Waldheim was assigned to the quartermaster's office of the Kampfgruppe Westbosnien (West Bosnian Combat Group), which carried out the brutal suppression of resistance in western Bosnia, most notably in the Kozara area, where some 3,400 were killed and more than

66,000 prisoners were taken. Many of the prisoners were transported to labor camps in Norway. Waldheim was decorated by the Croatian government "for bravery under fire" on 22 July 1942.

4. Waldheim was involved in the interrogations of British prisoners of war captured in Greece and therefore is liable to punishment as an accessory, if not a principal, for any mistreatment they received.

Rosenbaum and Herzstein devote much of their study to the horror of Nazi society and conquest. They produce the evidence that puts Waldheim in the pertinent German headquarters at times when that army was committing atrocities and war crimes. They emphasize the sensational discovery about Waldheim, although they do not compare it to the wartime experiences of others in comparable circumstances. Their analyses are highly readable and unfold like the text of a mystery.

They draw the conclusion that because Waldheim was part of the German army operations, he must have known what was going on and made no effort to stop them. Many documents place Waldheim on the spot. For proof Herzstein points to Waldheim's assigned responsibility for maintaining the staff war diary while serving the army in Greece. Waldheim's initials are on reports of the atrocities received by his office.

Herztein also points out that all of the occupying powers knew of Waldheim's complicity and used the information to establish leverage over him. He argues that the British and American cochairmen of the United Nations War Crimes Commission imposed the standards of evidence that destroyed the credibility of the Yugoslav "evidence" against Waldheim. Thus, they conspired with him to cover up the record. Herzstein acknowledges that Waldheim had no choice but to serve in the German military, but he categorically rejects any claims Waldheim has made of ignorance of the facts and of his innocence. Waldheim was an accessory to war crimes and should be treated as such.

Disagree:

Waldheim is neither a great man nor a totally honest man: he was ambitious and made personal compromises to get ahead in his career. But he was not a war criminal. Close examinations of the evidence immediately after the war and again in the mid-1980s are ambivalent. The ICH formulated the following conclusions:

In his various staff positions, Waldheim had duties which may have effected [sic] the fate of prisoners or refugees.

The transmission of interrogation reports containing statements given by Allied commando members was causally connected with their subsequent fate.... Activity of this kind can be qualified as action in accordance with orders, in clear knowledge of the fact that the order was criminal in intention....

> Waldheim was in the immediate proximity to criminal acts, especially in Banja Luka. . . . There is to date no concrete evidence pertaining to the manner of Waldheim's direct involvement in questions of transport and camp problems.
>
> . . . [I]n Athens, Waldheim was aware of the practice of transporting Italian prisoners to Germany in September 1943. . . . [He] had only limited practical possibilities of influence the course of such events.
>
> His role . . . in Arsakli [and] the framework of his function as intelligence officer for reports on the enemy situation can also be characterized in a similar manner.
>
> The picture which emerges is one of differing proximity, depending on position, to measures and orders which were incriminating in terms of the laws of war. . . .
>
> The Commission has not noted a single instance in which Waldheim protested or took steps—to prevent, or at least to impede its execution—against an order to commit a wrong that he must doubtlessly have recognized as such. On the contrary, he repeatedly assisted in connection with unlawful actions and thereby facilitated their execution.
>
> . . . One circumstance in Waldheim's favour is the fact that he had only extremely modest possibilities of any sort of opposition to the wrongs being committed. . . . In all probability, such actions would not have led to any concrete result.[17]

The British inquiry reached the same mixed conclusions: there was no evidence that Waldheim had any command authority over the way British prisoners of war were handled, although he certainly had knowledge of them. There was no evidence that he was a "professional intelligence officer" or an "espionage officer." His initials on headquarters documents "did not carry any responsibility for the substance of the contents." There is no evidence that he conducted interrogations; his duties were to collate and assess the information obtained from them. There is no evidence that he had any responsibility for orders about how the prisoners should be handled. Based on the information the British investigators reviewed, their report states: "The above summary of Lt. Waldheim's involvement contrasts with the presence of Kurt Waldheim's name on lists of persons sought on war crimes charges. The significance of such listings has not proved to be self-evident."[18]

If these independent reports and the certain review of Waldheim's wartime activities by the U.S. CIA and Justice Department failed to find the smoking gun, why, then, did President Reagan order Attorney General Edwin Meese to place Waldheim on the Watch List? For the answer to that, we must look to President Reagan himself. In May 1985 Reagan made a goodwill trip to Germany. Scheduled on his itinerary was a visit, together with West German chancellor Helmut Kohl and a general from each country, to the German military cemetery at Bitburg, in which 48 Schutzstaffel (SS, security echelon) soldiers were among the 2,000 interred there. Strong criticism to this visit arose well before Reagan left, especially from veterans' and Jewish organizations. Reagan wanted to characterize the event as "a time of healing." It could in no way, however, minimize the sacrifice of the U.S. military forces or the Holocaust. Reagan said, "The evil war of Nazism turned all values upside down. *Nevertheless, we can mourn the German war dead today as human beings crushed by a vicious ideology.*"[19] The outrage of the American public over this visit and Reagan's remarks continued well after his return. The condemnation of Waldheim was a public way of demonstrating his contrition without offending powerful and important German allies.

Kurt Waldheim was not a war criminal. It is amazing how many nations and interests have used the strategy of accusation to seek their own advantage. Ironically, he might be characterized as the quintessential victim of the war and of postwar world politics.

The Waldheim Controversy Is Still Relevant Today

Agree:

In Austria the legacy of the Waldheim controversy affected attitudes toward the FPÖ, which emerged as a powerful alternative party in 1986. Although the Greens also gained their first seats in the Nationalrat (National Council) in those elections, they did not threaten the "grand coalition" of Christian conservatives and socialists. Austrian politicians are using the politics of guilt to attack the FPÖ as neofascist and guilt by association to condemn Jörg Haider, its most prominent spokesman. The questions over Waldheim's possible culpability for Nazi war crimes helps them continue to equate the FPÖ with fascism.

The fact that Austria elected Waldheim in spite of the accusations against him is undoubtedly a factor in the action by the European Union (EU) to curtail relations with Austria in 2002. The EU condemned the appointment of FPÖ ministers to the cabinet after the 1999 elections because of the ongoing charges from the traditional parties that these ministers were neofascists. That unprecedented EU action opens the door to continuing interference in the domestic politics of member nations and to the possible rejection of popular democracy within them.

The hostilities raised in the United States by the Waldheim controversy have been perpetuated by Jewish organizations as the foundation of their efforts to reclaim Jewish property and assets confiscated by the Nazis after the Anschluss. Although Germany initiated compensation payments to German Jews and, later, to Holocaust survivors in Israel, no similar restitution was made in Austria. The country did not even erect a Holocaust memorial to the 65,000 Austrian Jews who died there.

The Waldheim controversy helped the WJC pressure the U.S. government to pass the War Crimes Disclosure Act in 1998. President William Clinton implemented this act with an Executive Order on 11 January 1999. It set the director of the Holocaust Memorial Museum, the historian of the Department of State, the archivist of the United States, and other appropriate department heads to work searching U.S. documents for all information on war crimes, including "assets taken from persecuted persons during the period beginning on March 23, 1933, and ending on May 8, 1945, by, under the direction of, on behalf of, or under authority granted by the Nazi government of Germany *or any nation then allied with that government.*"[20] This act required the declassification of many documents.

The new documentation helped the WJC pressure Austria into a settlement of Holocaust survivors' claims against the Bank of Austria and its subsidiary, the Creditanstalt. This was the first class-action suit in the United States over Nazi war crimes. The Bank of Austria assumed "moral responsibility" and expressed "profound regret" for the "Aryanization of Jewish property" during the Holocaust, and it agreed to an award of $40 million. The Austrian government, which early in 2000 had offered around $550 million, offered to augment that sum with another $215 million in December 2000.

Disagree:

Waldheim is no longer an active figure in either Austrian or world politics. Austria does not need to be confronted constantly with his story in order to act responsibly. The government has moved to construct a memorial to the Holocaust and to compensate Holocaust victims. The political controversies within contemporary Austria, especially over the FPÖ and Austria's role in the EU, have contemporary causes. The FPÖ complains about the Waldheim legacy because the party is trying to deflect scrutiny of its own activities and goals. It has not inherited Waldheim; it has created new undesirable leadership all on its own.

QUESTIONS AND ACTIVITIES

1. Using the Web and other sources, find out about the Nuremberg War Crimes Trials that followed the German surrender. For what crimes were the defendants tried? Write a short report on the definition of various types of war crimes. Did the Nuremberg Tribunal deal with Austrian war criminals?

2. Using the Web or other sources, find out about the Moscow Declaration of 1943. Who made the declaration, and why was Austria a focus of discussion? Write a short paper on the conference that drafted the declaration and what its goals were.

3. Read a book about Kurt Waldheim. Find out more about the author and the author's motives for writing the book. Write a short report on the book's narrative and analysis of Waldheim.

4. Read about the history of the United Nations. What does Waldheim's election to the United Nations leadership suggest about his reputation before 1986? Who were some of the other secretaries-general? What was their role? Report how Waldheim's terms as secretary-general compare with the leadership of some of those other men.

5. Using the Web and other sources, learn more about the WJC. What are its goals and activities? What does it report on the Waldheim controversy? Is the Wald-

heim controversy the only issue it has addressed? Make a list of the issues it has addressed. Discuss them with the class.

6. Review the U.S. press of late 1986 and the spring of 1987, when the Reagan government put Waldheim on the Watch List and barred him from entering the United States. What were the issues addressed in the press at that time? Compare these issues with the charges made by some investigators that the United States and Great Britain "covered up" Waldheim's war record. Write a short statement of your conclusions about the U.S. involvement with Waldheim. Discuss it with the class.

7. Was Kurt Waldheim a war criminal? Write a short paper explaining your opinion and supporting it with historical fact.

NOTES

1. For good summary biographies, see "Kurt Waldheim (Austria) Fourth United Nations Secretary General," http://www.un.org.Overview/SG/sg4bio.html; "Waldheim, Kurt (1918)," http://www.xrefer.com/entry/171951; and the Web site http://www.encyclopedia.com/html/W/Waldheim.asp.

2. Robert Edwin Herzstein, *Waldheim: The Missing Years* (New York: Arbor House/William Morrow, 1988), 50–59.

3. Kurt Waldheim, *In the Eye of the Storm: A Memoir* (Bethesda, Md.: Adler and Adler, 1986), 17–18. (The German-language title: *Im Glaspalast der Weltpolitik* [In the glass palace of world politics]).

4. Eli M. Rosenbaum, with William Hoffer, *Betrayal: The Untold Story of the Kurt Waldheim Investigation and Cover-up* (New York: St. Martin's Press, 1993), appendix, 476–83.

5. Herzstein, *Waldheim,* 66–75. Rosenbaum, *Betrayal,* appendix, 476–83; Jack Saltman, *Kurt Waldheim: A Case to Answer?* (London: Robson Books, 1988), 18–21.

6. Rosenbaum, *Betrayal,* 1–8.

7. Herzstein, *Waldheim,* 21–23.

8. Ministry of Defence, *Review of the Results of Investigations Carried Out by the Ministry of Defence in 1986 into the Fate of British Servicemen Captured in Greece and the Greek Islands between October 1943 and October 1944 and the Involvement, If Any, of the Then Lieutenant Waldheim* (London: Her Majesty's Stationery Office, 1989).

9. International Commission of Historians (ICH), *The Waldheim Report Submitted February 8, 1988 to Federal Chancellor Dr. Franz Vranitzky,* authorized English translation of the unpublished German report (Copenhagen: Museum Tusculanum Press, University of Copenhagen, 1993), 27–28.

10. Kate Connolly, "CIA Knew about Waldheim's Nazi Past," *Guardian Unlimited,* 2 May 2002, http://www.guardian.co.uk/elsewhere/journalist/story/0,7792,482019,00,html.

11. Michael Palumbo, *The Waldheim Files, Myth and Reality* (London: Faber and Faber, 1988), xiv.

12. Matthew Paul Berg, "Challenging Political Culture in Postwar Austria: Veterans' Associations, Identity, and the Problem of Contemporary History, *Central European History* 30, no. 4 (1997), 513 ff.

13. "Statement in Support of H.R. 4007 by Professor Robert E. Herzstein before the Subcommittee on Government Management, Information, and Technology of

the U.S. House of Representatives," 14 July 1998 [105 Cong., 2nd sess.], http://www.fas.org/sgp/congress/hr071498/herzstein.html (FAS stands for the Federation of American Scientists).

14. Hella Pick, *Guilty Victims: Austria from the Holocaust to Haider* (London: I.B. Tauris, 2000), quoted in Connolly, "CIA Knew about Waldheim's Nazi Past."

15. Herzstein, *Waldheim,* 49.

16. Palumbo, *The Waldheim Files,* xiii.

17. ICH, *The Waldheim Report,* 209–13.

18. Ministry of Defence, *Review,* 95–100.

19. Ronald Reagan, "Remarks at a Joint German-American Military Ceremony at Biturg Air Base in the Federal Republic of Germany May 5, 1985," http://www.reagan.utexas.edu/resource/speeches/1985/50585b.htm, emphasis added.

20. "Nazi War Crimes Disclosure Act. Public Law 105–246," Section 3, Nazi War Crimes (A), http://www.accessreports.com/statutes/nazi.htm, emphasis added. See also "Implementation of the Nazi War Crimes Disclosure Act: An Interim Report to Congress," October 1999 [106 Cong., 1st sess.], http://www.fas.org/sgp/news/1999/11/naraiwg.html.

SUGGESTED READINGS

The logical starting point is Waldheim's memoir, *In the Eye of the Storm: A Memoir* (Bethesda, Md.: Adler and Adler, 1986). Based heavily on his work as United Nations secretary-general, it reflects how most of the world perceived Waldheim before the accusations were made.

The accusatory works resulting from the WJC inquiries present the most vivid charges against Waldheim. See Robert Edwin Herzstein, *Waldheim: The Missing Years* (New York: Arbor House/William Morrow, 1988), and Eli M. Rosenbaum with William Hoffer, *Betrayal: The Untold Story of the Kurt Waldheim Investigation and Cover-Up* (New York: St. Martin's Press, 1993). Other accusatory books may be better written, but they are heavily influenced by these two works and the sources they uncovered.

The two official inquiry reports are written in bureaucratese but are vital to show how the sources can lead to other interpretations than those of the WJC scholars. See Ministry of Defence, *Review of the Results of Investigations Carried Out by the Ministry of Defence in 1986 into the Fate of British Servicemen Captured in Greece and the Greek Islands between October 1943 and October 1944 and the Involvement, If Any, of the Then Lieutenant Waldheim* (London: Her Majesty's Stationery Office, 1989), and International Commission of Historians, *The Waldheim Report Submitted February 8, 1988 to Federal Chancellor Dr. Franz Vranitzky,* authorized English translation of the unpublished German report (Copenhagen: Museum Tusculanum Press, University of Copenhagen, 1993).

Most of the German-language sources on Waldheim are in archives or in print. The bibliographies of the works mentioned previously identify most of these sources. No current Austrian newspaper Web pages discuss Waldheim.

8

AUSTRIAN NEOFASCISM

BACKGROUND

Although a small, landlocked nation located along the Danube River in southeastern Europe, Austria has deep historical roots. It began with the Roman Empire, which founded the cities of Vienna (Vindobona) and Salzburg (Iuvavum) and had other settlements east of Vienna. After Rome fell, the region was subjected to wave after wave of migrations, including both Germans and Magyars (Hungarians), and later the Slavs. In A.D. 995 the German Holy Roman Emperor, Otto the Great, conquered the region. The following year, 966, the area was identified in a document for the first time as *Österreich* (eastern empire). Its population grew as the empire established settlements and colonies of Christians among the pagan population. In 1156 it was designated as a duchy with some degree of autonomy and began to expand toward the east. In 1273 Rudolf Habsburg of German Bayern (Bavaria) became Holy Roman emperor and gave the duchies of Austria and Styria to his sons.

The Habsburg Empire

For the next 600 years the Habsburg emperors strengthened their hold over these Austrian duchies and used them as a power base for expansion into Bohemia, Hungary, Italy, and Spain. They successfully turned back the efforts of the Ottoman Turks to move into Europe after the fall of Constantinople. They sided with the pope against Martin Luther and the Protestants in the sixteenth century. In 1555 the great Habsburg emperor Charles V divided his family's holdings in two, separating the holdings of the Spanish Habsburgs and the Austrian Habsburgs. His younger brother, Ferdinand, took over the Austrian realm and the imperial title. At that time the Austrians controlled territory reaching from the Bodensee (Lake Constance) eastward to the Carpathian Mountains, and from the Tyrolean Alps northward through Bohemia and Silesia along the lower reaches of the Oder River. By the late eighteenth century Austria had expanded into northern Italy, along the coast of the Adriatic, and eastward to the Carpathian Mountains, incorporating the Kingdom of Hungary.

Austria as a Great Power

In the late eighteenth century Napoleon had early success in wresting the Italian and Adriatic provinces away from the Habsburgs and brought the German states under his own control in 1804. Emperor Francis II was forced to change the name of his remaining realm from the Holy Roman Empire to the Austrian Empire, which he then ruled as Francis I. The change was humiliating. But together with England, Prussia, and Russia, Austria defeated the French emperor in 1814 and met in Vienna (1815) to decide the map of Europe. It emerged with its territories restored and, as the presiding authority over the new Deutsches Bund (German Confederation), added those 35 German states of central Europe to its control. The Habsburgs were at the height of their modern power. With Vienna as their capital, they controlled the great European regional cities of Prague, Pressburg (current-day Bratislava), Budapest, Trent, Trieste, and Sarajevo, each the hub of a non-German ethnic region.

The Austro-Hungarian Empire

But the Revolutions of 1848 began to undermine this imperial dignity. They also aroused the nationalism of the German states. Austria's German rival, the Kingdom of Prussia, used a war within the Bund successfully to challenge Austria's authority. When Austria attempted to retaliate, Prussia defeated it soundly at the Battle of Sadowa (1866). The Prussians prudently stopped short of invading Austria and used the peace treaty only to expel Austria from the German Bund. Prussia then created a new Norddeutsches Bund (North German Confederation) under its own control. With their involvement in central Europe ended, the Habsburgs had to turn to the eastern portions of their realm. The Magyars and Slavs now comprised the majority populations of the empire. To assure the continuation of the Germanic Habsburg dynasty, the emperor conceded a new constitution that shared powers with the Magyars, giving them virtual autonomy in domestic affairs. The name of the country changed officially in 1867 to the Austro-Hungarian Empire.

The Minorities Problem

The concession to the Magyars angered and excited the envy of the empire's many minority ethnic populations: the Slavic Bohemians, Slovaks, and Poles in the north; the Italian Tyroleans in the southwest; and the Slavic Slovenians and Croatians of the southern Adriatic districts, to name the most prominent of them.

Because the German Austrians controlled the government and finance, and the Magyars controlled the vast and fruitful farmlands, the Slavic ethnic groups were politically and economically disadvantaged. Although they were not politically unified, a nationalistic wave of Pan-Slavism swept the eastern and southern minorities of the empire. They hoped for autonomy or even independence from Austria. This impulse was encouraged by the Serbs, who had won independence and nationhood from the Ottoman Empire. Russia, the largest Slavic nation of all, was also supportive. Austria's annexation of Bosnia and Herzegovina in 1908 led to a major crisis with Russia. The Balkan Wars (1912–13) strengthened Serbia and intensified its support for the Slavic minorities in southern Austria, including its support of ethnic terrorism.

The assassination of the Austrian archduke Franz Ferdinand, heir to the throne, by a Slavic terrorist, Gavrilo Princip, on 28 June 1914 ignited World War I. Austria was sure that Serbia had sponsored the act and thus was determined to punish that country. It called on Germany, with whom it had had a defensive alliance since 1879, to back it. Although Germany had no obligation to aid Austria if it attacked another country, the impetuous German kaiser, William II, sent his assurances. When Russia began to mobilize to prevent the Austrian attack (a six-week process), Germany realized it could face a two-front war, with Russia and France, its alliance partner. Austria declared war on Serbia on 28 July 1914. Germany decided to launch a preemptive strike to take out France before Russia could attack. It declared war on Russia (1 August) and then against France (3 August) and launched its westward invasion on 4 August 1914.

Disintegration and Defeat

During the war years the Austro-Hungarian Empire began to crumble. Emperor Franz Josef, who had reigned since 1848, died in 1916. His grandnephew, Charles, succeeded him, but the young man was relatively unknown and commanded no allegiance from the restive minorities. On 10 April 1918 the Congress of Oppressed Austrian Nationalities met in Rome. Motivated by U.S. president Woodrow Wilson's "Fourteen Points," the Slavic delegates called for self-determination and resistance to the Habsburg government. By early June the western powers were supporting the idea of statehood for Poland, Czechoslovakia, and the region populated by the southern Slavs. As the war turned against Austria, Czechoslovakia (28 October) and Yugoslavia (29 October) declared their independence. After William II abdicated in

Germany on 9 November 1918, young Emperor Charles vacated the Austrian throne two days later (although he did not formally abdicate). On 12 November the new Austrian Republic was declared to be part of the new German Republic. The Hungarian Republic was proclaimed on 16 November, and on 24 November the Serbs, Croats, and Slovenes united to form a new kingdom in the Balkans.

The Treaty of Saint-Germain, 1919

The western peacemakers at Paris verified the disintegration of the Austro-Hungarian Empire. Like the new German Republic, the new Austrian Republic was punished for the nation's role in World War I. Thus, the Treaty of Saint-Germain forbade the desired union between the Austrian and the German Republics. Moreover, Austria had to recognize the independence of the new eastern European "successor" states carved from it: Hungary, Poland, Czechoslovakia, and the new kingdom of the Serbs, Croats, and Slovenes, which came to be known as Yugoslavia (*yugo* means "south" in Slavic languages). Austria could have an army of no more than 30,000 and was required to pay reparations for a period of 30 years. The 750-year-old empire, long the cornerstone of southeastern Europe, retained only its core population of 8 million Germans and appeared as only a small lozenge on the new complex map of Europe, separated from Hungary and actually smaller than the new Slavic states.

Troubles for the Austrian Republic

The Austrian Republic was centered in Vienna, the administrative and financial hub of the former empire, where approximately one-quarter of its population resided. Postwar inflation and unemployment plagued the city because its successor states had taken its basic agricultural and industrial hinterland. Until favorable relations were established with them, Austria lived in economic distress and on the verge of famine. This situation raised popular demands for unification with Germany, but the western powers refused to hear of it. By the mid-1920s, even though the economy had stabilized, domestic politics remained turbulent. They were troubled by the conflict between the urban socialists and the rural conservatives, and by the emergence of a new Grossdeutsche Volkspartei (Greater German People's Party), a nationalist body that agitated for union with Germany.

To calm the situation, in 1922 the League of Nations stepped in to back financial aid for Austria. The terms required the government to pare back civil service and expenditures and to raise taxes significantly. They also introduced a new currency, the schilling, but this did little to stimulate the economy. When the League ended its oversight in 1925, there was still massive unemployment and unrest. The urban Socialists clashed with the more conservative rural Christian Socialists, each of which had formed militias, the Republikanisches Schutzbund (Republican Protection League) and the conservative Heimwehr (Homeland Defense), respectively. The militias increased tensions by bloody street warfare that resulted in a number of deaths.

The Impact of the Depression of 1929

In September 1929 a new coalition cabinet led by conservative Christian Democrats and nationalist Grossdeutsche parties came to power. This coalition amended the Constitution to give more emergency powers to the president and vowed to restore order. As the depression struck, however, once again unemployment skyrocketed. A strong cry for union with Germany arose, and again the western powers refused to allow such a union. As a result, Austria's greatest bank, the Creditanstalt, collapsed in 1931, bringing down the government. The conservative parties began to call for reforms like those taken by Benito Mussolini's fascist government in Italy.

What Is Fascism?

Fascism is an extreme conservative political movement with three characteristics: (1) it is based on mass popular support, usually winning significant elections with promises addressing mass grievances; (2) it is aggressively nationalist, often looking to past glories; and (3) it is authoritarian, elevating the state above the rights of the individual.[1] *Doctrine of Fascism,* which Mussolini published in 1932, spells out the specific concepts. A one-time socialist and postwar newspaper editor, he called upon the public to demand that the French and English fulfill their wartime promises to Italy, promises of territorial expansion at the expense of the Germans and Austrians. Disappointed that the treaties of Paris did not award Italy the city of Trieste and the eastern Adriatic coastline of the Austro-Hungarian Empire, Mussolini capitalized on the sense of grievance. He harked back to the glories of the Roman Empire and promised that Italy would be great again if the Italians backed the state. Long before Adolf Hitler made the same types of promises to the Germans, Mussolini won popular support in Italy and built Europe's first fascist dictatorship in Europe in 1922.

Fascism Moves to Austria

Fascism is explicitly antiliberal and antisocialist. This same strategy animated the conservative Christian Socialist Heimwehr in Austria after the depression. It attempted to set up a fascist government in the province of Styria; in the end, it took the army to oust them. In the spring elections of 1932, nevertheless, the National Socialist candidates proved to be very popular.

The National Socialists in Austria

Following Hitler's takeover of Germany in January 1933, the Austrian fascists looked to his example. In March 1933 the Austrian National Socialist Party led massive demonstrations against the Austrian government. In April the Social Democrats tried to overthrow the increasingly conservative government. This civil war opened the way to dictatorship. To suppress the opposition, Prime Minister Engelbert Dollfuss declared a state of emergency, which allowed him to suspend the Parliament and freedom of the press and assembly. Dollfuss formed a Fatherland Front government of loyal officials, which in January 1934 outlawed all parties except for the Fatherland Front. The street violence continued, however, and Dollfuss turned to Italy. In April 1934, with Italy's help, Dollfuss put through a new constitution. It introduced a corporate state in which all sectors of society were organized under government oversight. In July the National Socialists assassinated Dollfuss, but once again the army saved the state, which made it possible for a new government to be formed by Kurt von Schuschnigg, who consulted with both Mussolini and Hitler. Like Hitler, he broke the 1919 peace treaty in 1936 to expand the military.

The Anschluss

Despite cooperating with Nazi Germany, Schuschnigg insisted on the independence of Austria. Hitler appeared to respect this condition with an agreement in July 1936 pledging to respect the sovereignty of Austria. But in November 1937 he held a meeting with his military staff, whom he told to prepare to annex Austria and to take Czechoslovakia. On 24 February 1938 Hitler called Schuschnigg to his mountain hideaway in Berchtesgaden, near the German-Austrian border, and ordered him to include some National Socialists in the Austrian government.

Schuschnigg responded on 9 March by calling a plebiscite for 12 March on Austria's independence. The Germans countered with the demand that Schuschnigg cancel the plebiscite and then resign. When no country would respond to his call for assistance, Schuschnigg did resign on 11 March, turning power over to Arthur Seyss-Inquart, a National Socialist, who invited Germany to help him to "maintain law and order." The following day German troops crossed into Austria, cheered by the bystanders. On 13 March Hitler returned to his birthplace, the city of Linz in western Austria, and announced the Anschluss, the unification of Germany and Austria. Simultaneously, Jews and members of the political opposition were arrested throughout Austria. All of these actions were ratified in a rigged plebiscite conducted in Germany and Austria on 10 April 1938.

World War II: Defeat and Restoration of the Republic

As part of the Third Reich, Austria sent troops to the German armies that spread out across Europe and implemented the anti-Semite laws. Many of its troops were caught and imprisoned by the Soviet armies once the Germans began their retreat in 1943. The Allies, however, decided at a Moscow meeting of their foreign ministers in October 1943 to separate and restore Austria after defeating Germany. Their Declaration on Austria was significant for Austrian postwar attitudes:

The governments of the United Kingdom, the Soviet Union and the United States of America are agreed that Austria, the first free country to fall victim to Hitlerite aggression, shall be liberated from German domination.

They regard the annexation imposed on Austria by Germany on March 15, 1938, as null and void. They consider themselves in no way bound by any charges effected in Austria since that date. They declare that they wish to see re-established a free and independent Austria and thereby to open the way for the Austrian people themselves,... to find that political and economic security which is the only basis for lasting peace. Austria is reminded, however that she has a responsibility, which she cannot evade, for participation in the war on the side of Hitlerite Germany, and that in the final settlement account will inevitably be taken of her own contribution to her liberation.[2]

Soviet troops reached Vienna and conquered it on 13 April 1945. Like Germany, Austria was divided into four zones subject to the occupying forces of the United States, France, Britain, and the Soviet Union.

Political Parties in the Second Austrian Republic

On 27 April 1945, even before the defeat of Germany, a provisional government was formed in Austria. Headed by the Social Democrat Karl Renner, this government announced the restoration of the prewar political parties and reinstated the 1920 Constitution of the federal republic. The Allies initially permitted only three antifascist political parties—the conservative Christian Österreiche Volkspartei (ÖVP, Austrian People's Party), the Socialistische Partei Österreichs (SPÖ, Austrian Socialist Party), and the Kommunistische Partei Österreichs (KPÖ, Austrian Communist Party). In the provisional government the three parties were relatively equally represented. The first free elections in the Austrian Second Republic took place in November 1945, with victory going to the ÖVP, which established a coalition government with the SPÖ. The KPÖ elected only 4 of the 165 representatives, but there was one Communist minister in the cabinet during the first electoral period. The ÖVP generally commanded a majority in the Nationalrat (National Council) until 1966.

After a four-year interlude (1966–70) when the ÖVP ruled alone, the SPÖ won the majority in 1971 and held it until 1983. Then, having lost the absolute majority, it formed coalition governments together with the Freiheitliche Partei Österreichs (FPÖ, Austrian Freedom Party). The FPÖ had its roots in the Verband der Unabhängigen (VdU, Association of Independents), formed in 1949 as a liberal-independent faction. In 1955 the FPÖ succeeded this rather loosely organized group but retained its anti-Marxist ideology. Thereafter, it was the only opposition voice to the ruling coalitions until it joined the Socialist government in 1983. When its candidate, Jörg Haider, was elected governor of the province of Carinthia in 1989, the party took on a more militant tone.

Post–World War II Austria

As a former part of the Third Reich, Austria seemed to be building a parallel history with the reestablishment of a constitutional republic, traditional political parties, de-Nazification, division, and occupation by the victorious allies. But, unlike Germany, it was not on the frontline of the Cold War. Austria regained its sovereignty through the State Treaty of 15 May 1955, accepting certain restrictions on its military. On 26 October 1955 it established permanent neutrality as the foundation of its foreign policy, not joining either the North Atlantic Treaty Organization (NATO) or the Warsaw Pact. That December it became a member of the United Nations, serving on many of its committees and special commissions. Since then, Austria has been active on the international scene, as a member of the United Nations, the Conference on Security and Co-operation in Europe, and the Council of Europe. It has successfully worked with the emerging nations of eastern Europe to collaborate in resolving economic and transportation issues. In 1994 it became a member of the European Union.

ISSUES

Austria Was a Willing Partner to National Socialist Fascism

Agree:

In pre–World War I Vienna Mayor Karl Lueger had built Austria's most powerful prewar mass political party, the Christian Socialists, on the basis of anti-Semitism. This accomplishment, in fact, may have inspired Adolf Hitler's ambitions: he spent six years in Austria before the outbreak of World War I. The Austrian Republic that was proclaimed at the end of that war was a humiliating remnant of the former nation, economically weak and politically divided, incapable of building stability. Post–World War I Austria thus shared with Germany the core causes of National Socialism: deeply rooted German nationalism, aggressive anti-Semitism, the humiliation of the post–World War I treaty, and economic collapse. The desertion of the ethnic minorities from the Austro-Hungarian Empire strengthened the Germanic core of the new republic. The goals of National Socialism in Germany appealed strongly to many Austrians. During the Anschluss Austrian chancellor Arthur Seyss-Inquart invited the German forces into Austria, and they were cheered as they came.

There is strong evidence for Austrian participation in Nazi activities following the Anschluss. Evan Bukey's study of Austria in the Nazi era points out that the Austrian population was only 8 percent of the German Reich, but that Austrians made up almost 15 percent of the Schutzstaffel (SS, Hilter's security echelon) forces and some 40 percent of the personnel involved in carrying out the genocide. Willing Austrians destroyed 267 synagogues and 7,500 businesses and homes, and they rounded up more than 26,000 Jews (murdering 91 of them) for Kristallnacht on 9–10 November 1938.[3] These were hardly the acts of "victims."

Austria has never fully confronted its participation in Hitler's war. There has been virtually no prosecution for war crimes in Austria. In the decade immediately following the foundation of the Second Austrian Republic, war crimes cases were submitted only to Volksgerichte (People's Court Tribunals) established under the Verbotsgesetz (Nazi Prohibition Law) of 8 May 1945. These courts consisted of two professional judges and three laymen responsible to the Department of Justice. The Kriegsverbrechergesetz (War Crimes Law) of 26 June 1945 identified "crimes against humanity, torture and acts of cruelty, violation of human dignity, expropriation, expulsion and resettlement" as the basis for prosecution. There was a shortage of judges, however, owing to the fact that many had been disqualified because of their collaboration with the Nazis. Some 137,000 individuals were indicted; but only approximately 28,000 were brought to trial, and only 13,607 were sentenced. These courts were dissolved on 20 December 1955, after the State Treaty returned Austrian sovereignty, with 4,742 cases still unheard. In 1947 the Nazi Amnesty Law ended the prosecution of all but a few cases. Only 39 war crimes verdicts were handed down in Austria by juried courts between 1955 and 1975.[4] Meanwhile, veterans' organizations sprang up across the country, receiving respect and considerable attention from politicians.

The "victim" myth established by the Moscow Declaration has been exploited cleverly to mask the reintegration of former Nazis into Austrian society. One study reports that there were 536,660 registered Nazi Party members by 1946, including 22,729 who had served in the SS and 61,198 who had served in the Sturmabteilung (SA; Nazi Party Storm Troopers); 135,000 civil servants lost their positions after the war because of their Nazi ties.[5] The "victim" myth allowed them to be reintegrated into society without major conflict, however. On 21 April 1948 the Bundesrat (National Council) decided to grant amnesty to "less incriminated" Nazis. They were allowed to vote after 1949. Many of them helped found the VdU. According to the Documentation Centre of Austrian Resistance, "the main influence on Austrian political life in the 1940s and 1950s was not exerted by anti-Fascists or those persecuted or driven into exile by the Nazis, but by those who had taken part in the war on Germany's side or had been members or supporters of the NSDAP [Nazi Party]."[6]

It is readily apparent that many Austrians collaborated with the Nazis during the era of the Third Reich. After the war they successfully used their influence to reduce the importance of such activities and to evade punishment. They were fully reintegrated into Austrian society without significantly changing their viewpoints.

Disagree:

The historical evidence is clear. Successive Austrian governments were against any unification with Germany. When the Austrian National Socialists' assassination of Dollfuss failed to achieve the desired Putsch, Hitler signed the agreement to respect Austrian sovereignty. But soon he was plotting with his military chiefs to take over Austria.

Meanwhile, German Nazi Party agents were active in Austria, infiltrating social organizations and religious groups with the messages of German nationalism and anticommunism. They hid behind the label of "Nationalist Opposition" and worked to be brought into the Fatherland Front. Hitler ordered these groups to remain in secret contact with the Third Reich. Seyss-Inquart, who was a National Socialist, was one of their contacts and relayed discussions with his chancellor to Berlin. But even then there was no mass support for the Nazis. Electoral support for the German National Party, which garnered 18.4 percent of the votes in 1919, had declined to 12.8 percent in 1930, the last parliamentary election before the Anschluss. Together, the Nazis and the Fatherland Front block, which campaigned for the first time in 1930, managed to gain only 9.2 percent of the votes. They tallied only 339,028 ballots out of the 4,121,282 votes cast.[7]

With the Nazi domestic subversion and masses of German troops on the Austrian border, Schuschnigg had no option to stepping down in order to prevent a massive civilian disaster. Seyss-Inquart, his National Socialist successor, was clearly a traitor. The letter he sent to invite the Nazis to enter Austria was actually written in and announced from Berlin.[8] The post-Anschluss referendum staged by Hitler was a typically cosmetic event. It was conducted throughout both the German and Austrian sectors of the Reich on 10 April 1938, with both populations intimidated by the Nazi forces. Austrians did not support it, but they were outvoted by the Germans.

Austria was thus the first free country taken over by the Germans. Dollfuss was its first martyr. Its young men were drafted; its youth were forced to join Nazi organizations. The small population was powerless in the face of Nazi military pressure; resistance was virtually impossible. Austrians were forced to obey the Germans in both the civilian and military sectors. The Allies, who knew their enemy well, were clearly insightful and correct when they drafted the Moscow Declaration. Austria did not accept National Socialism willingly.

Austria Is Taking Another Dangerous Turn to the Political Right Today

Agree:

After World War II the ÖVP and the SPÖ provided skilled and stable leadership for Austria. Like the two major political parties in the United States, they were umbrella parties that incorporated a wide range of opinions and worked for consensus among them. Moreover, the two parties cooperated with each other for the first 35 years of the Second Republic, with the ÖVP claiming the chancellorships (1945–70) but incorporating SPÖ ministers in the cabinet. In 1970 the SPÖ won more seats in the Nationalrat but continued the coalition format of the cabinet. The two major parties operated on the principle of Proporz (proportionality), in which they balanced public offices and patronage between themselves, successfully excluding nonmembers from participation and patronage. It was a cozy partnership but one prone to abuse. The rise of opposition parties was inevitable.

Whereas the KPÖ had little success in Austria, the nationalist VdU, with strong support from veterans' organizations, began to organize the political right. It was succeeded by the FPÖ, which Anton Reinthaller, a onetime Nazi government minister, chaired from 1955 to 1968. His successor as head of the party from 1958 to 1978 was Frederich Peter, a veteran of the German Waffen SS (combat troops often differentiated from Heinrich Himmler's SS troops in charge of the German concentration camps). The FPÖ served mainly as an alternative party to those unhappy with the exclusiveness of Proporz. Its core principles were German nationalism, individual rights, and laissez-faire capitalism rather than welfare socialism. Its program was classical liberalism; the problem was with its fascist founding fathers, so it was regarded with suspicion. The FPÖ had modest success, garnering somewhere between 5.5 percent and 7.5 percent of the votes in federal elections. In the early 1980s a more liberal leadership emerged that attracted support from the working classes. In 1983 the SPÖ asked the FPÖ to join the government coalition.

Thus, it appeared that the FPÖ was moving toward the center. But in 1986 Jörg Haider became party chairman and reversed its direction. Haider not only strengthened the nationalist message, but also began a strongly antiforeigner/anti-immigration campaign that echoed the anti-Semitism of the Nazis. A charismatic campaigner, he attacked the cozy Proporz coalition of the major parties as corrupt and appealed to the discontent of the working classes. But he has also made worrying comments that approved of the employment policies of the Third Reich, and he has praised the veterans of the Waffen SS. Under his leadership the FPÖ grew from a small third party to a major political force in the republic and joined the ruling coalition in 2000 (see Table 8.1).

Table 8.1
Results of the General Elections for the Austrian Nationalrat

Year	Party	% Votes	Seats
1986	SPÖ	43.13	80
	ÖVP	41.29	77
	FPÖ	**9.73**	**18**
	Greens	4.82	8
1990	SPÖ	42.79	80
	ÖVP	32.06	60
	FPÖ	**16.64**	**33**
	Greens	4.78	10
1994	SPÖ	34.9	65
	ÖVP	27.7	52
	FPÖ	**22.5**	**42**
	Greens	7.3	13
	LIF	6.0	11
1995	SPÖ	38.1	71
	ÖVP	28.3	53
	FPÖ	**21.0**	**40**
	Greens	4.8	9
	LIF	5.5	11
1999	SPÖ	33.1	65
	ÖVP	26.9	52
	FPÖ	**26.9**	**52**
	Greens	7.4	14
	Others	5.6	-

Source: Austria: Facts and Figures (Vienna: Federal Press Service, 1994), 56; "Amtliches Endergebnis Österreich," 17 December 1995, http://www.idv.uni-linz.ac.at/wahl95/docs/oetab.htm; "Austrian Nationalrat Elections of 3 October 1999," http://psephos.adam-car.net/austria/austria1.txt.

This FPÖ, under Haider's leadership, is not simply a populist movement; it is a dangerous throwback to the Nazi past. It is perceived as such in the rest of Europe. In fact, the president of the European Union (EU), Portuguese prime minister Antonio Guterres, took the unprecedented action of warning Austria against including Haider and his party in the ruling coalition:

Governments of the fourteen member states will not promote or accept any bilateral official contacts at the political level with an Austrian government which includes Jörg Haider's Freedom Party.

If a party which has expressed xenophobic views and which does not abide by the essential values of the European family comes to power, naturally we won't be able to continue the same relations as in the past however much we regret it. Nothing will be as before.[9]

Disagree:

A certain disgruntled air has pervaded world politics since the disintegration of the Soviet system. The western European nations, expecting some major results from "winning" the Cold War, have found themselves confronted with mass immigration owing to the explosions of ethnic nationalism in southeastern Europe and the Middle East, and with problems of lagging economies and high unemployment. In these nations the welfare state has been the norm since World War II. Now the costs of government social insurance programs for citizens are rising at the same time as welfare costs for the masses of refugees and political asylum seekers from eastern Europe.

The current condemnation of Austria by the EU is a malicious echo of the Kurt Waldheim controversy in the mid-1980s.[10] Austria's FPÖ and Jörg Haider have been singled out for their articulation of antiforeigner/anti-immigration policies that extreme right politicians in other countries are pressing just as hard. Gianfranco Fini leads Italy's National Alliance, described as a "direct descendant" of Mussolini's Fascists and now part of a coalition government. Gerhard Frey founded the Deutsche Volksunion (German People's Union) in Munich in 1987, an extreme right party based on antiforeigner/anti-immigration programs, and he even denies aspects of the Holocaust. This party is having success in German state elections. Jean-Marie Le Pen of France heads the National Front, which wants to expel immigrants, and which won approximately 15 percent of the vote in France. Le Pen was a run-off candidate for the presidency. Consider, too, the extremist secessionist party in the Flemish section of Belgium; the anti-immigration party in Denmark; and the Schweitzerische Volkspartei (Swiss People's Party), whose leader praised a book that denied the Holocaust. Yet none of these nations have been singled out by the EU as dangerous.[11] Yet if the EU is going to demand democracy, then it must respect the choices made by the Austrian voters as well as those within their own countries.

Haider does lead the largest of the far right parties in Europe. He has been branded a neo-Nazi because of remarks he made about the favorable impact of Hitler's employment policy, because he praised the Waffen SS veterans, and because of his strong antiforeigner stance. He has apologized often in public for the Hitler comment and called it a mistake. His honoring of Austria's veterans is not unusual for a politician, and, after all, Austria has not fought in any other war since World War II. It must be remembered that U.S. president Ronald Reagan paid the same respect to German soldiers, including Waffen SS, buried in the cemetery at Bitburg, Germany. Haider's anti-immigration stance is not unlike that taken by California's governor Pete Wilson in his losing electoral campaign or by Pat Buchanan in recent U.S. presidential elections.

In fact, Haider has resigned from the party chairmanship in light of the controversies over his statements. He remains the elected governor in the state of Carinthia, but he has not sought to enter the government coalition.

Although he undoubtedly would enjoy being chancellor, there is no indication that he will attempt to destroy Austrian democracy to get there. It is incorrect to brand a quarter of Austria's voters as dangerous because of the imprudent remarks of one politician.

It is clear that other aspects of domestic policy led to the strong FPÖ vote. Austria's comfortable old "grand coalition" of Christian conservatives and Socialists is crumbling. It is not handling the influx of Balkan refugees well, and the population wants limits on immigration. Many voters are also outraged at the corrupt Proporz system and want to open up the political system. The FPÖ has been joined by the Greens and the Liberal Forum, both parties of the left, in the past decade. It is more likely that the established parties exaggerate the dangers from the right in hopes of enhancing their own electoral results, and that politicians in other European countries—which also face similar problems—are focusing on Austria in order to divert attention from their own national concerns.

Austria, like many European countries and like the United States, is moving toward the right in its politics. As a small country with minimal military capacity, it is hardly a danger to the world community.

QUESTIONS AND ACTIVITIES

1. Read about Austria in the twentieth century. Report to the class on the history of the Nazi Party there. What aspects of the Nazi program gained support in Austria?

2. Go to the Web site of Austria's ultraconservative FPÖ (http://www.fpoe.at/bundneu/index.jhtml). Read how it presents itself and its programs. Identify those aspects that you can agree with and those that you find questionable. Have a class discussion on the party's political orientation. Does it resemble the Nazi Party in its views?

3. Go to the Web site of the ÖVP (http://www.oevp.at/) and the SPÖ (http://www.spoe.at/). Make a list of their major party programs. Compare these programs with those of the FPÖ. How similar are they? How different are they? Make a classroom display to show the differences among the major Austrian political parties.

4. On the FPÖ Web site, read about Jörg Haider. What political influences have shaped his viewpoints? Compare him with one of the other "extreme right" politicians in Europe, such as Jean-Marie Le Pen of France, Pym Fortuyn of the Netherlands, Gianfranco Fini of Italy, or Gerhard Frey of Germany. Do these men have any views in common? Lead a classroom discussion about the emergence of ultraconservatism in Europe.

5. Many of the accusations against Haider and his party have arisen because they are against unlimited immigration into Austria. Some other prominent politicians, such as former governor Pete Wilson of California and Chancellor Gerhardt Schröder of Germany, have also taken strong stands against open immigration. Find out their views and compare them with Haider's. Does an anti-immigration stance automatically mean that the speaker is a neofascist?

6. Identify other countries in the EU that have implemented programs to check immigration. Prepare a presentation explaining how their policies resemble or differ

from those proposed by the FPÖ. Explain why there is such concern over Austria's discussion of the issue.

NOTES

1. For a comprehensive definition of fascism, see the History Guide Lectures on Twentieth Century Europe, "Mussolini, *Doctrine of Fascism* (1932)," http://www.historyguide.org/europe/duce.html.

2. "The Moscow Conference; October 1943," the Avalon Project at Yale Law School, http://www.yale.edu/lawweb/avalon/wwii/moscow.htm, emphasis mine.

3. Evan Burr Bukey, *Hitler's Austria: Popular Sentiment in the Nazi Era, 1938–1945* (Chapel Hill: University of North Carolina Press, 2000).

4. Winfried R. Garscha and Claudia Kuretsidis-Haider, "War Crimes Trials in Austria," paper presented at the Twenty-first Annual Conference of the German Studies Association, Washington, D.C., September 1997, http://doew.at/thema/thema/_alt/justiz/nachkriegforsch/warcrime.html.

5. F. Parkinson, "Epilogue," in *Conquering the Past: Austrian Nazism Yesterday and Today,* ed. F. Parkinson (Detroit: Wayne State University Press, 1989), 323.

6. The Documentation Centre of Austrian Resistance. See the discussion at http://www.doew.at/english/history/content.html.

7. "Eighth Day, Thursday, 29 November 1945," *International Military Tribunal "Blue Series,"* 2, no. 394. See http://www.holocaust-history.org. Gerhard L. Weinberg, *Germany, Hitler, and World War II: Essays in Modern German and World History* (Cambridge: Cambridge University Press, 1995), 105. Thomas T. Mackie and Richard Rose, *The International Almanac of Electoral History* (New York: Free Press, 1974), 30–31.

8. Weinberg, *Germany, Hitler, and World War II,* 106.

9. "EU Issues Unprecedented Warning against New Austrian Government," *Europe* 393 (February 2000), 24.

10. Waldheim is an Austrian diplomat who covered up his service in the German army during World War II. After completing two terms as the secretary-general of the United Nations, he returned to Austria to run for the presidency. The World Jewish Council revealed his service record in order to prevent his election. When he was elected, the international community isolated Austria throughout his term (1986–92). See chapter 7.

11. Barry Came, "Europe's Hard Edge," *Maclean's* 113, no. 8 (21 February 2000), 30 ff.

SUGGESTED READINGS

Most of the general histories of Austria are rather academic in nature. Many are out of print, so a trip to a library for background information is probably warranted. Richard Luther and Peter G. J. Pulzer, eds., *Austria 1945–1995: Fifty Years of the Second Republic* (Aldershot, Hauts, UK; Brookfield VT: U.S.: Ashgate, 1998), offer various perspectives. Anton Pelinka's *Austria: Out of the Shadow of the Past (Nations of the Modern World, Europe)* (Boulder, Colo.: Westview Press, 1998) is a comprehensive overview of the nation's government, politics, and economy, and discusses the "darker side" that differentiates between neo-Nazism and right populism. Evan Burr Bukey's *Hitler's Austria: Popular Sentiment in the Nazi Era, 1938–1945* (Chapel Hill: University of North Carolina Press, 2000) is particularly pertinent to this discussion.

Writing about the Kurt Waldheim controversy became virtually a cottage industry in the late 1980s, involving independent authors and a variety of official inquiries. Jörg Haider is beginning to attract similar attention. There are many opportunities to read about him in the Austrian press. This is one of the best ways to explore the subject. The MIT Libraries Web site (http://libraries.mit.edu/guides/types/flnews/german.html) offers an excellent list of German-language press to sample.

9

THE JÖRG HAIDER CONTROVERSY

BACKGROUND

Jörg Haider is a major spokesman of the Freiheitliche Partei Österreichs (FPÖ, Austrian Freedom Party) and governor of the state of Carinthia. Haider's leadership has helped make the FPÖ the second-largest party in Austria. The controversy over the man is inseparable from the controversy over the party he leads.

Why Is the FPÖ Controversial?

The FPÖ's origins are in the Verband der Unabhängigen (VdU, Association of Independents), founded in 1949 by a minister in the former Nazi government of Austria. Its second chairman was a former officer in the German Schutzstaffel (SS), an elite military force that swore allegiance directly to Hitler. In 1955 the VdU began to crumble, and it was reorganized into the FPÖ, which, at the time, was considered to be more of a liberal party. As a third party it gained less than 8 percent of the national vote against the Christian conservatives and the socialists, until Haider took its chairmanship in 1986. Under his charismatic leadership and vigorous campaigning the FPÖ has grown from 11 seats in the Austrian Nationalrat (National Council) in 1979 to 52 seats in the 1999 election. In 1983 it joined briefly with the Socialistische Partei Österreichs (SPÖ) government in the so-called small coalition, but in 1986 the socialists resumed their grand coalition with the

Jörg Haider, former leader of the right-wing Freiheitliche Partei Österreichs (Austrian Freedom Party), February 2000. (AP/Wide Worlds Photo)

Christian-conservative Österreiche Volkspartei (ÖVP). These partners had governed Austria since the formation of the Second Republic (1945).

The FPÖ campaigns for constitutional reform to improve basic civil rights, social support for the needy, the removal of special interests from influence over government and the economy, lower taxes, family values, and a strong federally-normed education system. It supports equal pay for women. It wants Austria to become a member of the North Atlantic Treaty Organization (NATO) with its own military forces. It campaigns against political party patronage and privilege, against unlimited immigration, and against domination of the Austrian economy by the European Union (EU).[1]

Today, as the second-largest political party in the nation, it is a strong challenge to the grand coalition of the two parties that have been ruling Austria and carving up its political prizes since 1945. These parties have warned that the FPÖ and Haider are neofascists, especially in their antiforeigner stance, which has been equated with Hitler's anti-Semitism. Haider has commented on what he considers to be the effectiveness of Hitler's employment policies, comments for which he has apologized, and he has paid tribute to Austria's veterans who served in the armies of the Third Reich, which absorbed existing Austrian units after the Anschluss (German annexation of Austria). In 2000 Chancellor Wolfgang Schussel (SPÖ) invited the FPÖ to join the new coalition government in 2000. Currently FPÖ members serve as vice chancellor; minister of justice; minister of finance; minister of national defense; minister for transport, innovation, and technology; and minister for social security and generations. Across Europe, where there is a revival of right extremist parties, strong concern has arisen from this development, and the EU has imposed sanctions against Austria.

Who Is Jörg Haider?

Haider was born in Bad Goisern, Upper Austria, on 26 January 1950. His political critics have characterized his parents as "out-and-out Nazis," "minor but enthusiastic Nazi officials," and "leading member[s] of the Austrian Nazi Party."[2] There were no serious charges filed against them after the war, however, which was not unusual for Austrian attitudes at that time. Upon completing his basic education, Haider, like other Austrian young men, did a year of military service in the federal army in 1968. Then he went on to study law at the University of Vienna in 1969. In 1970 he served as a member of the Federal Army Committee on Reform. After Haider received his doctorate in 1973, he served for the next three years as assistant professor at the Institute for State and Administrative Law of the University of Vienna.

Haider's political interests emerged early in his life. From 1970 to 1974 he was a member of the Ring Freiheitlicher Jugend, the Austrian chapter of the International Federation of Liberal and Radical Youth, a leftist international political youth organization founded in 1947. Austria was one of its founders.[3] He was also a member of the FPÖ, and after 1974 served on the party's executive committee. Between 1976 and 1983 he was the secretary of the party's organization in the state of Carinthia and became its leader in 1983. From 1979 to 1983 he was an elected representative in the Nationalrat and served as the FPÖ's spokesman on social issues. According to his party biography, he was regarded as a "liberal" at this time. From 1982 to 1983 he was also chief editor of the *Kärnter Nachrichten,* a newspaper circulating in Carinthia. For the next three years he served as an elected member of the Carinthian Diet (state legislature) and took particular interest in tourism and highways. In 1986, the FPÖ, at its annual conference, elected him their party chairman. He also began another three years in the Nationalrat before winning the governorship of Carinthia with 33.3 percent of the vote. In 1991 the ÖVP and the SPÖ combined in the Carinthian Diet to vote him out of office. Yet he was elected again the following year to the Nationalrat. He served there as the floor leader for the FPÖ faction. In 1994 he helped his party to gain 9 new seats in the federal legislature, and, despite the loss of 2 seats in 1994, the party grew again with 1999 elections to become the second largest in Austria, with a faction of 52 representatives. (The ÖVP polled virtually identical numbers, according to official figures.) After the national and international controversy about including the FPÖ in the governing coalition, Haider resigned his position as its chairman. But in 1999 he successfully campaigned to regain the governorship of Carinthia. Winning that election with 42.1 percent of the vote, he continues to serve in that capacity.[4]

ISSUES

The FPÖ Is Neofascist and Therefore Dangerous to Austria and to European Stability

Agree:

The FPÖ is a populist party that capitalizes on the fears of the people in exactly the same ways as Hitler's Nazi Party. Like the twentieth century fascist parties, it is antiestablishment, attacking the stable party coalitions that have led Austria so successfully since World War II. It raises discontent, charging the main parties with corruption and mismanagement despite Austria's excellent record of peace and economic growth. For example, in the 1999 parliamentary elections it directed a message of economic distress to the working classes, claiming high unemployment and low wages owing to the flood of immigrants despite one of the lowest unemployment rates in Europe (4.4 percent in that year). Clearly, this party will make any claim and distort any truth to seize power.

Like the pre–World War II fascist parties, the FPÖ is extremely nationalistic. Chapter 3 of its *Party Program* is entitled "Austria First!" It recognizes that ethnic minorities live within the state but *"emphasizes the affiliation of Austrians to the cultural community shaped by the mother tongue which for the overwhelming majority of Austrians is German."*[5] This seemingly benign formula echoes the anti-Semitism of fascism and could be translated into highly discriminatory racist laws should the FPÖ ever take power in Austria. But the FPÖ's language nationalism does not stop at its borders. It calls for cooperation with the other German-speaking counties of Europe to promote the "cultivation and dissemination" of German as the "*official* language in international organizations and [the] language of economics and the sciences."

This nationalism is also reflected in its rejection of the EU. Its *Party Program* states:

The independence of states should be restricted only by what is absolutely necessary to reach specific goals....

The European Union shall not become a European federal state but a confederation.

...We categorically reject the creating of artificial regions independent of historically grown communities and structures, and anything which ignores the independent right of self-determination by the population concerned.[6]

This same document also proclaims that it is time to end Austria's traditional neutrality and the 1955 State Treaty, which "restricts" its sovereignty. It asserts that Austria "should be a full member of the North Atlantic Treaty Organization (NATO) and the Western Europe Union and should actively participate in building up a European Security and Defense System." This assertion is coupled with the demand for replacement of the current compulsory military service with a standing army, augmented by militia. These clearly militaristic steps ominously violate the basic premises of the State Treaty, especially in that they are immediately followed by the assertion of Austrian rights to "protect" the German populations of Italy's South Tyrol and the "numerous members of the German groups now living in the former territories of the Austro-Hungarian Monarchy."[7]

Populist appeals, extreme nationalism, and latent expansionism were all the hallmarks of classical fascism. The FPÖ clearly has not lost the fascist elements of its VdU past and should be regarded with watchful suspicion.

Disagree:

The FPÖ gains its strength not from any latent Austrian fascism, but from a voting population fed up with the back-scratching corruption of the two traditional parties. For almost 50 years these parties have operated the Proporz (proportionality) system, deciding among themselves who, besides themselves, will gain benefits from party appointments. The ÖVP and SPÖ gain support through this expanding and grateful bureaucracy, as well as from opening the door to favored and well-heeled business and special-interest patrons. They have worked this system for so long that they are virtually indistinguishable from one another.

The FPÖ's mass appeal, by contrast, comes from the general public, which inspires its demand to eliminate "privileged groups and monopolies, party-political control of whole branches of industry, domination by officials in the fields of social insurance, of public economy, and of the politicized bank sector." To that end it wants to set up an independent governmental audit office to assure efficiency and honesty in government activities. It wants to take politics out of the control of entrenched party hierarchies by voting for candidates, not party lists for the Nationalrat.[8] These are the points that have so disturbed the two traditional parties and that have sent them into making wild accusations of neofascism and latent anti-Semitism.

The FPÖ grounds its conception of freedom in the basic rights of "freedom of opinion, of assembly, of association, religious freedom, freedom of conscience as well as freedom of the press and media." It demands equal rights and equal pay for men and women. It stands for family values and "the Christian consensus of common values." It wants to eliminate the party controls of the judiciary and maintain the system of trial by jury. These clearly stated, firmly held principles are quite opposite from fascist doctrines.

It is only necessary to compare the FPÖ's program with Italian dictator Benito Mussolini's *Doctrine of Fascism* to illustrate the most obvious contradictions:

> 6. Against individualism, the Fascist conception is for the State.... It is opposed to classical liberalism....
>
> 7. Liberalism denied the State in the interests of the Particular individual.... Therefore, for the Fascist, everything is the State, and nothing human or spiritual exists, much less has value, outside the State. In this sense Fascism is totalitarian....
>
> 8. Outside the state there can be neither individuals nor groups (political parties, associations, syndicates, classes). Therefore Fascism is opposed to Socialism....
>
> 9.... the State... is not to be thought of numerically as the sum-total of individuals forming the majority of the nation. And consequently Fascism is opposed to Democracy, which equates the nation to the majority, lowering it to the level of That majority.[9]

The obsolete grand coalition is trying to link the FPÖ to the controversy that arose over the Kurt Waldheim affair, which also became prominent in 1986. Waldheim, a longtime diplomat and two-term secretary-general of the United Nations, ran for the presidency of Austria on the ÖVP ticket. Although he had acknowledged service with the German army in Russia and France, he had tried to cover up his wartime service with the German army in Yugoslavia and Greece. Evidence surfaced during the election campaign to show that he was a lieutenant in the German army headquarters there at the time. He was accused of knowing about German army atrocities against civilian Slavs and Jews in these areas without trying to stop them.

World opinion was sharply critical of Austria for having been so eager to play the victim of the Nazis, thus ignoring its own record of complicity rather than conscientiously pursuing the war criminals in its midst. (One 1946 study indicates that nearly 600,000 Austrians were members of the Nazi Party, approximately 8 percent of the population of the time.)[10] The coalition was embarrassed. How convenient it was that the new, vigorously growing political party that threatened the coalition's control had feet of clay—the VdU, with its links to the Third Reich. How convenient it was for the coalition parties to be able to deflect criticism from themselves and from Kurt Waldheim, whom they had elected to the presidency. And given the subsequent growth of the FPÖ at the coalition's expense, the misleading propaganda has grown only louder. That, however, did not stop the SPÖ from inviting the FPÖ to join the coalition in 2000; at least in that case the SPÖ did respond to the will of the Austrian voters.

Moreover, the FPÖ is not the only new party that reflects Austrian discontent with the long-standing coalition partners. In that 1986 election the leftist Green Party emerged, and in 1994 the Liberal Forum. (Political parties must obtain 4 percent of the national vote to gain representation in the Nationalrat.) The old duopoly is now confronted with lively campaign debates over alternatives and is trying to regain its control.

No, the only danger the FPÖ poses is to the complacent, self-perpetuating grand coalition and to the Proporz system that has made the coalition so comfortable. The FPÖ has grown so rapidly because it articulates a program that promises to end corruption, strengthen the vitality of Austria in post-Soviet Europe, and to offer young, educated, and informed new leadership to the Austrian people.

Jörg Haider Is a Right Extremist and Is Leading the FPÖ in Dangerous Directions

Agree:

Born to and raised by former Nazis, Haider has deliberately chosen a path to political power. Instead of working to rejuvenate one of the traditional parties, he has moved outside them and is clearly to the right of them. Although he started with the Liberal Youth movement, he left that for the more extremist FPÖ, with its roots in fascism.

To be sure, he has modernized the exterior of this right extremist party by helping to develop a party program that speaks in the words of liberalism. But the true core of his beliefs is revealed in his public remarks. He praised Hitler's "orderly" employment policies and identified the concentration camps as "punishment camps," implying that only criminals were placed there. He later apologized for these remarks. On another occasion he said that the veterans of the Waffen SS (combat troops that some differentiate from the SS that Heinrich Himmler put in charge of the German concentration camps) deserved "honor and respect." His call for constitutional reform, the "Third Republic," is a blatant appeal to Nazi nostalgia.

A socialist critic may point out how Haider has reorganized the FPÖ along the top-down "Führerprinzip" (leader principle) lines of the Nazi Party. He tolerates no criticism and has replaced party officials who do so. The true liberal wing of the party, which flourished before he took over, split off to form the Liberal Forum in 1993. Indeed, he has allegedly met with members of the banned fascist National Democratic Party. Although he resigned as the party chairman in 2000 after the public protest against including the FPÖ in the new government coalition, it was merely a cosmetic gesture. Susanne Riess-Passer, who replaced him, follows his orders completely. And now she will bear the heat for the coalition rather than he.[11]

The most dangerous element in Haider's rhetoric is his strong anti-immigrant, antiforeigner stance. This is as racist as anti-Semitism ever was. In October 2000 he called for a total halt to immigration: "There are far too many illegal immigrants, crimes and drug dealers—none of them have a place here in Austria. This has to be our priority, to eliminate them uncompromisingly."[12] Austria has absorbed many of the refugees and asylum seekers from the Balkan Wars. Haider is stirring up hatred for them as a way of garnering votes. He is subtly transferring this hatred to the country's resident minority population as well.

Haider is a neofascist, a political opportunist, and a dangerous man. As governor of Carinthia he has tried to stifle opposition from the left: "Since I've taken office in Carinthia, no leftwinger has dared to demonstrate there any more."[13] He is becoming more overtly anti-Semitic as well. During the March 2001 municipal elections he referred to Ariel Muzicant, the leader of the Jewish community in Austria, in a derogatory way to a beer hall meeting of party faithful: "How can a man with such a name ("Ariel" is the brand name for a detergent product) have such dirt on his hands?" Later he accused Muzicant of "unclean business practices."[14] Haider's cultural affairs advisor, Andreas Molzer, was the editor of the anti-Semitic *Zur Zeit* newspaper in Vienna. He and his brand of politics must be exposed and constantly combated. To allow him to come to power either directly or indirectly will encourage a resurgence of fascism all across Europe.

Disagree:

If being the child of former Nazis is a criterion for being dangerous, then a large segment of the Austrian public must also be so condemned. Because Austria did not come to grips with its past until the Waldheim controversy in 1986, many former Nazis and their children still live there. Haider and his post–World War II generation represent a segment of the Austrian population that has an especial burden for dealing with both the past and the future. It is not surprising that many of them have moved into opposition to the coalition responsible for the war crimes cover-up, against the Waldheim generation and the parties he represents. Even most of Haider's critics do not call him a neo-Nazi. As one notes, "He wants a presidential system and plenty of plebiscites, and has consistently opposed the corporatism of fascist ideology. . . . he sacks followers who publicly deny the Holocaust."[15]

Haider understands the working classes in Austria and is weaning them away from the socialists. He is confronting the old coalition and their Proporz, which divides up among a chosen elite all the appointed offices from chancellor to schoolmaster. Many in the business community support Haider as well in the hope that he will repeal the speculation tax on stock held for less than 12 months. They are pleased that his choice for finance minister, Karl-Heinz Grasser, is pushing vigorously to privatize the state-owned companies such as Tabak, Austrian Airlines, and Telekom.[16] The trade unions, business associations, chambers of commerce, and other interest groups are all tied into the Proporz. They are most unlikely to sponsor such reforms.

The grand coalition leaders are working to discredit Haider in any way they can, even while incorporating his party into the government. In many ways this situation is a replay of the Waldheim circumstances. But as British analyst Anne Applebaum notes, Haider's leadership is not really dangerous, even though he has adopted extremely distasteful tactics:

> According to just about every intelligent observer of the Austrian system, his supporters are largely voting not for his bursts of Anschluss nostalgia, but for his anti-establishment, anti–status quo, tax-cutting and red-rate-slashing appeal, and for the youth and outsider status of the ministers he has just appointed to government. No doubt that it is this, just as much as those suggestive phrases about Adolf Hitler and his employment policies, that has made the rest of Europe so suspicious.
>
> ...Although he hotly insists he has been misinterpreted, Haider is undoubtedly a master of the suggestive phrase, well-designed to appeal to those to whom it is meant to appeal, and equally well-designed for its worst interpretation to be unclear or deniable to outsiders.... How sad that he was unable to find another form of patriotism to which he could appeal. And how much sadder that no one from within the system, from the mainstream right or even the mainstream left, had the courage to push for the political and economic reforms the country desperately needed years back.[17]

Haider's concern about Überfremdung (too many foreigners) reflects concern that Austria has already absorbed so many immigrants and asylum seekers from the Balkan Wars that the economy is suffering. His home state of Carinthia is right on the front lines of the former Soviet bloc; many migrants from Hungary, Slovenia, and the former Yugoslav states have headed for Klagenfurt as the entry point to Austria. Because the EU has required budget cuts and controls deficit levels within its member states, handling these newcomers is a real problem for a small state. Haider calls attention to the issues correctly. His attempt to define the problem is neither racist nor fascist. Nor is Haider an anti-Semite. Even the great Nazi hunter Simon Wiesenthal said: "he [Haider] represents no threat to democracy in Austria. He is not a pro-Nazi, but a right-wing populist."[18]

Haider's own willingness to step down from the party when he became controversial was an act of statesmanship. The six ministers who are now part of the ruling coalition in Austria are working effectively. Applebaum's observation, that the rest of Europe is the source of the real protest, is important. Status quo governments in other countries are equally threatened by nationalist movements. She states that the anti-Haider movement was being led by the Belgian foreign minister, whose own government is currently being challenged by a Flemish separatist movement. She also points to the fascist National Front, which the Italian government briefly included in a coalition, and to Jean-Marie Le Pen's National Front in France. The rise of the right threatens these governments more than Haider's leadership threatens the

Austrians. These governments want to make an example of Austria in order to try to quell the opposition in their own states.

The EU Was Correct to Place Sanctions on Austria So Long As Austria Has Members of the FPÖ in the Governing Coalition

Agree:

Haider leads the largest right extremist party in Europe. His anti-immigrant campaign directly undercuts an important new policy proposal of the EU: the right of citizens from member states to move and reside freely in other member states.[19] This proposal is key to the efforts to expand the EU toward the east. (Applications from Poland, the Czech Republic, Hungary, Estonia, Slovenia, and Cyprus are currently under consideration; Latvia, Lithuania, Slovakia, Bulgaria, Romania, and Malta are the most recent applicants. Turkey is also a candidate.) Haider is an extreme nationalist, probably a neo-fascist, who is using hatred of foreigners as his vehicle to achieve power. Even his use of the term Überfremdung comes straight from the lexicon of Joseph Goebbels, the vicious Nazi propagandist. Europe is on the cusp of unprecedented cooperation and unity. Allowing extreme national parties such as the FPÖ to enter member governments without criticism is irresponsible and wrong. Europe let it happen once before in 1933 in Germany. It cannot afford to let that happen again.

Disagree:

The EU's imposition of sanctions against Austria in February 2000 is anti-democratic: it wishes to overturn the decisions of 27 percent of the Austrian electorate and of the nation's legally elected chancellor. That is an unprecedented interference in the domestic affairs of a member nation and introduces an ominous example of how large nations can gang up on a small one. Moreover, it is hypocritical: there are extreme right and nationalistic parties in Italy, France, Belgium, Denmark, the Netherlands, Germany, and Britain, but these nations, which voted for sanctions on Austria, do not seem ready to clean their own houses. Italy's National Front wanted to deport 3 million immigrants, but no complaint was raised from the EU when it joined the government coalition.

The FPÖ program respects the rights of resident minorities. Its concern is with the unlimited immigration and settlement proposed by the EU. If the good old boys of the Austrian grand coalition will not take on the issue, then should not some voice in Austria reflect the legitimate concerns of the people?

The EU played right into the hands of Austria's grand coalition by accepting their accusations that Haider and the FPÖ are fascist neo-Nazis. The facts do not bear out these accusations. The sanctions against Austria simply identify FPÖ members as martyrs and the EU as an overbearing big brother who intends to use supranational power to bully small states. Thus, they have neither weakened the right nor strengthened the traditional parties in Austria.

QUESTIONS AND ACTIVITIES

1. Select a spokesperson for each of the major Austrian political parties and, using the information available from the parties' Web sites, stage a mock election debate focusing on the major issues of each party.

2. Study the map of Austria to identify the province of Carinthia, Haider's home base. Locate information about the population and economy of this region. Using this information, write a short report to explain why the voters there are so supportive of Haider.

3. Research Austrian history to learn about the events that influenced Haider's parents. Compare them with events since World War II that influenced Haider's youth and development as politician. Discuss whether his current politics reflect Austria's past or if he is just an opportunist capitalizing on current problems.

4. Read some articles about Haider in both the Austrian and the foreign press. (See Suggested Readings for the MIT Libraries link to the foreign press.) Prepare a short report listing and explaining the opinions you find there. Are there particular sources of his support? Are there particular groups who criticize and accuse him?

5. Review the information on the FPÖ Web site (http://www.fpoe.at). See if you can find out more about the party's leaders in the press and on the Web. Are they like Haider in origin and purpose? Prepare a display showing the FPÖ leaders and their positions in national and local government.

6. Immigration is one of the major issues in contemporary Austrian politics. Identify the origins of the largest groups of immigrants. Role play as an immigrant from one of those regions. Write a response to refute Haider's anti-immigration arguments.

7. Analyze the recent election statistics for Austria. Predict the trends in Austrian politics. Will the extreme right FPÖ continue to demonstrate strength? Put the election data on a graph and share it with the class.

NOTES

1. *Program of the Austrian Freedom Party as Adopted October 30, 1997* is available in its 34-page English version on the FPÖ Web site, http://www.fpoe.at.

2. Haider's father, Robert, became a member of the Hitlerjugend (Hitler Youth) when he was 15. He violated the 1933 ban on National Socialists (Nazis), was arrested, and fled to Bayern. He served in the German army for two years and joined the Nazi Party. He returned to Austria with the Anschluss and worked with the district Labor Office in Linz until he was drafted in 1940. He was wounded and discharged. He married Dorothea Rupp in 1945. She worked with the Bund Deutscher Mädchen (League of German Girls) and as a teacher. Robert Haider was arrested at the end of the war and forced by U.S. troops to work on opening the mass graves in concentration camp Glasenback. Dorothea was sentenced to work as the cleaning woman in a nursery school and barred from teaching for a number of years. Both par-

ents received amnesty as "less implicated" in any war crimes. See http://www.smoc.net/haiderwatch/bio.html. See Anne Applebaum, "Austria Ostracized," *The Weekly Standard Newsletter,* 23 April 2000, http://www.weeklystandard.com/Content/Public/Articles/000/000/001/164nsfik.asp?Zoom....; David Pryce-Jones, "Heil, Haider?" *National Review* 52, no. 4 (3 June 2000), 26; Christopher Hitchens, "Déjà Vu All Over Again," *Salon Daily Clicks: Newsreal,* http://salon.com/news/news961111.html.

3. The International Federation of Liberal and Radical Youth, made up of 51 national organizations, characterizes itself as "a federation of liberal and radical organizations ('Liberal' and 'Radical' are two names for the same thing....) For IFLRY, liberalism is more than an ideology of freedom and market economy. It is also the ideology of human rights, tolerance, social justice, and equal opportunities." Its current Web site (http://www.weijers.net/articles/iflry.html) indicates that it is embarrassed by Haider's "expression of sympathy for right-wing issues and his intolerance against foreigners."

4. This biographical information is taken from the official FPÖ home page, http://www.fpoe.at/.

5. *Program of the Austrian Freedom Party as Adopted October 30, 1997,* 5, 10, 30, emphasis added.

6. Ibid., 10.

7. Ibid., 12–13.

8. Ibid., 21, 17, 16.

9. The History Guide Lectures on Twentieth Century Europe, "Mussolini, *Doctrine of Fascism* (1932)," http://www.historyguide.org/europe/duce.html, 2.

10. F. Parkinson, "Epilogue," in *Conquering the Past: Austrian Nazism Yesterday and Today,* ed. F. Parkinson (Detroit: Fort Wayne University Press, 1989), 323.

11. Rich Kuhn, "The Threat of Fascism in Austria," *Monthly Review: An Independent Socialist Magazine* 52, no. 2 (June 2000), 21 ff.

12. Quoted in Kate Connelly, "All Illegal Migrants Out, Says Haider: Special Report: The Austrian Far Right in Power," *Guardian Unlimited Special Report,* 25 October 2000, http://www.guardian.co.uk/austria/article/0,2763,387506,00.html.

13. Ibid.

14. Quoted in Kate Connelly, "Haider Rallies the Racist Vote in Vienna Elections," *Guardian Unlimited Special Report,* 22 March 2001, http://guardian.co.uk/austria/article/0,2763,460885,00.html. Muzikant filed 12 different legal actions against Haider for defamation and anti-Semitism. In May 2001 the courts ruled that Haider had to stop making such direct remarks. Kate Connelly, "Vienna Jew Wins Ban on Haider Slur," *Guardian Unlimited Special Report,* 19 May 2001, http://www.guardian.co.uk/austria/article/0,2763,493090,00.html.

15. "Red, Black, and Blue Danube," *The Economist* 337, no. 7944 (12 September 1995), 51.

16. Matthew Karnitschnig, "Haider's Secret Weapon: Austria Inc.," *Business Week* 3670 (2 February 2000), 56.

17. Applebaum, "Austria Ostracized."

18. "Jorg Haider, an Austrian Conundrum," *The Economist* 354, no. 8157 (1 December 2000), 54.

19. See this proposal on the official EU Web site, http://europa.eu.int/scadplus/leg/en/lvb/133152.htm.

SUGGESTED READINGS

Haider is so controversial and so contemporary that the Web links listed in the Notes are good places to start. The FPÖ home page (http://www.fpoe.at/) provides his biography and current statements, lavishly illustrated with photographs. There are also links to the party's program, history, and leadership. This information gives the flavor of the party's energy and agitation and helps to explain others' concern about its statements and its potential appeal to Austrian voters.

A body of political and historical analysis is emerging in the effort to deal with the Haider phenomenon. For English-language studies see Melanie A. Sully's *The Haider Phenomenon* (New York: East European Monographs, Columbia University Press, 1997) and Lothar Hobelt's *Jorg Haider and the Politics of Austria, 1986–2000* (West Lafayette, Ind.: Purdue University Press, 2002). A basic German-language study is Gerd Kräh's *Die Freiheitlichen unter Jörg Haider: Gefahr oder Hoffnungsträger für Österreich* (Frankfurt am Main: P. Lang, 1996). This book was originally Hobelt's doctoral thesis.

A Web search, with Haider as the subject, will deliver a multitude of press comments. It is important to identify the source of these comments, however. Haider has become the darling of some of the revisionist sites that deny the Holocaust. It is important to understand their points of view within the context of the broader discussion.

The MIT Libraries Web site (http://libraries.mit.edu/guides/types/flnews/german.html) offers an excellent list of German-language press to sample.

SWITZERLAND

10

SWISS BANKING AND THE HOLOCAUST

BACKGROUND

The Swiss Law on Secret Bank Accounts

After World War I most European countries had laws in place that prohibited their citizens from trading in currency abroad. But when the depression began to shatter the European economy, numbers of wealthy elite from across the continent began to look to the Swiss banks, widely considered stable and secure, as a safe haven for their funds. The Swiss law permitted secrecy about such accounts, and any banker who violated that law was fined. Accounts came from all over Europe. In 1932, for example, more than 2,000 private French accounts were protected in the Baseler Handelsbank.[1]

After Adolf Hitler took control of Germany in 1933, he made it a crime for any German to have money in a non-German bank. One of the responsibilities of the Gestapo (Geheime Staatspolizei, Secret State Police) was to sniff out such money criminals and bring them to punishment. They naturally made inquiries of the Swiss banks. But after three Germans were executed for having bank accounts in Switzerland, the Swiss enacted new legislation in 1934 to protect the secrecy of their banking clients. Revealing information about a secret account was defined as a crime and subject to judicial punishment. This law protected Swiss banking clients, including both private citizens and the Nazi government, even under the pressures of war. Much later, in a 1984 national referendum, 73 percent of the Swiss voters approved continuing the practice.[2]

What makes this banking law so significant is that many Jews from across Europe deposited their assets in Swiss banks as Hitler threatened to implement his genocidal campaign against them. The security of the banking laws and the impeccable Swiss neutrality combined to offer the most secure haven for the funds of the persecuted. After World War II many of the account holders were dead, and the money lay in the bank vaults unclaimed. The destruction of European Jewry meant that there was an unusually high number of unclaimed accounts in Swiss Banks after the war. The Swiss were able to find the owners of some of them, but hardly all.

Besides Switzerland, the nations of Portugal, Spain, Sweden, and Turkey were also neutral noncombatants during World War II. They, too, received personal accounts and German government assets. After the war the Allies established policies and systems for obtaining the assets that the Nazi government had hidden in these countries' banks. A good portion of this wealth had been looted from the countries conquered by Germany or taken from individuals, especially from the Jews it persecuted and killed. Some of the deposits even consisted of melted dental gold taken from victims of the Holocaust. For the most part Portugal, Spain, Sweden, and Turkey cooperated with the Allies. Switzerland, however, objected to the invasion of bank privacy; it stalled and only reluctantly gave to the Allies some of the funds held in its bank vaults. This chapter discusses two aspects of the Swiss banks' handling of the "Holocaust accounts": the Allies' efforts to obtain the Nazi government's assets through negotiation; and the claims of Holocaust victims, survivors, and their heirs to secret accounts in Swiss banks.

The Impact of War on International Finance

Banks are often active if unwilling participants in hostilities. Nations at war generally make their banks freeze, or block, any enemy funds that they hold. When it became apparent during World War II that the German armies were looting the assets of the countries they conquered, the United States declared on 22 February 1944 that it would not recognize any transfers of looted gold from Germany and would not buy gold from any country that still had diplomatic relations with the Germans. Great Britain and the Soviet Union took similar action. As the defeat of Germany appeared inevitable, the international Bretton Woods Conference of July and August 1944 asked the neutral countries—Portugal, Spain, Sweden, Switzerland, and Turkey—to prevent any of the assets in their banks from being transferred to the enemy. In the following months the Allies established the Klaus Mission in Europe to find out if the Germans were trying to find safe places to hide looted assets. They requested that other governments try to prevent the Germans from doing so.

The Big Three Decisions

At the Yalta Conference in February 1945 the Big Three—Winston Churchill (United Kingdom), Franklin Roosevelt (United States), and Josef Stalin (Soviet Union)—agreed that Germany would have to pay reparations and that Germany's foreign assets could be seized in order to help pay them. The Potsdam Conference in August 1945, the last meeting of the Big Three, further agreed that Germany's external assets could be used to help refugees who could not be repatriated. They also agreed to restore any monetary gold to the European countries from which it had been looted. On 30 October 1945 the Allied Control Council, established to govern occupied Germany, assumed responsibility for all German external assets.

The Washington Accord, May 1946

In January 1946 the Paris Reparations Agreement set up a $25 million fund for refugees. The funds were considered as reparations and were to come from German holdings recovered from neutral countries. There was to be no safe haven for looted German assets. In May 1946 the Allies and Switzerland completed difficult negotiations that resulted in the Washington Accord. The Swiss initially maintained that international law gave Germany the right to the assets of countries it conquered and that their own banking laws prevented them from turning accounts over to the Allies. The Allies did not want to test international law, so they argued that preventing the return of assets to Germany would eliminate any opportunity for the Nazi movement to recur in Germany. They followed this argument with an appeal to Switzerland's sense of morality, pointing out that the assets should be used to help the victims of the Nazi war. The Allies estimated Germany's external assets to be $579 million in monetary gold and $750 million in other forms of wealth. They asserted that the Swiss National Bank had purchased $276 million from the Germans and that "an additional $138 million was 'washed' through the Swiss National Bank and eventually re-exported to Portugal and Spain."[3]

The Allies were reluctant to impose sanctions on the Swiss and eager to resume commercial activities with the only intact country left on the European continent. This reluctance gave the Swiss some latitude for negotiating the Washington Accord settlement. They finally came forward with two proposals. First, they agreed to turn over $58.1 million in 1946 to the newly established Tripartite Commission on the Restitution of Monetary Gold. Second, they conceded that there were probably some $250 million in other German external assets in Swiss banks. They would divide these assets, 50 percent to the Allies and 50 percent to be retained in Switzerland, but they would not open their records to the Allies to try to identify the accounts. Legitimate German owners were paid in German currency in order to unblock the accounts in the Swiss banks.[4]

The Swiss pledged to consider "sympathetically" the funds in accounts for which there were no heirs and thus that might be transferred to the Allied Intergovernmental Committee on Refugees. In 1947 the Inter-Allied Reparations Agency estimated that there were some $233 million in German assets in Switzerland, not including the personal accounts of individuals who held dual nationality or of those persecuted by the Nazis. Despite repeated efforts, however, the Allies were unable to force Switzerland to account for the heirless accounts; they gave up the effort after a last try in 1960. In 1963 the Swiss enacted a law that required banks and individuals to report any property they held that had belonged to victims of the Nazis, but the results were not revealed to the Allies.[5]

Revision of the Washington Accord

Discussions continued for the next four years over the appropriate rate of exchange for the involved currencies. And there was another issue to consider. The fledgling West German government, founded in 1949, feared the political fallout if the Swiss started returning funds to some claimants but not to others. Therefore, the 1946 Washington Accord was not implemented. Meanwhile, the West Germans had begun a program to pay reparations to the Jewish victims of the Nazis and wanted to use repatriated funds. Finally, in August 1952, the participants agreed to a settlement of $28 million from the Swiss, a considerable reduction of the amount agreed upon in 1946. Because Switzerland had already paid $4.7 million to the International Refugee Organization in 1948, that payment was included in the total. In order to secure even this resolution Germany agreed to reimburse Switzerland for the $28 million and even arranged a Swiss loan to meet its obligation. This agreement seemed to be the limit of what diplomacy could achieve with the Swiss.

U.S. Efforts to Compensate Victims

Shortly after the end of the war the U.S. government allocated to the War Claims Fund approximately $495 million in assets confiscated from the enemy. This fund was intended to compensate U.S. victims for losses sustained because of the war. The Harry S. Truman government also supported the passage of legislation to return assets to the survivors of persecution in enemy lands. This law did not deal with the assets of those persecuted who did not survive and had no heirs, which was a sticking point in negotiations with the Swiss, who would not give any estimate of the amount under consideration. In 1954 U.S. legislation amended the 1914 Trading with the Enemy Act to designate charitable organizations as the administrators of the assets of Nazi victims who died without heirs. Congress allocated some $3 million for the organizations to use to resettle and assist Jewish survivors in reclaiming their stolen assets. There were stringent requirements for proof of ownership, however, and initially only approximately 500 claims qualified. In 1962 Congress reduced the requirements and reduced the available amount to $500,000. In 1963 U.S. president John F. Kennedy, through Executive Order 11087, allocated the $500,000 from the War Claims Fund to the recently formed Jewish Restitution Organization (JRO). There seemed to be little more that diplomacy or direct governmental action could achieve.

The Survivors and Their Heirs (and Their Lawyers) Begin to Act

In the 1960s, the Israeli government began to record petitions from citizens who wanted help tracing private funds that had disappeared in Swiss banks. Some petitions came from survivors; others came from their heirs. Approximately 7,000 Jews from Israel claimed that they knew of funds transferred to Swiss banks either by themselves or by individuals known to them. By the 1980s the World Jewish Congress (WJC) had collected written testimony that some 17,000 Polish Jews had sent their money to Swiss bank accounts. As the claimants began to seek lawyers, the pressure to investigate the Swiss banks grew. These claims became all the more pertinent after 1986. In that year Austria came under fire for electing Kurt Waldheim as president. The WJC accused him of abetting war crimes as an officer in the German

A woman displays a photo of her late father, a World War II death camp victim, during a news conference in New York, May 1998. She is announcing that she has reached a settlement with Credit Suisse over her claim on her father's account. Behind her is Senator Alfonse D'Amato, who as chairman of the Senate Banking Committee led an inquiry into charges that the Swiss banks diverted millions in Jewish-owned assets to the Nazis during World War II. (AP/Wide Worlds Photo)

army. At the same time Austria's far right-wing Freedom Party seemed to signal the rise of neofascism in Austria. One result of this controversy was the leverage it gave to Austria's Jews in their demands for compensation. The Austrian government agreed to pay compensation to individual Austrian Jewish victims of the Nazi regime, which made it inevitable that the spotlight would next turn toward Switzerland and its alleged holdings of Jewish assets. The WJC again led the way. In 1993 it began to work with the JRSO to coordinate the efforts of a number of Jewish organizations.

The Governments Become Involved

In February 1996 the Swiss Bankers Association reported that it had identified only 775 dormant accounts set up by Jews for which there were no heirs. Jewish organizations protested that the report was incorrect. U.S. courts received a number of class-action lawsuits from Jewish depositors against the largest three Swiss banks that had branches in the United States: Credit Suisse, United Bank of Switzerland, and the Swiss Bank Corporation. In May 1996, bowing to the pressure, the Swiss agreed with leaders of the Jewish community to establish a commission to examine Swiss government and bank records for Jewish deposits. Paul Volcker, former chairman of the U.S. Federal Reserve, agreed to chair the commission. The Swiss Federal Council also set up a working group to study the issue. The politicians fell into line. In the U.S. Congress, New York senator Alfonse D'Amato of the Senate Banking Committee opened an investigation of the ways that Swiss banks had dealt with Holocaust victims and the dormant accounts. On 13 December the Swiss legislature unanimously passed legislation permitting an end to bank secrecy on this specific subject for the next five years. A week later the Swiss government appointed the Independent Expert Commission, with historian Jean-François Bergier as its chair, to investigate the subject of the Holocaust assets.

Swiss Dissent at High Levels

Not all Swiss agreed with this action, however. On 31 December Swiss Federation president Jean-Pascal Delamuraz, in a press conference marking the end of his term, expressed his concern that the whole controversy was an "attempt at ransoming and blackmail . . . a willingness to destabilize Switzerland." His remarks set off a storm of protest, especially in the Israeli Knesset (Parliament). As a result, on 8 January 1987 the Israelis set up their own commission for the recovery of Jewish funds. Delamuraz later apologized to Edgar Bronfman, the president of the WJC. Two weeks later the Swiss newspaper *Sonntagszeitung* printed excerpts from a 19 December report by the Swiss ambassador in Washington that described the Jewish organizations as "adversaries." The report further characterized the controversy as a "war that must be won." The ambassador was forced to hand in his resignation the following day.

The Swiss Give In

In February 1997 the three aforementioned Swiss banks placed 100 million Swiss francs (currently $76,182,290) in a special fund to be distributed to Holocaust victims. A rush of private contributions added another 165 million. The Federal Council concurred and began discussing its own action to set up a special fund for Holocaust victims and a foundation to administer it.

In a public act of contrition the presidents of the 26 Swiss state governments visited the Auschwitz concentration camp in early April. Shortly thereafter the government established the Committee for the Special Fund. In early May the new president of the Swiss Federation, Arnold Koller, proposed a 7 million Swiss franc fund that could be distributed half to Swiss victims of disasters and half to foreigners who had suffered disasters or human rights violations. That same day the government sent letters to the legislatures of 25 European and North American countries, including the Israeli Knesset, to inform them of the actions taken.

There were vocal protests from the far right Swiss People's Party, the smallest contingent in the government coalition. Its leader, Christopher Blocker, told cheering crowds that Switzerland did not need to apologize and that it had already allocated funding for Holocaust victims. In May it became apparent that this reversal in policy was not going to become a celebration of Swiss honor by the Allies, either. Stuart E. Eizenstat, cochairman of the Washington Conference on Holocaust-Era Assets, had worked with State Department historian William Z. Slaney to dig out the facts. The publication of the *Eizenstat Report* on Allied efforts to recover assets taken by the Germans revealed that the Swiss apparently held enormous amounts of unreported German assets during the war (see Table 10.1).

This report intensified the efforts to gain accurate information; public pressures on Switzerland and its banks multiplied. The Volcker Commission announced in March that it would focus on the activities of five banks. The Simon Wiesenthal Center of California, famous for its efforts to assist Holocaust victims, staged a conference in Geneva in June 1997, entitled "Property and Restitution—A Moral Responsibility in History." The House Banking Committee of the U.S. Congress invited Volcker to testify at hearings in late June. He revealed that the Swiss banks had agreed to publish the names on accounts that had gone unclaimed since the beginning of World War II.

The End of Banking Secrecy

Thus, on 23 July 1997 the wall of secrecy around the Swiss banks finally tumbled. Together, the JRO and the president of the Swiss Bankers Associa-

Table 10.1
Estimated German Assets Held in Switzerland 1939–45

German Assets	
Estimates used for the 1946 Washington Accord negotiations	
U.S. Treasury Department	$500 million
U.S. State Department	$200-500 million
Turned over to Inter-Allied Refugee Assistance	$ 28 million
Actually paid to Allies, 1948	4.7 million
Lump Sum renegotiated payment, 1953	23.6 million
Monetary Gold Estimates	
German gold reserves and movements 1939-1945	$781-785 million
The amount of it which was looted gold	579 million
Gold traded by Germany to Switzerland	$398-414 million
The amount of it which was looted gold	185-289 million
Amount of Belgian gold Swiss admitted to receiving	$ 88 million
Amount of gold Swiss agreed to transfer to Allies	**$ 58 million**

Source: "Switzerland: German Assets," *Eizenstat Report,* n.p.

tion published a list of 1,872 Jews who had opened individual accounts in Swiss banks before 1945, but with whom there had been no contact for at least 10 years. Although Swiss law allowed the banks to close the accounts and retain the assets, this unprecedented move to publish the names on the accounts made it possible for the account holders, their heirs, or their agents to claim them. Moreover, the banks promised to publish the names on accounts of Jews who were presumed to have died in the Holocaust, thus making them available as well. By October they also identified 64,000 dormant accounts that were held in the names of Swiss citizens, but that, in fact, might have been the assets of Jews for whom the Swiss citizens were account trustees.[6]

Charges That the Swiss Assisted Nazi Germany

But the investigators did not limit their scope to banking processes, however. Some began charging that the Swiss had hardly been neutral during the war. These charges were explicit in the *Summary of the May 1997 Preliminary Report* by the Eizenstat Committee. It asserted that "'Monetary gold' looted by Germany from the central banks of occupied nations of Europe had an important role in financing and prolonging the German war effort." Germany had confiscated some $579 million from 11 of the countries it had occupied, of which between $389 to $414 million had been transferred to the unquestioning banks of Switzerland. Despite Allied warnings about such transfers at the time, Switzerland had accepted the German transfers and afforded them secrecy. The report continued with even more serious allegations:

> Germany's war effort depended significantly upon its imports of raw materials and goods from the neutral nations. Switzerland was Nazi Germany's banker and financial facilitator, taking and transferring German gold—most of it looted—and providing Germany with Swiss francs to purchase needed products. Switzerland also supplied Germany with key war materials such as arms, ammunition, aluminum, machinery and locomotives. Moreover, Germany was able to mitigate slightly the effect of Allied bombing by moving some arms production to safety across the Swiss frontier....
>
> Switzerland resisted Allied efforts to reduce or halt its exports to Germany and to curb, if not end, the transshipment of German materials across its borders. Surrounded by Axis forces, Switzerland's financial relationship with Germany clearly exceeded that of other neutral countries.[7]

Another investigation, using Swiss archives in Bern, was supported by the Simon Wiesenthal Center. Alan Morris Schom, professor of history at the University of California, Berkeley, issued a 128-page report on 10 June 1998 entitled *A Survey of Nazi and Pro-Nazi Groups in Switzerland, 1930–1945.* This report charged, among other things, that in 1942 Swiss cabinet member (and future president) Eduard von Steiger worked with anti-Semitic groups to halt the flow of Jewish refugees into Switzerland. Schom also discovered that Swiss medical teams sent to help the Germans on the eastern front learned about the murder of Jews in Smolensk. One doctor who later tried to protest about that genocide was brought up on charges before the Swiss Parliament and condemned for violating Swiss neutrality, a judgment supported unanimously by senior government ministers. Moreover, the U.S. Library of Congress held photographs of Nazi rallies held in Basel, Zurich, Lucerne, and other Swiss cities.[8]

The Swiss began a program of damage control to defend the nation's honor and image. Indeed, among the first to respond were Swiss Jewish leaders. According to Mitchell Danow with the Jewish Telegraphic Agency, Jewish and Swiss government leaders together "lambasted" the Schom report. Swiss president Flavia Cotti denounced its findings as "wrong." Ambassador Thomas Borer, the point man on Swiss affairs for the U.S. government, called the Schom report "absurd and wrong," and accused the report of using "McCarthy guilt-by-association tactics." Danow pointed out that although Switzerland expelled more than 30,000 Jews during the war, it also gave refuge to 25,000 others. He compared that with the record of the United States, which accepted only 21,000 Jewish refugees, and of Canada, which accepted only 9,000. Although Jewish refugees in Switzerland had to be sponsored and paid for in advance by Jewish groups (estimated to have cost $40 million), some 300,000 non-Jewish refugees in Switzerland were sheltered at government expense.[9]

The Associated Press (AP) reported from Switzerland that the *Israelitisches Wochenblatt* of Zurich charged the Schom report with deliberately ignoring the strong anti-Nazi movement in Switzerland. The *Jüdische Rundschau* of Basel criticized the report for being full of "exaggerations and falsifications." The AP concluded by pointing out that even the U.S. State Department denied the Schom report, pointing out that Switzerland had sheltered some 50,000 Jews during the war.[10]

The Settlement

Britain's *Economist* (2 July 1998) reflected the speculation over the outcome of the class-action suits filed in the United States against the Swiss banks. One of the lawyers was Edward Fagan, who represented 31,000 clients. He estimated that the banks and insurers owed $54 billion to the survivors. The banks, however, had offered only $600,000, plus an amount equivalent to what a special team of accountants might find as incorrectly posted or wrongly paid. The banks believed that their offer was more than 10 times their actual liability. The lawyers indicated that they would probably accept around $1.5 billion. The WJC estimated that somewhere between $9 billion and $14 billion was actually taken from Jews during the war, although not all of that money ended up in Switzerland. Fagan was also involved in suits against Swiss life insurance companies and German banks.[11]

Two countries that held confiscated Jewish assets took action. In Norway, once a Nazi puppet state, the government established a $58.6 million fund to compensate Holocaust survivors. It was the first of the nations conquered by the Germans to do so. Even Great Britain allowed 25,000 Jews from abroad to claim accounts frozen during the war because they originated from hostile countries.[12]

On 12 August 1998 a settlement was announced by the U.S. District Court in Brooklyn, N.Y. There were four parts to the agreement. First, the defendant banks would pay $1.25 billion in four payments within three years; these payments would be credited to the dormant account claimants; in return, the claimants, on behalf of all claimants in all cases would provide "the broadest possible releases, for all claims of any kind arising out of a Nazi era World War II or its aftermath" for the defendant banks; the banks were not held responsible for any legal fees or costs of the settlement, which were to come out of the $1.25 billion. All other class-action suits against the banks would be dismissed.[13]

There was relief all around. Although the Swiss image was severely damaged, there would be no question of sanctions or trade wars in order to force Credit Suisse, the United Bank of Switzerland, and their subsidiary banks to take responsibility. The settlement also protected the Swiss government and all Swiss banks from further suits over their assets. The investigations continued, however, because there were still outstanding claims against insurance companies and banks in other nations.

ISSUES

The Accusations against the Swiss Were True; They Must Pay for Concealing the Jewish Accounts

Agree:

The Swiss considered the Washington Accord of 1946 to be the resolution of all claims against their banks and government for financial transactions during World War II. At the time the Allies took the Swiss negotiators at their word and even reduced the original settlement figure at Swiss insistence. But it has become glaringly obvious since then that the Swiss concealed their bank records and that they had not made a good faith effort to pay restitution. This concealment goes far beyond mere compliance with Swiss laws protecting the secrecy of accounts. Their denials amounted to a cover-up.

The many investigations—by the Volcker Commission, by the Independent Expert Commission, by the Eizenstat Committee, by Alan Schom, to mention only the most prominent of them—have exposed the magnitude of the banks' complicity with the Holocaust. Swiss banks engaged in money laundering and trade with the Nazi government, accepted assets in amounts that could only have come from the states looted by the Nazis, and then buried the accounts of the Holocaust victims so that neither they nor their survivors could claim them. The Swiss government also colluded with the Nazis by insisting that Germany stamp Jewish passports with a "J" so that the Swiss could keep out these unwanted refugees. Considering the hundreds of millions of dollars worth of German gold and assets that the Swiss banks held from the Germans and from Jewish depositors, the $58 million Switzerland finally paid in 1952 is more than insulting; it is almost fraudulent.

The WJC, its collaborating organizations, and the courageous lawyers who cooperated to confront the banks should be congratulated. Although no price can be calculated for the loss of lives and property caused by the Nazis, the exposure of the Swiss banks and the success in forcing them to assume responsibility through the $1.25 billion compensation to the depositors is an excellent start. It sets a precedent that warns other nations' banks, insurance companies, and those companies that used slave labor during World War II that their day is coming.

Disagree:

The Swiss and the Allies signed the 1946 Washington Accord in good faith and arrived at the $58 million figure collaboratively. The United States should acknowledge that binding agreement and defend it. Although the sum may seem small today, it is roughly the equivalent of $500 million in today's dollars. The Swiss at all times acted in accordance with Swiss banking law in maintaining the secrecy of accounts. Similarly, the Swiss government

New York author Norman Finkelstein promotes the German translation of his book *The Holocaust Industry,* a critique of Holocaust restitution, during a news conference in Berlin, February 2001. The author defends his efforts to expose Holocaust compensation claims as blackmail of European governments, though he acknowledges that his work might be seized upon by Germany's resurgent far right. Finkelstein claims that Holocaust restitution has developed into an industry that in turn encourages anti-Semites and Holocaust deniers. (AP/Wide Worlds Photo)

was entirely within its rights as a neutral nation to trade with and to continue banking transactions with belligerent powers during World War II. Other neutral nations did so as well. Surrounded by hostile nations—fascist Italy, Nazi Germany/Austria, and Vichy France—Switzerland had virtually no leeway to question or refuse the German transactions. As a nation of only 5 million at the time, it could well have been invaded if it had done so. If it had fewer transactions with Allied nations during the war, it was not out of policy choices, but because there were no ways to maintain such commerce while Europe was under Nazi control. It should be noted that all of the other neutral nations, which also dealt with the Nazi government, were on the fringes of the continent: Portugal, Spain, Sweden, and Turkey. They had the same interaction with Germany as Switzerland. Their restitution agreements after the war were calculated on the same bases as the Washington Accord.

The Swiss did not engage in the deliberate destruction of Jews like the European countries under Nazi control. Although they did refuse entrance to 30,000 Jews, they shielded 25,000 of their own Jews from Nazi predators and allowed more than 20,000 others to enter. They also shielded Allied soldiers who would otherwise have become prisoners of war. If Switzerland is to be penalized now for the 25,000 Jews it refused, then the United States should be similarly assessed for the 190,000 Jews it turned away, perhaps to their death.

This campaign against the Swiss banks has become more about the money than about the Holocaust. American businessmen and politicians recognize the leverage that guilt gives them. New York bank regulators recently required Germany's Deutsche Bank to be more diligent in exposing their Holocaust-era accounts before completing the takeover of Bankers Trust.

Writing in the *Washington Post,* Pulitzer Prize–winning columnist Charles Krauthammer asked: "Is this what honoring the Holocaust has come to: A shakedown of Swiss banks, Austrian industry, German automakers . . . that recalls the worst of racial hustling and class-action opportunism in the United States?"[14]

Monetary Restitution Is the Best Way to Compensate the Holocaust Victims

Agree:

World War II is two generations behind us, but European Jewry will never fully recover from it. Although the founding of the nation of Israel is an assurance of the continuation of the Jewish people, many Jews and their children still live desperate lives in poverty. It is not possible to restore all the stolen land and property to the survivors. Providing them with some monetary assistance is one way Europeans who collaborated with the Nazis can make amends for what happened during the Holocaust. The strategy adopted by the American Jewish organizations, initiating class-action suits and encouraging the necessary investigations and audits, is a productive one. It may embarrass the countries and industries targeted, but that is necessary. The $1.25 billion settlement is easily afforded by the Swiss banks today and will help them put an end to further litigation. Abraham H. Foxman, national director of the Jewish Anti-Defamation League, agreed that the two-year campaign by the American Jewish organizations, politicians, and officials was necessary: "Unfortunately, too many nations and individuals don't do the right thing on their own and pressure becomes necessary."[15]

Disagree:

The $1.25 billion seems like an enormous amount when considered in a block sum, but it will give very little aid and comfort to the individuals for whom it is intended. Although the Volcker report audit turned up only approximately 54,000 dormant Swiss bank accounts, a report in the *Jerusalem Post* suggested that approximately 600,000 survivors and heirs would file claims for their share in the settlement. If all were successful, each would receive only $2083.33 as his or her share.

Moreover, this scurrying of lawyers across the continents has raised false hopes among the individuals they recruit to sign on to the suit. One critic of the settlement reports that "[a]n independent tribunal of distinguished jurists has been at work evaluating claims against the Swiss banks and has already denied some 80 percent of them." The real beneficiaries of the Swiss bank settlement are the lawyers, auditors, and American Jewish organizations. The accounting firms of Arthur Andersen, KPMG, and Price Waterhouse were chosen by the Volcker Commission in 1996 to audit the Swiss accounts. In July 2000 the Israeli newspaper *Haaretz* revealed that these firms had charged $400 million for the audit. Given the typical hourly auditing fee of $200, it must have taken them six hours for each of the 350,000 accounts they reviewed. The banks knew they were going to have to pay those fees in addition to the actual settlement. The Israeli government believed that the banks might have offered more had the auditing fees been more reasonable. The lawyers fared well also. For example, Edward Fagan, who filed a class-action suit on behalf of 31,000 claimants, submitted his bill for $4 million to the court, a bill that the banks also had to pay. That is equivalent to $640 per hour, considerably more than the $640 per year that Israeli Holocaust survivors receive from the German government. The benefit to the American Jewish organizations cannot be overlooked, either. The *Jerusalem Report* revealed that the Conference on Jewish Material Claims Against Germany (known as the Claims Conference) was inadequately informing the actual claimants and their heirs of their rights and was then disposing of that property as it saw fit. Significantly, Israel Singer and Edgar Bronfman, two of the WJC's most dogged Swiss bank accusers, sit on that board. The *Jewish World Review* claimed that Bronfman had stated that a third of the funds from the Swiss banks should be used to create "an international foundation that would benefit both Israel and the rest of the world Jewish community with massive amounts for Jewish education and communal continuity."[16]

QUESTIONS AND ACTIVITIES

1. Using the Web and other sources, research the WJC and the Simon Wiesenthal Center. Prepare a report on how they have worked to discover and recover assets taken from Jewish victims of the Holocaust.

2. Have each member of the class select a book from the list of Suggested Readings to review. Find out about the authors of these books. Explain each author's major reason for writing his or her book.

3. Download a copy of the *Eizenstat Report* and review the conclusions it reaches. Discuss in class how the Germans, the Jews, and the Allies were affected by the Swiss banking laws. Consider whether, in general, banks should examine every depositor to determine whether or not to accept an account. What sorts of criteria should be used for making that decision?

4. Research the official Swiss responses to the charges against the banks. Identify the actions the Swiss took and the conclusions they reached. Write a brief presentation about their responses and actions. Indicate whether you think they acted in good faith.

5. Discuss the methods used to force the Swiss to acknowledge their responsibilities and make restitution. Who were the major leaders of the strategy? Explain why the U.S. courts were involved.

6. Using the Wiesenthal Center Web site or some other site, examine the process that an applicant had to go through in his or her attempt to gain restitution from the banks.

7. Reviewing the facts provided in this chapter and in other sources, discuss whether the Holocaust survivors or heirs really benefited from the restitution by Swiss banks in any significant way. Was the process the end in itself, or was money the object? How did the sponsoring agencies expect to benefit from the process?

NOTES

1. "Historical Origins of Swiss Bank Secrecy," Micheloud & Cie., http://switzerland.isyours.com/e/banking/sefcrecy/history.html. This company provides Swiss bank account services for investors.

2. Ibid.

3. A list of the diplomatic activities with Switzerland and other countries can be found in "Tables and Charts," in *U.S. and Allied Efforts to Recover and Restore Gold and Other Assets Stolen or Hidden by Germany during World War II: Preliminary Study,* prepared by William Z. Slaney, U.S. Department of State, May 1997, http://www.ess.uwe.ac.uk/documents/asetindx.htm. This report is generally known as the *Eizenstat Report.*

4. Ibid., 5.

5. Ibid., 10.

6. Itamar Levin, *The Last Deposit: Swiss Banks and Holocaust Victims' Accounts,* trans. Natasha Dornberg (Westport, Conn.: Praeger, 1999), xiii, 2–3.

7. "Annex II. Summary of the May 1997 Preliminary Report," *Eizenstat Report,* 1–2.

8. This lengthy report is accessible through the Simon Wiesenthal Center. It has a 14-page summary conclusion that can be found at the center's Web site (http://www.wiesenthal.com) using the search process identifying the author. At this site see also Marvin Hier and Abraham Cooper, "At Best, Selective Neutrality," *Los Angeles Times,* 17 June 1998. Both Hier and Cooper are administrators at the Wiesenthal Center.

9. Mitchell Danow, "Swiss Deny Report on Entry of Jewish Refugees," *Jewish Bulletin of Northern California,* 12 June 1998, http://www.jewishsf.com/bk980612/usdeny.htm.

10. Cited in "Swiss Jewish Newspapers Denounce Report," *Shawnee News-Star Online* (Oklahoma), 13 June 1998, http://www.news-star.com/stories/051398/new_swissjew.html.

11. "Swiss Banks and Nazi Gold," *Economist.com,* http://www.economist.com/PrinterFriendly.cfm?Story_ID=139987. July 2, 1998.

12. Ibid.

13. "August 1998 Settlement: Transcript of Settlement before the Honorable Edward R. Korman, United States District Judge," in *Switzerland and the Holocaust Assets—Documents* (12 August 1998), http://www.guissani.com/holocaust-assets/documents/settlement.html. This is an archived Web site and cannot be accessed directly. It can be accessed through a search for "Switzerland & the Holocaust Assets."

14. "Putting a Price on the Holocaust," *Economist.com,* 25 November 1999, http://www.economist.com/PrinterFriendly.cfm?Story_ID=326811. Charles Krauthammer, "The Holocaust Scandal," *Washington Post,* 4 December 1998, A29.

15. Abraham H. Foxman, "Lessons from the Swiss Bank Settlement," *Anti-Defamation League* (July 1999), http://www.adl.org/opinion/swiss_bank_settlement.html.

16. "Unsettling," *Economist.com,* 17 August 2000, http://www.economist.com/PrinterFriendly.cfm?Story_ID = 318493; "Insurance and the Holocaust," *Economist.com,* 13 March 1997, http://www.economist.com/PrinterFriendly.cfm?Story_ID=369353; Gabriel Schoenfeld, "Holocaust Reparations—A Growing Scandal," *Commentary* (September 2000), locate by title at: www.Findarticles.com/cf_dls/PI/index.jhtml; Jonathan Tobin, "The Bottom Line of the Holocaust," *Jewish World Review Insight,* 13 December 1999, http://www.jewishworldreview.com/cols/tobin121399.asp.

SUGGESTED READINGS

Much of the controversy and most of the documents used in this chapter originated in the efforts of American Jewish organizations and the U.S. government. Therefore, most are in English, and the readings are easily accessed through the Web. Some of the Web sites used as documentation in the Notes are inactive. These materials can be accessed, however, through a browser search by subject, title, or author. The recommendations that follow identify where this process is necessary.

To understand the claims against the Swiss banks for concealing assets of Nazi gold, read *U.S. and Allied Efforts to Recover and Restore Gold and Other Assets Stolen or Hidden by Germany during World War II*, prepared by William Z. Slaney, U.S. Department of State, May 1997 (http://www.ess.uwe.ac.uk/documents/asetindx.htm), otherwise known as the *Eizenstat Report* (the name of the committee's chairman). This lengthy document was compiled, at the request of President Bill Clinton, from the examination of more than 800,000 pages of the archived records of 10 U.S. government departments and agencies and of the Holocaust Memorial Museum. The foreword introduces the project and summarizes its major findings. The individual sections of the report discuss the findings in considerable detail.

Adam LeBor's *Hitler's Secret Bankers: The Myth of Swiss Neutrality during the Holocaust* (Secaucus, N.J.: Carol Publishing Group, 1997) focuses on the international aspects of wartime banking. Marilyn Henry's *Switzerland, Swiss Banks, and the Second World War: The Story behind the Story* (New York: American Jewish Committee, 1997) is a short and revealing accusation. Jean Ziegler's *Schweiz, das Gold und die Toten* [The Swiss, the gold, and the dead] (New York: Harcourt Brace, 1998) is a work by a Swiss man who was charged by his government for false reporting. Tom Bower's *Nazi Gold: The Full Story of the Fifty-Year Swiss-Nazi Conspiracy to Steal Millions from Europe's Jews and Holocaust Survivors* (New York: HarperCollins, 1997) is an especially hard-hitting study.

To understand the difficulties of trying to research the individual accounts of Holocaust victims in the Swiss banks, see the preliminary report of the Volcker Committee: *Report of the Independent Committee of Eminent Persons (Volcker Committee)* (http://www.house.gov/international_relations/crs.volcker.html). The final 351-page report of this committee, published by Staempfli Publishers, Bern, is not accessible on the Web. Mitchell Danow's article "Final Report on Swiss Banks Finds 54,000 Accounts of Nazi Victims" can be accessed on the *Jewish Bulletin of Northern California* site (http://www.jewishsf.com/bk991210/iswissbanks.shtml). The strongly accusatory Schom report on Nazis in Switzerland during World War II is available through the Simon Wiesenthal Center Web site (http://www.wiesenthal.com). This site also contains all the necessary forms and documents for individuals to apply for funds from the Swiss banks' settlement fund and offers the reader the opportunity to experience the requirements and process.

The "Switzerland & the Holocaust" Web site is archived and therefore not directly accessible. A browser search under that title will provide a comprehensive chronology of the pursuit of individual accounts and transcripts of other important documents. This collection also identifies links to important reports or commentaries. Although some of these links are inactive, a browser search by title or author is often successful.

Gabriel Schoenfeld's *Holocaust Reparations—A Growing Scandal* is a balanced and thoughtful critique of the methods to recover the individual accounts. It is best accessed through a browser search by author and title. A more scholarly, but also more biased analysis is Itamar Levin's *The Last Deposit: Swiss Banks and Holocaust Victims' Accounts* (Westport, Conn.: Praeger, 1999).

11

SWISS NEUTRALITY

BACKGROUND

What Is the Concept of Neutrality?

Neutrality is a concept in diplomacy that is accepted by nations throughout the world. It has two basic parts generally recognized in international law: (1) that a nation proclaiming neutrality will not assist or interfere with either side in a time of armed conflict; and (2) that it will treat all parties to the conflict alike.

Why Is Swiss Neutrality in Question?

In recent years a number of accusations have been made about the accommodations Switzerland made to the Germans during World War II. The principal concern has been over Swiss banks' retention of Holocaust victims' assets, as discussed in chapter 10. A second concern has been the growing participation of Switzerland in various international organizations, culminated by Swiss admission to the United Nations in September 2002. Because some of these organizations impose an obligation to carry out various actions, many feel that the Swiss are violating basic principles of neutrality as they are defined in international law. This chapter sketches the history of neutrality as a concept and the history of Switzerland's move toward permanent neutrality before addressing these two major concerns.

The Historical Background of Neutrality

The concept of neutrality originated in the seventeenth century, during the European religious conflict known as the Thirty Years War (1618–48). This war over religion began in the Holy Roman Empire, which consisted of more than 300 autonomous German states in central Europe, nominally ruled by the Austrian Habsburg emperor. In the course of the war most of western Europe became involved, mainly to seek territorial gain, but some states sought to avoid the destructive military action by creating an army only to defend their territory. The signers of the Treaties of Westphalia, which ended that war in 1648, recognized this defensive strategy as the principle of neutrality. It was reaffirmed by the Congress of Vienna in 1815 and by the Hague Conventions of 1907. Although the Covenant of the League of Nations recognized that some nations would remain neutral while others were at war, it required all who were members to participate in certain types of economic sanctions (Article 16). Switzerland, however, was granted an exemption from all military activities carried out by the League. But the 1945 United Nations Charter obligates all members to carry out the decisions of the Security Council (Article 25). The only way to avoid this responsibility is to abstain from membership in the United Nations. Thus, Switzerland participated in some of the humanitarian activities of the United Nations but declined to seek full membership until 2002. The 1949 Geneva Conventions, relating to the proper care of wounded or sick military prisoners of war, recognized political neutrality. In the modern world neutrality means no participation in war by the government or by any of its citizens as mercenaries, equal treatment of the combatants, and a military force consistent only with self-defense.

When Did Switzerland Become a State?

Switzerland actually began as a group of cantons (like counties) of the southern European Duchy of Swabia. In the thirteenth century Rudolf I, the first Habsburg Holy Roman emperor, tried to take over the duchy. Resistance came from the so-called Forest Cantons of Schwyz, Unterwalden, and Uri, which wanted their autonomy. In 1291 they formed the Everlasting League for their mutual defense. Their soldiers still fought for the emperor in Italy, however. In the fourteenth century other Swiss cantons joined the Everlasting League and expanded its territory: Berne, Glarus, Lucerne, and Zurich. As a confederation they came to a truce with the Austrian emperor and by the end of the century had formed the Federal Diet, which was supposed to coordinate their activities and support their neutrality. But these cantons actually competed with each other, which led to a long civil war (1436–50). The Peace of Constance, which ended it, nevertheless reaffirmed the confederation.

During the fifteenth century a number of Swiss campaigns were conducted to extend the territory of the confederation. Some of these campaigns were successfully conducted against the emperor and the Austrians. The newly incorporated cantons included Appenzell, Basel, Fribourg, Schaffhausen, Solothurn, and, later, Zug. The Swiss diet of Stans drew up the Covenant, which structured the confederation. In the Treaty of Basel (1499) the emperor conceded the confederation's virtual autonomy.

The confederation had expanded by war. It sent mercenaries to the armies of the emperor, the Italians, and the French. It joined the Holy League in 1510, fighting against France to restore certain territories in Italy. They administered a resounding defeat to France, and, as a result, the Swiss confederation took over the cities of Locarno, Lugano, and Ossola. The Swiss were so successful militarily that they controlled most of the important passes in the Alps mountain range.

At the seeming height of its military power, however, the confederation was overwhelmed by the religious conflicts of the Reformation. In 1524 eight of the cantons followed the preaching of protestant Ulrich Zwingli broke with the Roman Catholic Church. The remaining five joined with the church to suppress the movement. The fighting was vicious and involved Catholic forces from other European countries. John Calvin's arrival in Geneva to establish his Protestant City of God in 1541 only intensified the struggle. One of the concerns for the neighboring European countries was over the Swiss control of the vital passes through the Alps. Thus, foreign powers intervened into the confederation's civil war to keep the passes open for their own troops.

How Did Switzerland Obtain Recognition as a Neutral State?

The Swiss domestic conflict continued intermittently, but in 1602, when Savoy launched an attack on the cantons, they reaffirmed their confederation. The Thirty Years War then renewed the Reformation conflicts in northern Europe in 1618. Although the exhausted cantons could agree on little else, they agreed upon a policy of neutrality regarding that conflict. This neutrality and Swiss independence from the Holy Roman Empire were formally acknowledged in the Treaties of Westphalia of 1648.

Neutrality afforded the Swiss a peaceful interlude in which to restore their economy and domestic order. Because the religious differences were not settled, the cantons insisted on relative autonomy within the confederation. Each could determine its own style of government. The 13-seat Diet (confederate legislature) was not strong enough to mediate the continuing disputes among the cantons, so numerous conflicts erupted before the Diet was dissolved in 1798. In that year the French Revolution expanded into Switzerland. Part of its territory was annexed and the rest was formed into the French-dominated Helvetic Republic. The cantons remained under French control until 1813, when Napoleon began his retreat after losing the Battle of Leipzig. They convened a new Diet in Zurich, which proclaimed Switzerland's armed neutrality for the remainder of the war against Napoleon.

Following the defeat of Napoleon in 1815, a peace conference was convened in Vienna, Austria. There the negotiations focused on returning the nations of Europe to the status they had prior to the French Revolution and Napoleon. During the March meetings of the Congress of Vienna the participants accepted, in principle, the concept of neutrality. Finally, as a result of the Paris agreement of 20 November 1815, the Great Powers determined that Switzerland should be "permanently neutral."

The concept of "permanent neutrality" relieves a nation from having to declare its position conflict by conflict. It also places obligations on the warring nations to avoid involving that nation in their conflict. The European powers also recognized the permanent neutrality of Belgium in 1831, following its independence from the Kingdom of the Netherlands. Following the establishment of the United Nations, Austria accepted permanent neutrality as a condition for ending occupation after World War II and for regaining its full independence in 1955. Laos gained the same status in 1962. In most cases, though, a nation limits its neutrality to a specific conflict. For example, the United States declared neutrality at the beginning of World War I and World War II, although it did not hesitate to send troops to Mexico in 1915 and 1916. But when U.S. ships were attacked by German submarines in 1917 and by Japanese planes in 1941, the United States was able to declare an end to its neutrality and enter the conflicts.

How Is Neutrality Conducted during Wartime?

Neutrality is a policy that certain nations have adopted in order to stay outside armed conflicts. It is based on the international law of neutrality established by the Treaties of Westphalia. For example, at the start of World War II, Ireland, Norway, Portugal, Spain, Sweden, Switzerland, Turkey, and the United States all declared themselves officially neutral after Adolf Hitler's armies invaded Poland in September 1939.

Both the nation proclaiming neutrality and the other states around it have to recognize the legality of neutrality. Thus, neutrality does not always protect the nation proclaiming it. Hitler invaded neutral Norway in 1940 and set up a puppet government there.

What Are the Current Issues about Neutrality?

Generally, when the wars are local in nature, as between France and Germany in 1871 or between Russia and Japan in 1905, neutrality was an obvious statement of principles. In that type of local conflict widespread neutrality actually helped to limit the scope of the war and, perhaps, to bring a more rapid end to the hostilities. However, in the first major war of the twentieth century, World War I (1914–18), the intense propaganda machines of the opposing powers identified grand causes in order to gain support. Grand coalitions were formed on both sides. Those nations that stayed out of the conflict were suspect.

This attitude only intensified and became more complex after the war with the foundation of the League of Nations as an instrument of peacekeeping. In the 1930s, when Italy invaded Ethiopia and Japan invaded Manchuria, the League imposed sanctions against them. These sanctions were not successful in halting the aggressors, however.

The many declarations of neutrality in 1939 after World War II (1939–45) began in Europe also had little effect. Indeed, the Axis powers (Japan, Germany, and Italy) simply ignored neutrality when it suited them. However, those nations that declared neutrality came under greater criticism than ever. It has been noted that "To remain neutral in 1914–1918 or 1939–1945 was to shrink from taking part in what the participants—amounting to a high proportion of the inhabitants of the globe—regarded as a crusade."[1] This was particularly so in World War II Europe, where both the war and the Holocaust generated such atrocities that neutrality was bitterly resented.

The principle of neutrality was severely eroded by World War II. Some neutrals, such as the United States, clearly tilted toward one side in the hostilities. Although officially neutral, for example, the United States set up the Lend-Lease Agreement (1941) with Britain, "lending" it warships for the war efforts in exchange for "leasing" British ports in the Caribbean. In October 1941 the United States also agreed to send war supplies to the Soviet Union, which Hitler had invaded in June of that year. It did not send supplies to the Germans.

Combatants on both sides routinely conducted espionage in neutral countries and sometimes against neutrals, intercepting communications or flying over their air space. Even the Vatican was not exempt from such incursions. But the neutrals were equally guilty, spying to gain information that might better help them protect their own neutrality.[2] After the war, the nations of the world again began to form international organizations, such as the United Nations, and military alliances and collective security arrangements, such as the North Atlantic Treaty Organization (NATO) and the Russian-led Warsaw Pact. The members of these organizations would be required to take military action under certain situations, such as in the name of peace. Neutrality became increasingly more difficult to define and maintain.

How Does Switzerland Define and Maintain Its Neutrality?

The Swiss are proud of their tradition of permanent neutrality and determined to maintain control over it. The Swiss government publishes a carefully prepared brochure that defines the nation's neutrality past and present and that relates it to the complexities of contemporary diplomacy. The brochure states: "A power is neutral when it does not take sides in war. Switzerland's neutrality is self-determined, permanent and armed."[3]

It explains that there are special Swiss circumstances that make the policy of neutrality necessary for both domestic and foreign policy. One of the major considerations is the diversity of the Swiss resident population. According to the census of 2000, 63.9 percent of the 5.8 million Swiss speak German, but the remainder speaks the other three official national languages: French (19.5 percent), Italian (6.6 percent), and Romansch (0.5 percent). Switzerland is also home to nearly 1.5 million foreigners who speak a variety of other languages.[4] The Swiss are sensitive to the fact that these minorities have their champions in France and Italy. (It is significant that the Swiss national census carefully avoids identifying citizens by their ethnic heritage.) The Swiss population is also divided by religions that have both historical and regional bases and that also have links outside the borders. The government maintains that "neutrality has always helped to guarantee internal cohesion. Thus, in the past, the principle of neutrality was also applied to conflicts within the Confederation.... External neutrality guaranteed internal cohesion."[5] Neutrality helps Switzerland avoid being dragged into European conflicts of importance to segments of its own population.

The Swiss maintain that "neutrality is seen as one way among others of ensuring Switzerland's external security," and they reserve to themselves the right to define how that definition is to be interpreted.[6] This "flexible" neutrality has given rise to the recent criticism of Swiss actions during World War II.

Swiss Neutrality and World War II

Status as a neutral does not prohibit Switzerland from defending itself. The Swiss have a modern standing army, and every Swiss man is prepared to serve in it. Boys begin training in military drill and gymnastics in most Swiss elementary schools, and men between the ages of 17 and 50 are liable to be called for service. When Swiss men are 20 years old, they are automatically registered in the Auszug (first level of military service) and each man must complete 45 days his first year and 16 days every other year after that until he is 32. After that he becomes a member of the Landwehr (First Reserve), serving 9 days every 4 years, until he is 44. Then he enters the Landsturm (Second Reserve). This lifelong obligation makes Switzerland, despite its neutrality, a nation of soldiers. (This is probably the reason why the Swiss army knife and Swiss army watch have become such popular and marketable objects.)

This attitude of militant defense served the Swiss well at the beginning of World War II. When the Germans invaded Poland on 1 September 1939, the Swiss immediately mobilized their army. When the Germans launched their attack on France in 1940, some of their planes crossed over Switzerland as a shortcut. The Swiss defended their neutral territory and status by shooting down the German planes (with Messerschmitts purchased from Germany). At the same time, the Swiss had interned members of the French army who fled into Switzerland to escape the Germans. The armed neutrality was apparently even-handed. The Germans later found evidence, however, that the

Swiss defense minister Adolf Ogi *(center)* poses with members of the Grenadier RS14/97 regiment in camouflage gear at the Isone shooting range of the Swiss army, May 1997. Fully armed, Switzerland sat out both world wars. Critics contend that collaboration with the Nazis rather than neutrality staved off German attack. Neutrality has prevented Switzerland from sending troops to United Nations peacekeeping or NATO operations. (AP/Wide Worlds Photo)

Swiss and French military chiefs had collaborated on plans to fight Germany had it invaded Switzerland.[7]

After June 1940 Switzerland was ringed by the Axis powers: Greater Germany (including Austria after the 1938 Anschluss), fascist Italy, and "Free" France, subject to German authority even if not fully occupied by German forces. In the effort to prevent a German attack the Swiss decided on the novel policy to emphasize their neutrality. Approximately two-thirds of the Swiss forces were demobilized, with the rest concentrated in the Alps to protect the mountain passes. Some have interpreted this demobilization as an action to appease Germany, especially in light of the German majority among Swiss citizens. The strategy worked, and none of the belligerents invaded Switzerland during the war.

Neutral status did not prevent Switzerland from trading with the belligerents, as long as it did not favor one side. Switzerland has been accused, however, of giving special favors to the Axis during the war. Although it is true that Swiss imports from Germany increased during the war, reaching their highest level in 1942, their trade with the United States followed the same pattern. Swiss exports to Germany also peaked in 1942; but their exports to France, Great Britain, and the United States continued throughout these years, albeit at a reduced level, despite the necessity of shipping them across Axis-controlled Europe.

ISSUES

It has been proven that the Swiss banks ignored the origins of funds, gold, and other assets placed in their vaults by the Germans during World War II. Because the Swiss government protected the secrecy of those accounts, the Germans found a safe haven for funds looted from the countries they conquered. But so did the Jews who were trying to hide their assets from the Germans. The Swiss banks later took over some accounts for which there were no legitimate claimants after the war. They are now paying compensation and penalties for these actions. (See chapter 10.) The recent controversies over Swiss neutrality focus on two issues: (1) Switzerland's relations with Germany and the Axis countries during World War II, and (2) the impact of full membership in the United Nations on Switzerland's status as a permanent neutral.

DID THE SWISS MAINTAIN NEUTRALITY DURING WORLD WAR II?

Switzerland Violated Its Neutrality by Discriminating against Jewish Refugees during the Second World War

Agree:

Questions have been raised about Swiss treatment of foreign refugees during the war. In August 1942 a police circular in Switzerland ordered closure of the nation's borders to all those trying to enter "only because of their race, Jews for example." This circular appears directly to have supported German anti-Semitic policies and the Holocaust. Marvin Hier and Abraham Cooper, writing in the *Los Angeles Times* (17 June 1998), charged that a Swiss government official collaborated with the anti-Semitic Swiss Fatherland Association to shut down the flight of Jewish refugees into Switzerland. They imply a connection between meetings held by Eduard von Steiger, a cabinet minister in 1942 (and later Swiss president), and the order that Swiss customs officials received later that year "that no Jew could be eligible for political asylum." In a recent television documentary, *Frontline: Switzerland: Neutral or Cowardly*, the Swiss were accused of refusing to permit entrance to 30,000 Jewish refugees who were fleeing from the Holocaust.[8] Moreover, it has been charged that those refugees whom Switzerland admitted were herded into camps, where they worked long hours.

Disagree:

It is truly unfair to say that because the Swiss closed their borders to individuals whom the Germans wanted to arrest, they were aiding the Germans. By 1942 Switzerland was surrounded by Germany and its allies. It is a small nation, with limited resources, and could not indiscriminately house all those fleeing the Germans. It did the best it could to cope with the relatively new concept of political asylum. In June 1942 it was accommodating 9,600 refugees. By December 1942 that number had burgeoned to 26,200. In April 1944, of 25,174 refugees recorded, 2,990 were in camps for quarantine and reception processing, 4,041 in labor camps, 5,206 in homes, and 5,329 in hotels or living with family members. For example, Swiss Protestants helped finance housing for 1,100 Jewish refugees with families and in homes. By the end of the war, May 1945, some 57,000 refugees resided in Switzerland. This number was in addition to approximately 40,000 interned soldiers, mainly French and Polish, who were under Swiss military authority in compliance with special rules of war. In comparison to the United States, which accepted only 21,000 Jewish refugees during the war, and Canada, which accepted only 9,000, Switzerland was a veritable haven. By the end of the war Switzerland had sheltered almost 300,000 individuals, the majority of whom were foreign soldiers. A number of Allied governments thanked Switzerland for their help.[9]

It was Swiss policy to put people to work rather than leave them idle and bored in the refugee camps. For their labor they received a small wage as well as housing:

> Men between age 16 and 50 who were able-bodied and healthy, were assigned to labor camps. Children were placed with families at age six. Women and frail males were housed in homes where they could perform light work. Those making use of their personal means or receiving aid from charitable organizations or family support had a chance to leave the camps and regain their independence. . . . [N]ot only Jewish organizations supported the refugees; nor did they have to finance the camps, as been assumed incorrectly. The same conditions applied to all. All people falling under the category of wealthy refugees had to pay a special tax.[10]

The refugees in the camps worked a 42–44 hour work week, with a three-day vacation every six weeks. But during the war all Swiss between the ages of 16 and 65 were obliged to provide labor service as well. Nearly 550,000 were called to additional work between 1941 and 1946.

The Swiss Violated Neutrality by Letting Germany Transport War Materials and Prisoners across Switzerland during World War II

Agree:

There are accounts of the Germans transporting Italians in cattle cars through Switzerland's Gotthard Pass. Said one Swiss eyewitness: "we knew they were going to Germany, we knew they were Jews, we knew about the concentration camps." Further investigation located an Italian who saw the Germans rounding up Italians by offering them free cigarettes. Records show German requests to permit trains carrying Italian workers to cross Switzerland. The Swiss refused to supply any trains, but they did not object to the movement of the workers. The Center for Documentation on Contemporary Jewish History has recorded unconfirmed stories that such trains went through Switzerland. It is known that the Germans also sent some 9,000 Jews through Austria's Brenner Pass to the eastern concentration camps. Moreover, documents in the U.S. Archives show a great deal of rail traffic through Switzerland by German trains after bombing closed the Brenner Pass in 1943. The Swiss government had signed a treaty with the Germans and Italians in 1909 to define the use of the Gotthard Tunnel through the Gotthard Pass. Transportation of soldiers and weapons through it were prohibited. But after Allied bombs closed the Brenner Pass, some short-term agreements did permit passage of German shipments until the autumn of 1944. These shipments could well have been Italian prisoners. It is well documented that the Germans forced some 23,000 Italians to work in Germany and deported more than 10,000 partisans between September 1943 and April 1944. A September 1943 memorandum by a Swiss police official indicates that some three to five German transports passed through his country per day. Eyewitness accounts report weapons and troops on those trains, not just the coal and nonstrategic materials listed in the official reports.[11]

Disagree:

For most of the war the Germans were capable of moving men and materials from Italy through the Brenner Pass into Austria. According to one expert, the only German troops permitted to cross Switzerland during the war were 3,000 men so badly wounded that Swiss medical authorities determined they would not be able to return to duty for a long time.[12]

As for the accusations about transporting Italians, the Swiss manager of Railway Operations categorically denied that they had transported Italian workers. In a memo to the General Head Office of the railroads he wrote on 30 October 1943:

Zur Anfrage des Eidg. Post- und Eisenbahndepartments betr. Verschwinden von 28. ital. Arbeitern aus einen plombierten Transportzuge durch die Schweiz teilen wir Ihnen folgendes mit:

Es sind seit 27. Juli 1943 keine Transporte italianischer Arbeiter mehr durch die Schweiz durchgeführt worden. Die in Frage stehende Meldung ist vollständig aus der Luft gegriffen. Unsere Untersuchung hat ergaben, dass auf unsern Linien kein Ereignis in der Meldung erwähnten Art stattgefunden hat. Wir haben nicht ermitteln können, was zu diesem Gerucht gegeben hat.[13]

"To the General Head Office. With reference to the inquiry to the Swiss Post and Railway Department regarding the disappearance of 28 Italian workers from a sealed transport train traveling through Switzerland, we would inform you as follows: Since July 27, 1943, there have been no further transportations of Italian workers through Switzerland. The notice in question is totally unfounded. Our investigation has proved that there has been no incident of the kind mentioned in the notice on our railway lines. We have been unable to establish what gave rise to this rumor. [signed] The Manager of Railway Operations Sallinari. Berne, October 30, 1943. O.B.C. Nr. 3726, 15/43.

The Swiss, landlocked in continental Europe, depended on trade with Germany, among other states. They did permit German goods that they had purchased to enter Switzerland. They also shipped to Germany goods that they had sold to the Germans. Under these circumstances it is not surprising that accusations of transporting prisoners arose. But at the end of a long investigation of the issue, the producers of the documentary *Frontline: The Train* concluded: "We were not able to locate anyone who may have been on forced transports through Switzerland during the war." So the accusations remain just that, unproven allegations.

The Swiss Violated Neutrality by Favoring German Trade during World War II

Agree:

A research report generated in 1997 by the U.S. Department of State makes allegations about Switzerland's economic cooperation with Germany:

Germany's war effort depended significantly upon its imports of raw materials and goods from the neutral nations. Switzerland was Nazi Germany's banker and financial facilitator, taking and transferring German gold—most of it looted—and providing Germany with Swiss francs to purchase needed products.

Switzerland also supplied Germany with key war materials such as arms, ammunition, aluminum, machinery and locomotives. Moreover, Germany was able to mitigate slightly the effect of Allied bombing by moving some arms production to safety across the Swiss frontier....

Switzerland resisted Allied efforts to reduce or halt its exports to Germany and to curb, if not end, the transshipment of German materials across its borders. Surrounded by Axis forces, Switzerland's financial relationship with Germany clearly exceeded that of other neutral countries.[14]

Indeed, Switzerland aided and abetted the German war effort and the Holocaust.

Disagree:

There is nothing in international law forbidding neutrals to trade with warring nations. The United States continued to trade with Great Britain after the start of each of the world wars even though it was officially neutral. The Swiss sold arms to both Great Britain and France in 1939 but halted trade with them once the war began, as the laws of neutrality dictated.[15] It is unreasonable to presume that Switzerland should have starved itself or shut down its industries rather than trade with the Germans and their allies during World War II. As one scholar concludes, Swiss trade with Germany during World War II "was not only legal, but also inevitable." To be sure, the war dislocated the traditional patterns of Swiss international trade. The data in Table 11.1 give some indication of how this dislocation occurred.[16]

In 1941 the drastic cut in imports to Switzerland from Great Britain and France reflected how their trade was blocked by German control of the western ports. This was balanced, to some extent, by a continuing high level of

Table 11.1
Swiss Foreign Trade with Selected Countries (millions of Swiss Francs)

Year	German Reich	Italy	France	Great Britain	United States	Other Countries	Total
				Imports			
1935	314.1	83.5	207.9	77.8	69.5	531.106	1,434.506
1938	373.1	116.7	229.2	97.2	125.3	666.403	1,606,803
1941	656.2	244.6	76.5	14.3	151.3	882.542	2,024.342
1943	532.2	131.3	78.4	3.6	56.4	925.179	1,727.079
1944	433.4	26.6	51.8	1.8	21.1	649.331	1,185,931
1945	54.3	47.1	129.8	22.6	136.8	834.767	1,225.367
				Exports			
1935	169.7	72.8	121.3	78.8	48.1	331.25	821.860
1938	206.1	91.2	121.4	149.7	90.7	657.472	1,316.572
1941	577.0	185.6	92.6	24.0	108.0	476.148	1,463.348
1943	596.4	93.5	51.5	37.8	152.8	694.949	1,628.949
1944	293.6	4.9	23.6	37.0	140.8	631.935	1,131.835
1945	11.2	11.1	165.8	37.5	385.3	863.497	1,473.697

Source: "The Swiss Economy in World War II. Swiss Foreign Trade with Germany, Italy, France," http://www.switzerland.taskforce.ch/W/W2/W2d/d1_e.htm.

imports from the United States and other countries who were not yet engaged in the hostilities. Similarly, the amount of Swiss goods exported to Great Britain plummeted, while those to Germany doubled. The Swiss had to make agreements with both the Allies and the Germans to continue to trade, and they kept both sides fully informed of the magnitude of that trade. In fact, despite all the allegations about Switzerland helping the Germans launder their looted gold, Swiss bankers bought nearly 30 percent more gold from the United States and Great Britain than it did from the Axis countries. This gold was held in New York rather than in Swiss vaults, however.[17] Considering that Switzerland was, by 1941, surrounded by regions under German control, the trade data do not give strong evidence that the landlocked nation was allying itself with Germany.

Indeed, Swiss relations with Germany were not particularly favorable. The German army had given the impression that it was going to invade Switzerland at the same time as it moved on the Netherlands and Belgium in 1940. After the fall of France, the army still had an invasion plan named Case Switzerland; the plan apparently was set aside in favor of the invasion of Russia. But Hitler banned any presentations of *William Tell* in the Reich and labeled the Swiss "the most despicable and wretched people, mortal enemies of the new Germany." Later he boasted that he would be "the Butcher of the Swiss."[18]

Under the banking laws of the time and the traditions of neutrality, the Swiss were within their legal rights to conduct trade and banking with the warring nations. It would have been a violation of neutrality, in fact, to reject such trade and deposits from the Germans while continuing to deal with the Allied states. Swiss neutrality was of benefit to both sides in the war because each relied upon the Swiss Red Cross to assist prisoners of war on both sides of the battle lines, to facilitate mail and food deliveries to them, and to deliver certain types of medical help to the wounded. It is clear that much of the controversy over the Swiss relations with German during World War II emerged in the 1990s with the efforts to recover Holocaust assets in Swiss banks. Part of that campaign was an attack on Swiss-German trade relations in order to gain punitive damages from the Swiss banks for holding "Nazi gold." Thus, the twenty-twenty ethical hindsight of the present is being imposed on the past. Those determined to prove Swiss guilt have distorted Swiss motives and their efforts to sustain their role as a neutral nation under the most difficult of wartime circumstance.

CAN SWITZERLAND REMAIN NEUTRAL AS A MEMBER OF THE UNITED NATIONS?

The second controversy centers on Swiss participation in international affairs. Following World War II Switzerland continued to cling steadfastly to its neutrality instead of taking sides in the Cold War. This stance has caused many to accuse Switzerland of practicing extreme isolationism or of pursuing a policy of crass economic opportunism. Yet Switzerland is active in many humanitarian organizations, and because of its neutrality many international organizations maintain their headquarters there. Although the United Nations did impose and execute military operations in some conflicts, Switzerland participated in many of its peaceful activities. The government's decision to apply for full United Nations membership sparked an intensive internal debate about the future of Switzerland's cherished neutrality. Switzerland became the 190th member of the United Nations on 10 September 2002.

The Decision to Join the United Nations Is Wrong; It Will Destroy Switzerland's Status as a Permanent Neutral

Agree:

It must be recognized that the United Nations Charter awards binding power to the Security Council to declare boycotts by the member nations, which means giving up trade and limiting communication with the offending nation. Similarly, the charter can require the member nations to send forces to discipline offending nations, as it did during the Gulf War and in Kosovo. Thus, as part of the United Nations, Switzerland will be forced to take sides in a military conflict. It will lose the right to remain neutral, which will affect its trade, its peaceful relations with other nations around the world, and potentially its freedom from attack by other nations. And it will put Swiss soldiers in harm's way abroad for the first time in centuries.

Switzerland has struggled since the sixteenth century to establish its neutrality. Its status as a permanent neutral has been recognized internationally since 1815, when the Congress of Vienna first defined that principle. Neutrality has been the cornerstone of both its foreign policy and its security policy. Swiss peaceful armed neutrality has kept the country free of invasion since that time. The trust and stability engendered by that scrupulous neutrality have aided the growth of Swiss prosperity. Even during the two devastating world wars in Europe, neutrality kept the battlefields at a distance, while permitting the Swiss to aid refugees and prisoners of war. At the same time, many international organizations headquartered in Switzerland were able to continue their humanitarian missions, and the diplomatic communities maintained some level of contact even among the belligerents. There is simply no good reason to surrender Switzerland's historical neutrality at this time. The world needs a trustworthy, peaceful, neutral nation.

Switzerland will gain little from being a member of the United Nations. Over the years the United Nations has become more like a military alliance than a peacekeeping organization. The determination of the United States to drag it twice into war in Iraq demonstrates that all too clearly. The argument that the United Nations gives the Swiss a clear voice in global peace processes is an exaggeration. Switzerland already participates in the peacekeeping activities of the Council of Europe, the Partnership for Peace, the Organization for Security and Cooperation in Europe, and the European Free Trade Association. Swiss representatives assist most of the United Nations' humanitarian agencies. Switzerland has long been a strong voice and role model for peace and can continue to be so without compromising its principles. It declined to join NATO and the Western European Union because both are military alliances. It was a mistake to join the United Nations.

Disagree:

In a 1986 referendum 75 percent of the Swiss public rejected United Nations membership and made a clear turn toward isolationism. But since the end of the Cold War in 1990, the world situation has changed significantly. It has not been able to attain peace. There have been conflicts across Europe, Asia, South America, and Africa. Many of these conflicts were internal domestic rebellions, but at least 10 armed conflicts erupted between and among nations between 1990 and 1998. Many were between some of the world's poorest nations. Switzerland remained a bystander in the United Nations' efforts to mediate these disputes. The United Nations often sent peacekeeping forces to keep the hostile parties apart while negotiations were conducted. On the sidelines Switzerland began to lose the respect and influence it had enjoyed in the past.

History has demonstrated that neutrality is not a static concept, but that it must be consistent with events. Thus, in World War II Switzerland declared its armed neutrality and backed it up by mobilizing some 450,000 men and women to defend its national territory. Despite some accidental bombing by both Axis and Allies, the belligerents respected the Swiss policy. No change in Swiss policy was required during the Cold War, as the world divided up behind two bristling military superpowers.

But at the end of the Cold War different kinds of conflict occurred. In 1990 the United Nations instituted sanctions against Iraq after it invaded Kuwait. It further authorized a coalition, led by the United States, to push the Iraqis out of Kuwait. When asked to participate in the sanctions, the Swiss Federal Council agreed to do so. It also permitted the coalition forces to move across Swiss air space to the war zone. It defined this situation as one of "differential neutrality" for humanitarian purposes.

In 1991 the Federal Council established a special task force to examine the changing circumstance for Swiss neutrality. Before the task force completed its deliberations, conflict began in 1992 after Bosnia announced its secession from Yugoslavia. War threatened Europe again. In 1993, after the task force had presented its reports, the Swiss government stated is changing policy in the *White Paper on Neutrality of November 29th, 1993.* It concluded that some of the obligations of neutrality are now outdated. "The Federal Council considers it important to adapt Switzerland's neutrality policy to present-day conditions." That might even include joining the European Union and demonstrating solidarity with United Nations sanctions.[19]

After the Dayton Peace Accords were signed in December 1995, NATO, with the backing of the United Nations, set up the peacekeeping Implementation Force (IFOR). They asked permission to transport this force across Swiss air space to deploy in Bosnia. The Swiss Federal Council again agreed. This action did not violate neutrality because all parties to the conflict accepted IFOR. Some members of the Swiss army volunteered to assist the mission by providing equipment repair and medical and postal services. They were distinguished by their yellow caps. It is clear that the United Nations and NATO are capable of cooperating for peace. But only the United Nations has an international mandate to do so.

The government of Switzerland has tried since 1986 to educate the population about the new dimensions of neutrality. In August 2000 it began to change the operating definition of neutrality in its *Report on Swiss Neutrality in Practice:* "Das Neutralitätsrecht gilt ausschliesslich in internationalen bewaffneten Konflikten, d.h. in gewaltsamen Auseinandersetzungen zwischen Staaten. Beschliesst hingegen die UNO wirtschaftliche oder militärische Sanktionen, findet das Neutralitätsrecht keine Anwendung" (Neutrality law applies only in the context of international armed conflicts, that is, in violent conflicts between states. By contrast, it is not applicable in situations where the United Nations imposes economic or military sanctions).[20]

However, the report continued, the law of neutrality would apply to any military conflict not sanctioned by the United Nations. The Defense Forces Administration's Directorate of International Law published a long statement on neutrality in December 2000. It documented the policy and participation changes in Swiss relations with the international community. It further stated that if in the future an international organization could offer the same reliable security as the neutrality policy, Switzerland might drop neutrality for that system. Switzerland has already supported nonmilitary sanctions against aggressive nations without sacrificing its neutrality. Its participation with the peacekeeping activities in Bosnia/Herzegovina and Kosovo exemplify that type of solidarity with international organizations.[21]

The Federal Council has argued a strong and appropriate case. It reserves the right to maintain the principle of neutrality within actions of the international peacekeeping organizations. It convinced the Swiss electorate and won the referendum support to join the United Nations. This change was no mistake. It is evidence of a dynamic security and foreign policy fully consistent with Swiss history and tradition.

QUESTIONS AND ACTIVITIES

1. In class discuss the implications of neutrality as it has been defined at the beginning of this chapter. Be sure you fully understand the responsibilities of the neutral country and of other countries toward it. Make a list of the advantages and disadvantages of neutrality for security and as a foreign policy.

2. Prepare a poster to list the nations that declared neutrality in World War I and World War II. Identify those that maintained neutrality throughout both conflicts. Identify those that abandoned neutrality to join the conflicts. Explain why they did so.

3. Read a book about the history of Switzerland. In a short essay explain your opinion on the importance of neutrality to Switzerland. Did this policy really protect the nation, or was it just an excuse to take advantage of wartime trade and profits?

4. Locate and read one of the articles or books that accuse the Swiss of violating neutrality during World War II. How does it prove its point? Who wrote it, and what was his or her purpose in publishing the accusation? Prepare a short presentation to the class that explains the strengths and weaknesses of the arguments and evidence.

5. Investigate one of the other European nations that remained neutral during World War II, such as Spain, Portugal, Sweden, or Turkey. Has this nation also been accused of violating neutrality? In a class discussion compare their behavior and activities during the war with those of Switzerland. Do the accusations against Switzerland single it out unfairly?

6. Using the Web and other resources, research the peacekeeping activities of IFOR and the United Nations since 1990. Pay particular attention to the role of the Swiss participants. Did their activities violate the requirement that neutrals deal with both sides of the conflict equitably?

7. Brainstorm to compile a list of humanitarian organizations, including those that are part of the United Nations, that are working for health, social concerns, and peace. Find out whether Switzerland is a member of any of them. Find out whether any of them have offices in Switzerland. Based on what you have learned, discuss whether joining the United Nations is a significant change in policy for Switzerland.

NOTES

1. Detlev F. Vagts, "Switzerland, International Law, and World War II," *American Journal of International Law* 91, no. 3 (July 1997), 466, http://www.asil.org/ajil/vagts.htm, 1.

2. An excellent bibliography on neutrals and World War II espionage activities is available at http://intellit.muskingum.edu/wwiieurope_folder/wwiieurother.html.

3. The Swiss Federal Department of Defence, Civil Protection, and Sports (DDPS) and the Swiss Department of Foreign Affairs (DFA), *Swiss Neutrality,* http://www.vbs.admin.ch/internet/e/vbs/pub/neutral-E/Active.htm.

4. Bundesamt für Statistik, "Ständige Wohnbevölkerung nach Heimat," in *Statistik Schweiz,* http://www.statistik.admin.ch/stat_ch/ber01/dufr01.htm.

5. Swiss DDPS and DFA, "Tradition," in *Swiss Neutrality.*

6. Swiss Department of Foreign Affairs, Directorate of International Law, "Swiss Neutrality," http://www.eda.admin.ch/sub_dipl/e/home/thema/intlaw/neutr.html.

7. Vagts, "Switzerland, International Law, and World War II," 2.

8. Marvin Hier and Abraham Cooper, "At Best, Selective Neutrality," in *Perspectives on the Swiss Role in WWII,* Simon Wiesenthal Center, http://www.wiesenthal.com/swiss/opedlatimes61798a.cfm. Rabbi Marvin Hier is the founder and dean of the Simon Wiesenthal Center; Rabbi Abraham Cooper is the assistant dean. *Frontline:*

Switzerland: Neutral or Cowardly, http://www.pbs.org/wgbh/pages/frontline/shows/Nazis/tv/.

9. André Lasserre, "Why Comparisons with Concentration Camps Are Odious," http://www.swotzerland/taskforce.ch/W/W2?W2c/c4_.htm; "Swiss Jewish Newspapers Denounce Report," *Shawnee News-Star Online* (Oklahoma), 13 June 1998, http://www.news-star.com/stories/051398/new_swissjew.html; "Refugee Camps in Switzerland during World War II," http://www.Switzerland.taskforce.ch/W/W2?W2c3_e.htm; "Switzerland in the Second World War: Nostra Culpa," *Economist.com,* 26 July 2002, http://www.economist.com.

10. Lasserre; "Why Comparison with Concentration Camps Are Odious."

11. *Frontline: Switzerland: The Train,* http://www.pbs.org/wgbh;pages/frontline/shows/nazis/train/.

12. Vagts, " Switzerland, International Law, and World War II," p. 2.

13. "An die Generaldirektion," *Frontline: The Train,* http://www.pbs.org/wgbh;pages/frontline/shows/nazis/train/5/html.

14. "Switzerland in the Second World War"; *U.S. and Allied Efforts to Recover and Restore Gold and Other Assets Stolen or Hidden by Germany during World War II: Preliminary Study,* prepared by William Z. Slaney, U.S. Department of State, May 1997, http://www.ess.uwe.ac.uk/documents/asetindx.htm. This report is generally known as the *Eizenstat Report.* "Annex II. Summary of the May 1997 Preliminary Report," 1–2.

15. By contrast, Vagts reports that during World War I the United States continued to sell arms to all the warring powers. The U.S. secretary of state told the Austro-Hungarian ambassador that if more arms reached the British than the Central Powers, he could complain to the British Royal Navy. See Vagts, "Switzerland, International Law, and World War II."

16. Ibid., 3.

17. Ibid. For information on these trade agreements, see the series of letters between Switzerland and Britain: "War Trade between Switzerland and the Axis Powers" dated 19 December 1943, 14 August 1944, 8 March and 5 April 1945. These letters are available online at the Web site of the Avalon Project at Yale Law School, http://www.yale.edu/lawweb/avalon/wwii/swiss/01.htm (through /04.htm).

18. Stephen P. Halbrook, "Target Switzerland," speeches given 16 July and 21 July 1998, http://www.stephenhalbrook.com/ts.html. *William Tell* celebrates the Swiss resistance to the invading Austrian emperor.

19. *White Paper on Neutrality of November 29th, 1993* (93.098), http://www.eda.admin.ch/eda/e/home/recent/rep/neutral.html.

20. *Bericht Zur Neutralitätspraxis der Schweiz—aktuelle Aspekte,* report of 30 August 2000 by the Interdepartmental Working Group, http://www.eda.admin.ch/eda/e/home/recent/rep/neutr.html.

21. DFA Directorate of International Law, "Swiss Neutrality," 12 December 2000, http://www.eda.admin.ch/sub_dipl/e/home/thema/intlaw/neutr.html.

SUGGESTED READINGS

A good place to start is with a basic history of Switzerland. Charles Gilliard's *A History of Switzerland* (Westport, Conn.: Greenwood Press, 1978) is dated but short and clear. Mike Graf's *Switzerland* (Mankato, MN: Bridgestone Books, 2002) is equally readable and up to date.

Stephen Tanner's *Refuge from the Reich: American Airmen and Switzerland during World War II* (Rockville Center, N.Y.: Sarpedon, 2000) offers some of the history of the Swiss and a dramatic account of the World War I soldiers who were interned there.

A number of works have attacked Swiss neutrality during the war. Jean Ziegler's *Switzerland: The Awful Truth* (New York: Harper and Row, 1979) is one of the earliest. Adam LeBor's *Hitler's Secret Bankers: The Myth of Swiss Neutrality during the Holocaust* (Secaucus, N.J.: Carol Publishing Group, 1997) and Tom Bower's *Nazi Gold: The Full Story of the Fifty-Year Swiss-Nazi Conspiracy to Steal Millions from Europe's Jews and Holocaust Survivors* (New York: HarperCollins, 1997) explain their viewpoints in their titles.

Switzerland also has its defenders. Stephen R. Halbrook's *Target Switzerland: Swiss Armed Neutrality in World War* (Rockville Center, N.Y.: Sarpedon, 1998) tries to put Switzerland's wartime activities in perspective. Angelo M. Coderilla's *Between the Alps and a Hard Place: Switzerland in World War II and Moral Blackmail Today* (Washington, D.C.: Regnery, 2000) is a more vigorous defense.

Switzerland has gone to great lengths to present all aspects of its neutrality in sites accessible on the Web. The best place to start is a well-written and illustrated pamphlet: The Swiss Federal Department of Defence, Civil Protection and Sports (DDPS) and the Swiss Department of Foreign Affairs (DFA), *Swiss Neutrality* (http://www.vbs.admin.ch/internet/e/vbs/pub/neutral-E/Active.htm). Other documents are identified with the links indicated in the Notes for this chapter.

Detlev F. Vagts's article "Switzerland, International Law, and World War II," *American Journal of International Law* 91, no. 3 (July 1997): 1–9 (http://www.asil.org/ajil/vagts.htm), offers a thoughtful analysis of the legal and diplomatic factors of neutrality, with special consideration of the Swiss case. For additional works on neutrals and World War II espionage activities, check the bibliography given at http://intellit.muskingum.edu/wwiieurope_folder/wwiieurother.html.

The transcripts of the two *Frontline* programs, presented as documentaries by the Public Broadcasting System, *Frontline: Switzerland: Neutral or Cowardly* (http://www.pbs.org/wgbh/pages/frontline/shows/Nazis/tv/) and *Frontline: Switzerland: The Train* (http://www.pbs.org/wgbh;pages/frontline/shows/nazis/train/), give the flavor of the current controversy, with narrative and eyewitness testimonies.

INDEX

About the Author

ELEANOR L. TURK is Professor of History emerita at Indiana University East. Her book *The History of Germany* (Greenwood, 1999) was named an "Outstanding Academic Title" by the American Library Association's *CHOICE* Magazine.